Augsburg College
George Sverdrup Library
Minneapolis, Minnesota 55404

WITHDRAWN

D1255674

WHEREAS—
A Judge's Premises

WHEREAS—
A Judge's Premises

ESSAYS IN JUDGMENT, ETHICS, AND THE LAW

Charles E. Wyzanski, Jr.

An Atlantic Monthly Press Book

LITTLE, BROWN AND COMPANY · BOSTON · TORONTO

COPYRIGHT 1944, 1946, 1947, 1951, 1952, 1953, 1954
© 1956, 1958, 1959, 1961, 1965, BY CHARLES E. WYZANSKI, JR.

ALL RIGHTS RESERVED. NO PART OF THIS BOOK MAY BE REPRO-
DUCED IN ANY FORM WITHOUT PERMISSION IN WRITING FROM THE
PUBLISHER, EXCEPT BY A REVIEWER WHO MAY QUOTE BRIEF PAS-
SAGES IN A REVIEW TO BE PRINTED IN A MAGAZINE OR NEWSPAPER.

LIBRARY OF CONGRESS CATALOG CARD NO. 65–10906

FIRST EDITION

"Constitutionalism — Limitation and Affirmation" is reprinted by permission of
the publishers from *Government Under Law,* Arthur E. Sutherland, editor, Cambridge, Mass.: Harvard University Press, © 1956 by The President and Fellows
of Harvard College. "The Future of the Bar" is reprinted by permission of *The
Chicago Bar Record.* "The Law and Its Compass" is reprinted by special permission of the *Northwestern University Law Review,* Vol. 55, No. 4, Copyright ©
1960, by Northwestern University School of Law. "The Open Window and the
Open Door: An Inquiry into Freedom of Association" is reprinted by permission
of the *California Law Review,* Copyright 1947 by the *California Law Review.*
"The Democracy of Justice Oliver Wendell Holmes" is reprinted by special ar-
rangement with the Vanderbilt University School of Law and the *Vanderbilt Law
Review.* "The Public Responsibilities of Lawyers" is reprinted by permission of the
American Law Institute © 1959 by the American Law Institute.

ATLANTIC–LITTLE, BROWN BOOKS
ARE PUBLISHED BY
LITTLE, BROWN AND COMPANY
IN ASSOCIATION WITH
THE ATLANTIC MONTHLY PRESS

*Published simultaneously in Canada
by Little, Brown & Company (Canada) Limited*

PRINTED IN THE UNITED STATES OF AMERICA

AUTHOR IN BCL 2nd ED.

KF
213
W9
1965

For Gisela — d.w.w.m. —

There is nothing conventional
about her, or my love for her, or
the dedication of this book to her.
And if this volume has any mes-
sages which reach readers they
will know that the thoughts were
carried on a current which flowed
from her, and were first coded in
the sparkle of her eyes and the
dash of her tease.

71035

In Petto

P.D. and M.C. have forbidden me fully to express the acknowledgment that is their due. They are unnamed princes of my church, whose views and support I treasure.

Avis au Lecteur

REREADING my speeches and articles I suffer the anguish of an egoist — a pain that could be adequately described by Dante, who rightly accepted the traditional ordering of sins which places pride first. Nonetheless, I am honored by the time my publishers spent on this collection. Yet let me candidly avow that I would not have made the same selection. I like what I said on my twenty-fifth reunion at Harvard, the words I chose in inducting President Pusey, what I told my fellow Examiners about the inside of the Ford Foundation, and the attempt I made at the Rockefeller Institute in *Both the Saying and the Thinking* to put a philosophical coating on my prejudices. Even so, my disposition is to admit that, though I am unconvinced, my publishers may be right. I have often seen how poor a judge of his own work an author is. Wordsworth's rewriting of his own poems, particularly *The Prelude*, is an illuminating example from the heights of Olympus. How often the first draft was best, and what critical errors he made in his excisions and additions; or so it seems to most of us.

The whole collection of these papers is, I believe, more than the sum of its parts. This is *not* because they reveal a personality. I have not that charisma or magnetism or essence which makes the room catch fire when I spill over. But the whole set of papers discloses a typical trained mind

moving with the stream that carried America, and especially American law, from the last vestiges of its colonial
period into a place of paramount power in the modern
world.

When I was born, 1906, and even when I was in law
school, 1927-1930, England set the style in ideas about law
as in the cut of men's suits. We Harvard students had a
curriculum which would not have seemed strange to a
member of the Inns of Court. Our casebooks had a generous sampling of judgments pronounced at Westminster and
in the Law Courts on the Strand. What was fair we decided with one eye to the conduct of an English gentleman,
and to the limitations that English judges (who knew not
Justice Hugo Black — the greatest influence on twentieth-
century American law) had told us were the appropriate
boundaries of judicial action.

All this has changed. Now American law has grown free
of its tutor. We are proud of our own history — maybe a
little too proud of the relation of courts to economics and
of practitioners to men of affairs and not proud enough of
Holmes and Shaw, who were so deeply influenced by England. Esoteric recitals of early suits in the Admiralty Courts
of New York, disclosures of the interpenetration of lum-
bering and law in Wisconsin, and the interplay of railroad
magnates and legislative minions have their merit. But law
is something far, far more than the push and pull of private
desires.

Lord Radcliffe is one of the few contemporary jurists
who have tried to keep our vision directed at more than the
earth on which we tread. He would find symbolic relevance in Aldous Huxley's observation that of all the glories
of this world none exceeds the sky: to look at it every day
is to discern a new beauty.

But what is the relation between the blue sky and the

practical execution of ideals we cherish? In two generations the law has moved in ways unforeseeable by any nineteenth-century lawyer. The center shifted from the common law adjudged in the courts, to enacted law administered by executive agencies subject to limited judicial reviews. Statutory regulations became the bulk of the law; and judges used their remaining freedom to rewrite the Constitution to effectuate what they conceived to be the unexpressed yet ultimate popular will.

At first this seemed to exalt the naked power of the majority — to make all law fit Thrasymachus's definition of "the interest of the stronger." Of course, the stronger were no longer the rich, the wellborn, the educated. The masses had successfully revolted and taken the lead. They had broken down local barriers and ancient "liberties," in the sense of licenses for special privilege. From the country's capital they enacted national laws which put labor in the saddle, gave the farmer more than a fair return for his produce (and indeed for his nonproductive land), protected the customer against deleterious and misbranded products, required sellers of securities to conform to rigid standards of disclosure, taxed all at high rates so that the moon might be explored and the Communists contained, and through excises, collected even from householders and charities, set up a system of welfare payments for the unemployed, the aged, and others thought not prudent enough to provide for their own safety in an economic world where disaster could strike with almost as little warning as in the world of nature.

This plethora of novel legislation, this rise of the welfare state, however, had deeper significance than the overturn of the post-feudal or Lockeian settlement. More was implied than the widening of law to reach goals beyond the suppression of force and fraud. What was at the heart of

the new order was an increased belief that man has great —
albeit not uncontrolled — power over his circumstances;
that the differences between men, between groups of men,
between races of men, between colors of men lie less in
innate factors than in cultural patterns and opportunities
which can be altered; and that, though much of man's motivation is selfish and in the sole interest of the first person
singular, few of us escape an awareness that our selfish delight (our pleasure in our own powers and potentialities) is
vastly enhanced when we include within our plans and
projects the enlargement of other men's capacities and performances.

It overstates the matter to claim that in our century there
has been an increase in fraternal feeling, or neighborliness,
or that kind of love which carries the Latin tag *caritas*. But
it is *not* an error to note that the law in our time has moved
from a primarily adversary to a primarily cooperative outlook.

Lawyers, law professors, law administrators, possibly
even judges spend far more of their time than they did of
old in studying and effectuating arrangements for "peace."
Of course, the turn is not complete. I have too often
quoted Heraclitus's maxim "Strife is the source of all
things" not to be mindful of the importance of law courts
as a place for resolving issues by examination, cross-examination, and debate by "warriors," or should I say "condot-
tieri." And I do not recant my frequent statements that out
of the struggle comes not truth, to be sure, but a workable
compromise, acceptable partly because the contestants have
learned that they are not strong enough to have it all their
own way.

All that I now emphasize is that the forensic part of the
law has dwindled in importance. Where the best talent
goes, for the most part, is to the chairs at law schools, to the

desks of power in Washington, and to the offices in the large cities where countervailing power does its best to keep the balance with official force. What goes on in these non-judicial centers is far more affirmative than a mere verdict, or settlement by agreement in open court. Attention is directed to the very largest issues of social and economic and ethical importance. And the cross-ruff between the academic and the practical players goes on constantly. Men shift from one kind of work to another, from one role to another; and the American law professor is as familiar to the Wall Street lawyer and vice versa as the English solicitor is to the English barrister. Together the professor and the lawyer, often with the aid of the economist, sit at conferences, sometimes for an immediate end, more frequently for the restatement of legal principles to guide a whole area, or even international relations.

This altered structure of the law as a calling has made it a far more philosophical enterprise. Value is not merely, as it always has been, inherent in the process. It is at the forefront of explicit considerations. This is underlined in each number of every law review.

From these declarations, of course, no table of values good *semper ubique* emerges. None would claim that now we know what is the good life which Plato sought. All we can say is that when men are overt in their search for value, when they enlarge the space they accord to reason, then there is less dissent than would have been predicted. Admittedly, in Learned Hand's phrase, some still prefer pearls, and others rubies. But if you can prove that pearls are more easily imitated, discolor faster, and need to be worn or lose their luster, there will be some who change their minds. Oh, of course, not at once. Was it not Morris R. Cohen who advised us that you should never try in an argument to make your opponent change his view forthwith? What

should be your aim is to have him on the *next* occasion
when he discusses the subject adopt some of your contentions as though they were his.

It is in that spirit that I submit the following pieces.
They have a few usable points, not sharp enough to be
quotable or even traceable. Take what there is; burnish it;
and grip it in your own hilt!

CHARLES E. WYZANSKI, JR.

Cambridge, Massachusetts
October 2, 1964

Contents

I

Judges and Judgment

A Trial Judge

I SUPPOSE that the first thing that a district judge tries to learn but never succeeds in learning is not to talk too much from the bench. The reason that most of us chatter so much is not because we suppose ourselves more competent than counsel. We fear that we shall go to sleep on the bench. We can hardly parade up and down our platforms like professors. How are we to keep our attention through the long morning and afternoon unless we have some form of physical exercise? But when I have been more tempted than usual to yield to the passion for interruption, I have had typed and put in front of me an old English story. A barrister was arguing before Mr. Justice Wills, the distinguished judge of the King's Bench and the son of the even more distinguished Chief Baron of the Exchequer. The Lord Justice constantly plagued counsel with questions. Finally the lawyer leaned forward and said, "Your Lordship is an even greater man than your father. The Chief Baron used to understand me after I had done, but your lordship understands me before I begin." Patience may not be the judge's greatest virtue but it is his most seemly.

Perhaps you think that the most revealing thing I could say would be to describe how I come to write my opinions. But frankly I doubt whether the job of a trial judge in connection with opinion-writing is as important as his job in

connection with presiding at a trial. When I was Judge A.
N. Hand's law clerk he used to say that a decent trial judge
ought to be affirmed about two-thirds of the time, and I am
sure that the judge of average intelligence and wisdom can
write opinions which will stand up on review in the overwhelming majority of cases. A high percentage of cases are
of a routine nature. In those which present real difficulties I
have no doubt that many judges do what I do — write
opinions two different ways and find which sticks the better. But the task of writing opinions is as nothing compared
with the duty of so conducting a trial, particularly a jury
trial, that the jurors, the parties, the witnesses, the counsel,
and the spectators not only follow the red threads of fact
and of law but leave the courtroom persuaded of the fairness of the procedure and the high responsibility of courts
of justice in advancing the values we cherish most deeply. A
judge who succeeds in that endeavor even half the time is an
extraordinarily good man. For in this aspect of his work the
judge is to be measured in comparison with the success of
the teacher with his students or the parent with his child.
Good as the instruction may be, there are so many intangi-
bles and imponderables that no one is ever entirely satisfied
that his performance merits more than a passing grade.

But I have always been willing to experiment. I read with
interest what that prolific appellate judge and Yale Law
School Professor Jerome Frank wrote about means of controlling juries in their determinations of fact. Obedient to
his proposals, I have tried on occasion to put before a jury
not a general verdict but a special verdict. When the matter
turns on technical problems of contract or commercial law
and when I have really understood the case, which is not so
often as I should like, I have found the special verdict of
some value in preventing the jury from exaggerating or
minimizing claims. But a special verdict often leaves lacunae

which a judge must fill. And this produces a hybrid and often curious result even in commercial cases. In ordinary tort litigation it is most ineffective. After all, there are certain types of controversy in which, as Pascal said, "The heart has reasons of which the reason knows not." And it is not necessarily undesirable to allow twelve men representing different points of view and different biases to come to a collective judgment pretty much unrestrained by the permanent official who is called a judge. This is true at least in those cases where the jury's experience is as extensive and as diverse as the judge's.

Perhaps you would like me to say something about different types of litigation. You may be surprised when I report to you that of the run-of-the-mill cases, the kind I like best are tax cases and patent cases. Tax cases are like law review work and you will readily understand that choice. About patent cases I must give an explanation. Perhaps it is because the patent bar, being small, carries on best the tradition of the eighteenth and early nineteenth centuries, a tradition of courtesy, thorough preparation, and free exchange of information before trial. But there may be a deeper reason why patent cases are so satisfactory to try. The patent lawyer understands better than most of us that the mystery of the universe lies in the detail. And to make his lesson clearer the patent lawyer gives me the benefit of the instruction of the topnotch professors from the finest technological institutes.

Leaving aside the run-of-the-mill cases, let me talk in the most discreet fashion about long and short cases, or big and small cases. Every week now somebody tells me how much he sympathizes with me for being caught in so long a litigation as my present antitrust proceeding where the United States has brought suit against the United Shoe Machinery Corporation. How little my commiserator appreciates what is truly wearisome and what is truly delightful in the work of the trial court! For what irks a trial judge most in this modern statutory, CCH service era is to feel himself operating in a very narrow area where all he can do is to define as best he can the words and the purpose of a statute or of an administrative regulation. As Learned Hand has observed, in such controversies the judge seeks to find, *and not to alter*, the compromise upon which competing interests have elsewhere agreed. But in antitrust matters the trial judge is given again as broad a scope as was enjoyed by the ancient judges who formed the law of tort and those who made the criminal law before the Victorian era. Congress in the widest-sweeping strokes has sketched a grant of almost unlimited authority to the federal courts. And in great cases such as that that I am now trying, the whole field of justice, of economics, of creative thought unfolds itself in daily panorama. Shall I interpret the antitrust laws in the sense of Lord Acton that all power corrupts and absolute power corrupts absolutely? Or shall I follow Ralph Waldo Emerson and say that when a corporation builds the best mousetrap in the world, the world will flock to that source regardless of competition? Shall I agree with Professor Schumpeter that invention is common but innovation is rare and that the great task of a democratic society is to further the heroes of the entrepreneur class who make possible industrial laboratories, or shall I go along with ex-professor, ex-judge Thurman Arnold in believing that modern industrial laboratories are successful merely in devising new gadgets and that fundamental invention and innovation come from the untrained, unfinanced outsider? How far is the creative process as described by Hadamard, the mathematician, or Graham Wallas, the political scientist, or Beveridge, the animal pathologist, characteristic of creative advance in the industrial world? These are the types of problems which no man of intellectual curiosity can say are of less than the first magnitude. They go far to explain why William Howard Taft, after having been Solicitor General, a state trial judge, a federal lower court judge, Governor of the Philippines, Secretary of War, President of the United States, and Chief Justice of the Supreme Court, said that there was no job in the world as satisfying as that of being a federal trial judge. There, he thought, a man's character, courage, and resourcefulness were subject to daily test against a variety of tasks without equal in the Anglo-American world.

And then the big case presents to the judge the constant challenge of technical dexterity. What can he do to bring the case within reasonable compass and make it understandable not only to himself in the first instance but to the appellate court and to the general public whose judgment is the one that finally counts? How far shall he force the parties to reduce the multitude of their exhibits? What rules shall he lay down for sampling evidence, rules that not merely will accomplish expedition but will satisfy the scientific canons worked out by statisticians in many fields? How far may he call to his assistance in or out of court in person or by literary proxy men with economic or other specialized training?

But you may ask, have I fairly summarized the work of the district judge? Looking at the reports of the Administrative Office on the flow of business to the district courts, don't I have to admit that much of the litigation is stale bread? To be sure, in any calling, even that of member of the Cabinet or president of a university, as Mr. Eliot long ago admitted, a substantial part of all that comes to one's desk is routine, ephemeral, and in one sense dull. But even the dryest crusts may be given an eternal worth if their sacramental value is understood. And the calling of a judge, more than most professional opportunities, gives one a chance to see the enduring significance of each aspect of the pattern of our society.

For the law is more than a historical review of the sediment deposited by the generations that have come before. The law is the instrument by which we keep the avenues open to the adventurous ideas that lie ahead. The technique of the lawyer is the indispensable skill by which the sovereignty of war has been reduced and the area of peace has been extended. It is the channel through which economic assistance has been furnished to the needy here and abroad. It is the constant teacher of the importance of giving form and style to ideas of right. It teaches more effectively than philosophy itself that process is the only reality, that the procedures of the past, the present, and the future are the ways in which our substantive ideals come to realization. But above all, law and the judicial function teach the moral responsibility of man. In his unforgettable words about authority and the individual in Greek civilization, Professor Werner Jaeger told us that the distinguishing characteristic of Greek thought was that it recognized that the ultimate authority did not repose in institutions but in men, and that the poets and the philosophers of ancient Athens were the enduring embodiments of the Greek spirit. Is it a fanciful notion, an extravagant example of self-praise for us to suppose that in the manners and habits of our age and our country it is given to the lawyers and to the judges as it was given in Athens to the poets and the philosophers to be the spokesmen of the fundamental values of the community?

Yale Law Journal, 1951

A Trial Judge's Freedom
and Responsibility

THE ethical test of a judge is not whether his judgments run parallel to the judgments of a moralist, but whether the judge administers his office true to its traditional limitations as well as to its aspirations. From the day he takes his seat he is aware that while he has more personal discretion than the books reveal, he is hemmed in by impersonal usages, canons, and legitimate expectations. While he has choice, he cannot exercise it even to his own satisfaction unless it is disciplined according to standards. The minima are supplied by reversals administered by appellate courts. Those, however, are necessarily negative in nature. What counts more is the establishment of affirmative norms of judicial behavior. One man knows the practices of his own and perhaps a few other courts; so, to evolve standards, he must become critical of his own shortcomings, attentive to the reactions of the bar, informed of the unrecorded practices of his colleagues, and, above all, reflective about subtle differences in the tasks assigned to him.

The trial judge's first problem is his relationship to the jury. Much of the debate about the jury system rests on political premises as old as the eighteenth century. Montesquieu, Blackstone, and their followers contended that lay tribunals with a plurality of members were the safeguard of liberty. Bentham and more modern reformers replied that when the rule of law itself is sound, its integrity requires that its application be entrusted to magistrates acting alone. In their view, responsibility is the secret of integrity, and a reasoned choice is the secret of responsibility.

Experience will not give a sovereign answer to these warring contentions. Yet the disagreement can be narrowed if the question of the jury's utility is subdivided with specific emphasis on separate types of suits.

The importance of this subdivision is concealed by Chief Justice Hughes's striking phrase that a federal judge is the "governor of the trial." Some regard this as an implied acceptance of the practice of English courts. They construe it as a broad invitation to exercise in all types of cases a right to comment upon the evidence, provided of course that the judge reminds the jury in his charge that they are not bound to follow the court's view of the facts or the credibility of the witnesses.

Such boldness is not the surest way to end disputes in defamation cases. In 1944 a discharged OPA official brought a libel suit against the radio commentator Fulton Lewis, Jr. At one stage in the examination I suggested that Mr. Lewis's counsel was throwing pepper in the eyes of the jury; and at the final summation I indicated plainly that, although the jury was free to reject my opinion, I thought Mr. Lewis had been reckless in his calumnious charges against the ex-OPA official. It makes no difference whether what I said was true; I should not have said it, as the reaction of the bar and public reminded me. A political libel suit is the modern equivalent of ordeal by battle. It is the means which society has chosen to induce bitter partisans to wager money instead of exchanging bloody noses. And in such a contest the prudent and the second-thinking judge will stand severely aside, and will act merely as a referee applying the Marquis of Queensberry rules.

Later a libel suit was brought by James Michael Curley against the publisher of the *Saturday Evening Post* because the *Post* had said that Mr. Curley was a Catholic of whom His Eminence Cardinal O'Connell would have no part. Who knew better than the Cardinal whether that charge was true? Mr. Curley, the plaintiff, did not call the Cardinal to the stand. The defendant's distinguished counsel did not desire to find out what would be the effect upon a Greater Boston jury if a Protestant lawyer should call a Catholic prelate to the witness stand. Should the court have intervened and summoned the Cardinal on its own initiative? The Fulton Lewis case gave the answer. In a political libel suit the judge is not the commander but merely the umpire.

Those cases which involve sordid family disputes also are better left to the jury without too explicit instructions. Plato implied and Holmes explicitly stated that judges are apt to be naïve men. If judges seem to comment on the morality of conduct or the extent of damages, they may discover that the jurors regard their own knowledge as superior to the judge's. At any rate when brother sues brother or when spouse sues paramour, the very anonymity of the jury's judgment often does more than the most clearly reasoned opinion or charge of an identified judge could have done to still the controversy.

What of the trial judge's role in accident cases? How far should he go in requiring available evidence to be produced, in commenting on the testimony, and in using special verdicts and like devices to seek to keep the jury within the precise bounds laid down by the appellate courts?

There are some who say that the trial judge has not fulfilled his moral obligation if he merely states clearly the law regarding negligence, causation, contributory fault, and types of recoverable damage. In their opinion it is his duty to analyze the evidence and demonstrate where the evidence seems strong or thin and where it appears reliable or untrustworthy.

Most federal judges do not make such analyses. They are not deterred through laziness, a sentimental regard for the afflatus of the Seventh Amendment, or even a fear of reversal. They are mindful that the community no longer accepts as completely valid legal principles basing liability upon fault. They perceive a general recognition of the inevitability of numerous accidents in modern life, which has made insurance widely available and widely used. Workmen's compensation acts and other social and economic legislation have revealed a trend that did not exist when the common-law doctrines of tort were formulated. And the judges sense a new climate of public opinion which rates security as one of the chief goals of men.

Trial judges cannot, without violating their oaths, bow directly to this altered policy. In instructions of law they must repeat the doctrines which judges of superior courts formulated and which only they or the legislatures can change. But trial judges are not giving "rein to the passional element of our nature" or forswearing themselves by following Lord Coke's maxim that "the jurors are chancellors." Traditionally juries are the device by which the rigor of the law is modified pending the enactment of new statutes.

Some will say that this abdication is not merely cowardly but ignores the "French saying about small reforms being the worst enemies of great reforms." To them the proper course would be to apply the ancient rules with full rigidity. They foresee that adverse reactions would then lead to a complete resurvey of accident law; to a scrutiny of the costs, delays, and burdens of present litigation; to a comparative study of what injured persons actually get in cash as a result of lawsuits, settlements out of court, administrative compensation proceedings, and other types of insurance plans; and ultimately to a new codification. To this, one answer is that in Anglo-American legal history reform has rarely come as a result of prompt, comprehensive investigation and legislation. The usual course has been by resort to fictions, to compromises with logic, to juries. Only at the last stages are outright changes in the formal rules announced by the legislators or the appellate judges. This is consistent with Burke's principle that "reform is impracticable in the sense of an abrupt reconstruction of society, and can only be understood as the gradual modification of a complex structure."

I am not at all certain that it would be a desirable reform in those personal injury controversies, known as tort cases, to substitute trial by judges for trial by juries. Just such a substitution has been made in the Federal Tort Claims Act. And experience under that statute does not prove that in this type of case a single professional is as satisfactory a tribunal as a group of laymen of mixed backgrounds. In estimating how a reasonable and prudent man would act, judges' court experience counts for no more than juries' out-of-court experience. In determining the credibility of the type of witness that appears in accident cases an expert tribunal is somewhat too ready to see a familiar pattern. Shrewdness founded on skepticism and sophistication has its place in scrutinizing the stories of witnesses. But there is a danger that the professional trier of fact will expect people of varied callings and cultures to reach levels of observation and narration which would not be expected by men of the witness's own background. Moreover, when it comes to a calculation of damages under the flexible rules of tort law the estimate of what loss the plaintiff suffered can best be made by men who know different standards of working and living in our society. Indeed, I have heard federal judges confess that in a Federal Tort Claims case they try to make their judgments correspond with what they believe a jury would do in a private case. And many judges would prefer to have such cases tried by juries.

In commercial cases and those arising under regulatory statutes there is reason to hold a jury by a much tighter rein than in tort cases. This is not because the rules of law are more consonant with prevailing notions of justice. In these controversies judges have a specialized knowledge. Parties have usually acted with specific reference to their legal rights. Departures from the declared standard would undermine the legislative declaration and would be less likely to produce reform than confusion and further litigation.

An extreme example will serve as an illustration. In a tax case tried before a jury at the suit of one holder of International Match Company preference stock, the issue was whether for tax purposes those certificates had become worthless in the year 1936. In another taxpayer's case the Second Circuit Court of Appeals had affirmed a ruling of the Board of Tax Appeals that similar stock had become valueless in the year 1932. Technically this adjudication did not bind the jury, though the evidence before it was substantially the same as that in the earlier case. To preserve uniformity on a factual tax problem of general application I had no hesitation in strongly intimating to the jury that they should reach the same result as the Second Circuit.

In sales cases something close to a scientific appraisal of the facts is possible; there are strong mercantile interests favoring certainty; and future litigation can be reduced by strict adherence to carefully prescribed statutory standards. These considerations sometimes warrant giving juries written instructions or summaries and often justify the use of special verdicts. Either method makes jurors focus precisely on the formalities of the contract, the warranties claimed to

have been broken, the types of damage alleged to have been sustained, and the allowable formulae for calculating those damages.

Indeed, except for tort cases, I find myself in agreement with Judge Frank that the trial judge ought to use special verdicts to a much larger extent, though it is more difficult than may at first be realized to frame questions to the satisfaction of counsel and to the comprehension of juries. Once when I used what I thought simple questions, a fellow judge, half in jest, accused me of trying to promote a disagreement of the jury and thus to force a settlement.

The arguments supporting special verdicts in commercial or statutory cases also support a trial judge in giving such cases a more detailed charge and more specific guidance in estimating the testimony. In complicated cases or those in fields where the experience of the average juror is much less than that of the average judge, there is a substantial risk of a miscarriage of justice unless the judge points rather plainly to the "knots" in the evidence and suggests how they can be unraveled. The only time I have ever entered judgment notwithstanding a verdict was in a private antitrust suit. The jury had awarded damages of over one million dollars as a result, I believe, of the generality of my instructions.

So far I have said nothing of federal criminal cases. About ninety per cent of all defendants in the federal court plead guilty. In those federal cases which come to trial the crime charged frequently concerns economic facts; and generally, though not invariably, the preliminary investigation by the FBI and other agencies of detection has reduced to a small compass the area of doubt. Often the only remaining substantive issue of significance is whether the defendant acted "knowingly." Indeed, the usual federal criminal trial is as apt to turn on whether the prosecution has procured its evidence in accordance with law and is presenting it fairly, as on whether the defendant is guilty as charged. All these factors combine to concentrate the judge's attention upon the avoidance of prejudicial inquiries, confusion of proof, and inflammatory arguments. Counsel can aid the judge to maintain the proper atmosphere by stipulation, by refraining from putting doubtful questions until the judge has ruled at the bench, and by other cooperative efforts. But if cooperation is not forthcoming, the judge should hesitate to fill the gap by becoming himself a participant in the interrogation and should not indicate his view of the evidence. For the criminal trial is as much a ceremony as an investigation. Dignity and forbearance are almost the chief desiderata.

I turn now to the freedom of the trial judge when he sits without a jury. In nonjury as in jury cases, a substantial part of the bar prefers to have the judge sit patiently while the evidence comes in and then at the end of the trial summarize the testimony. This seems the sounder practice in the great bulk of trials. But in cases of public significance, Edmund Burke admonished us: "It is the duty of the Judge to receive every offer of evidence, apparently material, suggested to him, though the parties themselves through negligence, ignorance, or corrupt collusion, should not bring it forward. A Judge is not placed in that high situation merely as a passive instrument of parties. He has a duty of his own, independent of them, and that duty is to investigate the truth. . . ."

Let me give some examples of when I believe the judge has a duty to elicit facts in addition to those that are offered by the parties. The plaintiff, an owner of a multiple dwelling, brought suit for a declaratory judgment seeking to have the premises declared a "hotel" and thus exempt from the rent regulations of the OPA. Only one of the numerous tenants was named as defendant. In the trial the plaintiff

offered evidence that showed the building was a hotel and not an apartment. Because of lack of funds or of forensic skill, the tenant's counsel failed to shake the stories of the plaintiff's witnesses or to offer adequate testimony to the contrary. Yet if the trial judge had called specialists and others familiar with the community and the property, the evidence would have demonstrated that in truth the building was a mere apartment house. I took no step myself to call witnesses or to interrogate those who did testify but, relying exclusively on what the parties offered, entered a judgment declaring the premises a "hotel" and thus exempt. Since this declaration of status became in effect a general rule binding on scores of persons not represented in the proceedings, would it not have been sounder if the court had taken a larger initiative in seeing that the record corresponded with reality?

A later controversy of even greater public importance posed a similar problem. The United States sued the United Shoe Machinery Corporation for violation of the antitrust laws. Among the issues that were presented was the effect of the corporation's acts upon its customers and its competitors. The government in its case relied exclusively on the corporation's documents and officers. The corporation planned to call some customers, though the method by which they were drawn was not disclosed to the court. This seemed an inadequate survey. So the court asked the parties to take depositions from forty-five customers, selected from a standard directory by taking the first fifteen names under the first, eleventh, and twenty-first letters of the alphabet; and the court itself called to the stand the officers of the principal competitor. In the summons the court listed topics appropriate for questioning the officers. The actual examination was conducted in turn by the competitor's counsel, the government's counsel, and the defendant's counsel. Both these types of testimony give a much clearer understanding of the total picture of the industries that will be affected by any decision.

Another problem in the United Shoe case has been to determine what have been the usual methods followed by the defendant in setting prices, in supplying services, and in suing competitors. An adequately grounded conclusion can hardly be based entirely on the plaintiff's selection of a few dramatic incidents and on the defendant's testimony of the general attitude of its officers. The critical point in determining liability and the form of relief may turn on what has been the typical pattern of the defendant's conduct and the typical effect of that conduct on outsiders. Here the judge can perform a useful function if he, through pre-trial conferences or at a later stage of the litigation when he is more aware of its dimensions, provides for appropriate samplings of the conduct and the effects. If the judge is fortunate, the parties may agree on the sampling. But where they do not, it seems to me to be the judge's responsibility first to elicit from witnesses on the stand the criteria necessary to determine what are fair samples and then to direct the parties to prepare such samples for examination and cross-examination. Sampling will make the record not merely more informative but shorter.

The question as to what has been the custom of the market and what would be the consequence of a judicial decree altering those practices arises not only in antitrust cases but also when the judge is faced with the problem of determining either the appropriate standard of fair competition in trademarks or the appropriate standard for fiduciaries. Usually, to be sure, diligent counsel offer in evidence enough relevant material. But where this has not been done, there have been times when a judge has tended to reach his result

partly on the basis of general information and partly on the basis of his studies in a library.

This tendency of a court to inform itself has increased in recent years following the lead of the Supreme Court of the United States. Not merely in constitutional controversies and in statutory interpretation but also in formulation of judge-made rules of law, the justices have resorted, in footnotes and elsewhere, to references drawn from legislative hearings, studies by executive departments, and scholarly monographs. Such resort is sometimes defended as an extension of Mr. Brandeis's technique in *Muller* v. *Oregon*. In Muller's case, however, Mr. Brandeis's object was to demonstrate that there was a body of informed public opinion which supported the reasonableness of the *legislative* rule of law. But in the cases of which I am speaking these extrajudicial studies are drawn upon to determine what would be a reasonable *judicial* rule of law. Thus the focus of the inquiry becomes not what judgment is permissible, but what judgment is sound. And here it seems to me that the judge, before deriving conclusions from any such extrajudicial document or information, should lay it before the parties for their criticism.

How this criticism should be offered is itself a problem not free from difficulty. In some situations the better course may be to submit the material for examination, cross-examination, and rebuttal evidence. In others, where expert criticism has primarily an argumentative character, it can be received better from the counsel table and from briefs than from the witness box. The important point is that, before a judge acts upon a consideration of any kind, he ought to give the parties a chance to meet it. This opportunity is owed as a matter of fairness and also to prevent egregious error. As Professor Lon Fuller observed, the "moral force of a judgment is at maximum if a judge decides solely on the basis of arguments presented to him. Because if he goes beyond these he will lack guidance and may not understand interests that are affected by a decision outside the framework."

The duty of the judge to act only on the basis of material debated in public in no sense implies that the judge's findings should be in the precise terms offered by counsel. Nor does Rule 52(a) of the Federal Rules of Civil Procedure require the judge always to recite all relevant evidence and to rely for persuasive effect exclusively upon mass and orderly arrangement. Yet in corporate cases or other litigation where the issues turn on documentary analysis and precise analysis of business details, and where appeal is almost certain to be taken, the trial judge may perform the greatest service by acting almost as a master summarizing evidence for a higher tribunal.

On the other hand, if a judge sitting alone hears a simple tort or contract case falling within a familiar framework and analogous to jury litigation, it is perhaps the best practice for him to state his findings of fact from the bench in those pungent colloquial terms with which the traditional English judge addresses the average man of common sense. When credibility of witnesses is the essence of the controversy, the parties and the lawyers like to have judges act as promptly as juries and on the basis of fresh impressions.

Where the search for truth is more subtle, the trial court faces the same stylistic challenge as the appellate court. Fortunate are those who, like Judge Learned Hand, have the gift of many tongues. His admiralty opinions breathe salt air, his commercial cases echo the accents of the marketplace, and his patent rulings reflect an industrial society developed by Yankee ingenuity. Even those whose narrower experience makes them stutter, occasionally strike a subject where they have both the sensitivity and the self-confidence to put the story simply and selectively. But in most cases we average judges can only try, without much hope, to make our summations of facts pithy, sympathetic, and illuminating.

While, in summarizing the facts, we trial judges may seek to imitate our superiors on the higher courts, when we wrestle with the substantive law we should not regard ourselves as the appellate judges writ small. Our freedom is inevitably more narrowly exercised. Most of the time we do not see the points of difficulty too clearly. With us the pace is quicker, the troublesome issues have not been sorted from those which go by rote, the briefs of counsel have not reached their ultimate perfection. Yet even when we have the clearest perception of the legal issues, certain inhibitions are peculiarly appropriate to restrain a judge who sits alone and subject to review by judges higher in commission.

If the trial judge is presented with the claim that a legislative act is unconstitutional, he ought to remind himself that every possible presumption is in favor of the validity of the legislation and that in certain constitutional controversies a district judge has no jurisdiction to act unless he is sitting with two other judges. Though in a constitutional case or any other case he must not surrender his deliberate judgment and automatically accept the views of others, he can ordinarily best fulfill his duty in a constitutional case by explicitly stating for the benefit of an appellate court any doubts he has, without going so far as to enter a decree against a statute which has commanded the assent of a majority of the legislature and, generally, of the executive.

If there is no constitutional question and the trial judge is presented with a judicial precedent or precedents contrary to his own view of what would be the sound rule of law, the problem is more subtle. First, take the situation where the hostile precedents are in the tribunals that sit on review of his own decisions. If the precedents have been so severely impaired by recent cases that it is reasonably clear they no longer represent the present doctrine of the appellate court, the trial judge is generally thought to be free to minimize their directive force, though there is strong opinion to the contrary. Where the precedent has not been impaired, the balance is in favor of the trial judge following it in his decree and respectfully stating in his accompanying opinion such reservations as he has. The entry of the decree preserves the "priority and place" which Shakespeare reminds us are indispensable to justice. Moreover, the reservation in the opinion promotes the growth of the law in the court where it most counts, for if the criticism of the precedent be just, the appellate court will set matters straight, and any trial judge worthy of his salt will feel complimented in being reversed on a ground he himself suggested. No trial judge of any sense supposes his quality is measured by a naked tabulation of affirmances and reversals.

Where the hostile precedents come from a judge of equal rank or a court not in the direct line of superior authority, I doubt whether there should be absolute rules of deference. If the precedent is from a sitting judge in one's own court and represents his mature reflection, the argument in favor of following it rests not only on the appropriate amenities, but also on profounder considerations of equality in the treatment of litigants. But the situation is different where the precedent comes from an inferior court sitting in another geographical area. In the federal system conflict of judgments between the inferior courts is one of the ways that the Supreme Court is led to grant review of legal questions. And the most effective method of getting a significant issue over the Washington threshold is to challenge overtly a court in another circuit.

We federal judges are told that in diversity jurisdiction cases our duty is to follow the state law. Most of the time that is readily discoverable. But what are we to do when no state law has been declared, or the state law has not been the subject of reconsideration for a generation or more? Take unfair competition cases, at least before the Lanham Act. Until the end of the rule of *Swift* v. *Tyson* the state law lay relatively dormant. Most of the important controversies in this field had always been adjudicated in the federal courts according to a general jurisprudence. What happens when these federal cases are not binding authorities? Shall we seek to evolve the state rules exclusively from state precedents, some of which are quite old, and ignore the federal precedents?

Shall we be equally conservative in corporation cases? A short time ago a policyholder brought a derivative suit in the United States District Court for the District of Massachusetts against an insurance company without first seeking to enlist the aid of his fellow policyholders. The reported Massachusetts cases involved stockholders' suits. None of them was precisely in point. Some of the rulings were not addressed to considerations recently stressed by other courts and by legislatures and administrative agencies. Should the federal court follow closely what the state has already said, or should it keep one eye on the national trend? Or look at the case of a stockholder seeking to procure an equity receivership for the purpose of liquidating a corporation. The only Massachusetts decisions are old and negative. The modern trend is favorable. Shall the federal court assume that the Massachusetts state court will follow its predecessors or its contemporaries?

The impression that I gather from the cases is that a federal judge sitting in a diversity jurisdiction case is less willing to depart from obsolete doctrines than when he sits in a purely federal case. Every time judges are called upon to apply the law of a foreign jurisdiction, are they not inclined to give undue weight to the recorded landmarks and to underestimate the mobile qualities and the thrusts of principle we discern in our domestic law?

And now, before I conclude, may I address myself to a doubt which should perhaps have been tackled at the outset. Are the usages followed by trial judges more than patterns of behavior; are they law in any sense; and even if they are law, are they too disparate and detailed ever to have an honored place in the study of jurisprudence?

Concede that the normative practices which we have been reviewing fall far short of the Austinian command of the sovereign. For a judge who chooses to depart from these particular standards does not lay himself open to reversal by courts of superior authority. And yet that which is generally approved as being good and being within the reach of average men does in time become law in the strictest sense. This, we all know, is how the law of fiduciaries and the law merchant have grown. And the principle applies in equal measure to the law governing trial judges. What is the whole law of procedure but the crystallization of judicial custom? The trial judges made the law of evidence by their usages; and perhaps now they are unmaking it by their usages. The revocation is hidden by appellate courts which treat departures from the proclaimed evidentiary rules not as though they represented new doctrine, but as though they were insignificant nonreversible errors.

What are the rules governing measure of proof? Today we say there exist in the federal courts only two standards: the criminal standard of proof beyond a reasonable doubt and the civil standard of the preponderance of the evidence. And yet already in some special classes of cases where fraud is the central issue, we seem to see the emergence of an intermediate rule, the requirement that the evidence shall be clear and convincing. This intermediate requirement reflects the unspoken practice of trial courts to move with extreme caution in fastening a finding of immoral conduct upon a party litigant.

What shall we say of remedies which trial judges have newly evolved in equitable suits founded on statutes? Novel remedies begin as permissible exercises of discretion by the court of first instance. They win approval and imitation by other similarly circumstanced courts. And in the end what was discretionary has become mandatory. Here is the common law at work — a progressive contribution by the judges, trial as well as appellate; less important perhaps today than formerly, and always less important than the additions made by legislative bodies; but more clearly ethical in its nature because the consent on which it rests has undergone a longer, more intimate, more pragmatic test.

Let us not suppose that because our jurisdiction is limited, because so much of our work goes unreported, because we are immersed in the detail of fact, we trial judges are clothed with small responsibility in relating law to justice. It is we who make the law become a living teacher as we transmit it from the legislature and the appellate court to the citizen who stands before us. It is we who watch the impact of the formal rule, explain its purpose to laymen, and seek to make its application conform to the durable and reasonable expectations of our communities. It is we who determine whether the processes of common-law growth shall decay or flower with a new vigor.

From the *Atlantic Monthly*, 1952

The Democracy of
Justice Oliver Wendell Holmes

IN planning this series of lectures there were selected as the
five exponents of American democracy four Presidents
of the United States — Thomas Jefferson, Abraham Lincoln, Woodrow Wilson and Franklin D. Roosevelt — and
one judge — Oliver Wendell Holmes. Why was a judge,
even if he be the only one who can claim an influence on
law, an effect on political theory and a world respect that
match Chief Justice John Marshall's, bracketed with four
heads of state as a representative of the fundamental creed
of our society?

To be sure, Holmes is everywhere recognized as a great
American. His life story has been depicted on the stage, in-
vestigated and popularized in biographies, and majestically
summarized in the *Dictionary of American Biography* by
his successor and disciple. Every undergraduate knows of
Holmes's wounds in three Civil War battles, his seminal lectures on *The Common Law* delivered at the Lowell Institute, his pioneer decisions in labor cases in the Supreme Judicial Court of Massachusetts, and his long and distinguished
tenure as Associate Justice of the Supreme Court of the
United States. But it is not the recital of his public offices
that brings Holmes to the level of the other four statesmen
in this series. Unlike them, he was not in title or in fact the
commander-in-chief of his own generation. He sought the

joy of the thinker "who knows that . . . men who never heard of him will be moving to the measure of his thought — the subtile rapture of a postponed power, which . . . is more real than that which commands an army."

And tonight, instead of reviewing with you the details of his biography or analyzing the precise contours of the cases he decided, I propose to concentrate on the democratic ideas which Mr. Justice Holmes embodies in three fields — the powers of popular government, the civil liberties of the citizen, and the dignity of man. These will be admittedly mere strands plucked from a pattern. I should not want anyone to suppose that I am attempting an essay on the man as a whole. All I seek is to assay certain of his ideas which, though they will be, nay have been, to some extent superseded, seem to me to have eternal relevance to democracy and therefore to be of constant interest to every American.

I come first to Mr. Justice Holmes's views of the powers of popular government. Etymologically this clearly belongs at the forefront of any discussion of democracy. For from the Greek days when the word was coined, democracy has at the least embraced the idea of that form of state in which the people as a whole share public authority.

In the United States "democracy" has sometimes been defined with its original literal significance — the classic example being the triad in Lincoln's Gettysburg Address. Yet during the first century of the history of the United States, the actual role of the people diverged from that in a Greek democracy.

Our orthodox eighteenth- and nineteenth-century view of popular government turned for philosophical justification not to Plato or Aristotle but to Locke and Montesquieu, and for practical techniques not to the colonies on the eastern Aegean founded by Athens but to those on the western Atlantic founded by England. The essence of the

traditional American theory is that democratic government
is limited in its methods and its objects, that the division of
powers amongst the executive, legislative, and judicial
branches is the core of Anglo-American liberty, that the
federal balance between the nation and the states is the secret of strength without tyranny and self-government
without provincialism, that the people express their wisdom
not in determining policies but in choosing representatives,
and that the maximum goal of the state is to prevent force
or fraud from interfering with the self-development of the
individual man.

Whether this theory be labeled constitutionalism or the
system of checks and balances or representative government or laissez-faire, it is the one set forth in most high-
school courses in civics. It is the picture of American government drawn by such serene and sophisticated observers
as the omniscient historian Lord Acton and the knowledge-
able ambassador Lord Bryce. More important, it was the
view of popular government which nineteenth-century
Justices of the Supreme Court proclaimed not only from
the bench but also from the platform, as the published lectures of Justices Miller, Brewer and Harland reveal.

How far did Holmes subscribe to the same theory?

Before I try to answer the main question I must not avoid
a preliminary hurdle. Does a judge in his official capacity
ever have a theory of government, or — to put it less in
psychological terms and more in philosophical form —
should a judge in his official capacity have a theory of government?

No informed observer supposes that a judge is a variety
of impersonal calculating machine who merely applies the
law. He does not automatically render an answer mechani-
cally derived from learning, first, the facts from the litigants
and, second, rules of law from books in a library. His judg-

ments are not predictable by lawyers as eclipses are predictable by astronomers. He does not, Mr. Justice Roberts to the contrary notwithstanding, decide a case by laying the text of a statute against the text of the Constitution to see whether it squares. Every constitutional judge to some degree, and self-conscious judges like Holmes to a large degree, apply in their judgments the policies which they believe represent the sober second thought of the community and are suited to its inarticulate needs. Of course, I have not meant to indicate that a judge is always free to rule according to his discernment of the long-term public interest. The area of his freedom is limited — perhaps the boundaries have never been better described than by Judge Cardozo in *The Nature of the Judicial Process* — but nonetheless, as the multitude of dissents in the Supreme Court have incontrovertibly proved to our citizenry, there are some cases where there is an area of choice and, when he is within it, the judge consciously or unconsciously reveals his theory of government. Even an abstention from decision is a revelation of choice — a choice to entrust power to other hands more competent, more flexible, or more responsive to popular will.

Before Holmes came to the Court, and during most of his tenure, the majority of the Justices were enforcing with full vigor and without abdicating much to the judgment of others what I have called the orthodox theory of American democracy. The majority held that the national government was severely circumscribed in its fields of interest. It had no right without an amendment to the Constitution to lay an income tax on individuals, or to prevent the shipment in interstate commerce of child-made goods, or to control monopolistic practices in manufacturing industries. The majority also held that both the national and the local governments must move warily where they trench on property rights. They could not in time of peace fix minimum wages or regulate maximum prices or preclude an employer from discriminating against union labor. And courts, if they were to be faithful to the Anglo-American tradition, must not allow the legislature to give administrative agencies a judicial power to find the ultimate facts in controversy and to enunciate and apply the governing rules of law.

The familiar decisions to which I have somewhat elliptically referred were, it is hardly necessary to say, superficially cast in terms of legal rather than political, economic or philosophical doctrines. The judges who wrote the majority opinions purported to find their reasons in the fundamental law of the land — in the scope of the taxing power conferred on Congress by Article I §8 cl. 1 of the Constitution or in the scope of the commerce power conferred on Congress by Article I §8 cl. 3 of the Constitution or in the limits imposed by the "due process" clauses of the Fifth and Fourteenth Amendments to the Constitution or in the implications of Article III that judicial power can be reposed only in what are formally designated as courts of the United States. But there were no precise words in the text of the constitutional provisions which compelled this logic. And, as Holmes's opinions illustrated, a quite opposite course of reasoning was possible for one who started with a more enlarged view of constitutional democracy.

The starting point with Holmes was his awareness that "the provisions of the Constitution are not mathematical formulas having their essence in their form; they are organic living institutions transplanted from English soil. Their significance is vital not formal; it is to be gathered not simply by taking the words and a dictionary, but by considering their origin and the line of their growth."

Our charter of government was intended to endure for

ages and to be adaptable to a changing world and to the growth of men's experience and enlargement of their vision. It did not, as Holmes said, "enact Mr. Herbert Spencer's *Social Statics*" or for that matter Locke's *Civil Government*. The provisions of the United States Constitution are not to be read as a petrification of past practice. They are set in a context calculated to remind us of the historical forces which originated, and of the contemporary allegiances which preserve, a balance between national and state governments. They are phrased in terms not of subject matters to be regulated by government but in terms of powers available to government. This is because just as individuals use their powers to create new forms of organization and to embark on new lines of activity to serve their own interests, so the people as a whole through their government are free to create new forms of regulation and to embark on new fields of welfare with the object of keeping all groups of private interests adjusted to each other. They are couched in language of utmost generality. For the Constitution excludes from the area of permissible regulation only a few topics, and those for the most part the so-called civil liberties. And even on the excluded topics the Constitution offers less an inflexible rule of limitation than a broad counsel of moderation — a constant appeal to the only half-articulated spiritual traditions that give substance to the promise of American life.

Applying these principles in litigation where the national government and the state governments conflicted, Holmes was one of the foremost in recognizing the overriding rights of the nation. Some may see in this the deeper impact upon his mind of his services as a soldier in the Union cause than of his services as a state judge. In any event, he was alert to invalidate state tax or police action that revealed discrimination against, or even much theoretical interference with, the commerce among the several states. He said in an oft-quoted passage: "I do not think that the United States would come to an end if we lost our power to declare an Act of Congress void. I do think the Union would be imperilled if we could not make the declaration as to the laws of the several States." And as a corollary to that observation, he was more willing than most of his contemporaries to allow the national Congress to reach its regulatory arm into what were once thought to be local business concerns. His opinion in the first child labor case and his extension of the Sherman antitrust statute to cover the packers' operations will serve as illustrations.

Of perhaps greater significance as an example of Holmes's democracy was the constancy with which as a judge he voted to allow governments both local and national to experiment with novel forms of regulation, of which as a voter or legislator he might have disapproved. The Supreme Court reports are replete with his explanations of these judicial votes; perhaps the most familiar is the statement in *Truax* v. *Corrigan:* "There is nothing that I more deprecate than the use of the Fourteenth Amendment beyond the absolute compulsion of its words to prevent the making of social experiments that an important part of the community desires, in the insulated chambers afforded by the several States, even though the experiments may seem futile or even noxious to me and to those whose judgment I most respect."

The temper of that quotation explains how Holmes voted to sustain minimum wage and maximum hour legislation, state laws which imposed compulsory insurance for banking deposits, public regulations of employment contracts and many other measures which in his private correspondence the Justice would have characterized as socialistic humbug.

Holmes's willingness to tolerate change, variety and experimentation accounts for his attitude toward another facet of orthodox democratic theory. He was as familiar as any statesman with the oft-proclaimed virtues of the separation of powers, and he was aware how many interpreters of our Constitution have found these virtues enshrined not merely in certain constitutional clauses but in the very textual structure of the document — Article I dealing with the legislative power of Congress, Article II dealing with the executive power of the President, Article III dealing with the judicial power of the Courts. Yet Holmes was receptive to the needs of modern society to establish agencies of government which mingled these supposedly separate powers. He showed this in his votes in cases involving the ICC, the FTC and the government of the territories we acquired after the Spanish-American War. In many of these cases, however, he was less the pioneer than the second to Mr. Justice Brandeis, the chief judicial expositor of the most original affirmative powers of our twentieth-century democracy — administrative agencies, governmental corporations and public authorities of mixed functions.

So far we have been considering Holmes's attitude toward the affirmative aspects of popular government — the powers which may be exercised by nation and state. But in a democracy, limitations upon governmental power are equally significant. "The wise restraints that make men free" are restraints upon public authority as well as restraints upon private persons. And it is, therefore, appropriate to consider now Mr. Justice Holmes's attitude toward civil liberties.

Even before we adopted our Constitution we announced

in the Declaration of Independence our belief in the inalienable rights of man — a doctrine whose genesis has
been so admirably studied in Professor Carl Becker's famous historical monographs. And this stress upon individual rights and civil liberties was carried further in the
habeas corpus provision in the Constitution of 1789 and the
first ten amendments of 1791. The safeguards of these
amendments, as Ambassador Thomas Jefferson's letter of
March 15, 1789, to Congressman James Madison reminds
us, were inserted because of "the legal check which it puts
into the hands of the judiciary." Thus, in the Jeffersonian
and Madisonian no less than in the Hamiltonian and in
Marshall's view, the judges of our courts were specifically
authorized to invalidate such public action as was repugnant to those particular civil liberties which are guaranteed
by the Constitution.

But when Holmes ascended the bench in Washington in
1902 this authority had been sparingly exercised in the
fields which most concerned Jefferson and Madison. A
1902 catalog of cases in which civil liberties had been successfully invoked would be surprisingly short. Property
rights, to be sure, had been protected in the nineteenth
century by invoking first the "obligations of contract"
clause of Article I §10 and later the "due process" clauses
of the Fifth and Fourteenth Amendments. But what we
ordinarily embrace within the concept of civil liberties or
human rights had hardly been appreciated as constitutional
rights subject to vindication by the Courts, as is convinc-
ingly shown in Professor Commager's slender though ex-
haustive volume on *Majority Rule and Minority Rights*.
Indeed Holmes himself, applying constitutional principles
as a Massachusetts state judge, had not been disturbed at a
New Bedford police rule which denied a policeman the
right to discuss political issues or at the Boston ordinance

which denied citizens the right to make a speech on the Boston Common without a permit from the Mayor.

The twentieth century, however, brought great changes in Holmes's viewpoint and later in that of the majority of the Court.

To my mind, the most important change was not in the field of free speech, as is sometimes asserted. It was the recognition that fair procedure in criminal trials conducted in state as well as federal courts is a civil liberty so fundamental to our democracy that it is covered by the constitutional assurance of "due process." When this point was first pressed it was denied by the Supreme Court of the United States. Indeed, as recently as 1915 in *Frank* v. *Mangum*, where the defendant had been convicted by a Georgia state jury which was terrorized by a mob surrounding the courtroom, only Justices Holmes and Hughes thought that the federal Supreme Court was warranted in invoking the due-process clause or any other constitutional provision to set aside the sentence. The majority view was that so long as the state authorities outwardly followed the established form of trial the defendant could not successfully assert that his constitutional rights had been impaired by what was in substance lynch law. Today the dissent of Holmes is regarded as almost self-evident. And from Holmes's doctrine have stemmed the myriad of cases which lay down as fundamentals of our democratic system protected by the Supreme Court the right of a defendant in any criminal court in the land to a trial which is open to the public and free of outside pressure, which admits no evidence secured by torture or by third-degree methods or by perjury known to the prosecution and which assures a defendant the right to the assistance of counsel in meeting a charge of undeniable gravity. Indeed Holmes's dissents go further than the law has yet gone in precluding the conviction of defendants upon the basis of evidence which had been procured by wiretapping or other methods which he described as "dirty business."

A second and much more widely known phase of Holmes's work in the field of civil liberties concerned freedom of speech. Here his influence not only on the law but on political theory and philosophy has perhaps been unmatched by any single American, although, as I shall say in a minute, it is not clear that this country now accepts his doctrines without qualification as adequate to meet the changed circumstances of the contemporary world.

It was in the aftermath of World War I that Holmes first faced a large volume of cases in which the free-speech issue was predominant. In one of these, the *Schenck* case, he stated in a sentence now familiar to every newspaper reader: "The question in every case is whether the words used are used in such circumstances and are of such a nature as to create a clear and present danger that they will bring about the substantive evils that Congress has a right to prevent."

This is not the occasion to trace the origin of that doctrine, to show how much it owed to Holmes's youthful studies of the common law of criminal attempts and how much it owed to his reading of Milton's *Areopagitica*, to his knowledge of the history of John Adams's administration, and to his personal friendship with John Stuart Mill, Frederick W. Maitland, Sir Frederick Pollock, and Leslie Stephen. Yet without drawing that genealogical tree, we must recognize that Holmes's doctrine of the limits of free speech is the final crystallization of nineteenth-century liberalism. The doctrine is an admirably consistent series of deductions from two initial premises—that man is a reasoning animal and that, given time and space, reason will dissipate not merely error but danger as well. These deductions have captured countless readers partly because of the undeniably superb logic with which they move from the assumed premises, but even more because of the haunting poetry in which Holmes enshrined them. Let us stand in the back of the courtroom and hear him read his immortal opinion in the *Abrams* case:

. . . when men have realized that time has upset many fighting faiths, they may come to believe even more than they believe the very foundations of their own conduct that the ultimate good desired is better reached by free trade in ideas — that the best test of truth is the free trade in ideas — that the best test of truth is the power of the thought to get itself accepted in the competition of the market, and that truth is the only ground upon which their wishes safely can be carried out. That at any rate is the theory of our Constitution. It is an experiment, as all life is an experiment. Every year if not every day we have to wager our salvation upon some prophecy based upon imperfect knowledge. While that experiment is part of our system I think that we should be eternally vigilant against attempts to check the expression of opinions that we loathe and believe to be fraught with death, unless they so imminently threaten immediate interference with the lawful and pressing purpose of the law, that an immediate check is required to save the country.

Who can doubt the practical wisdom, the noble philosophy, and the enduring strength of that passage — the most eloquent in all our court reports? Does it not belong with the two great memorial speeches of the democratic tradition — the one of 431 B.C. and the other A.D. 1863?

I am not prepared to deny the implication of these questions. Yet I want to invite you before applauding to consider carefully whether you agree not with Holmes's deductions but with his premises. Is man a reasoning animal and, given time and space, will reason dissipate not merely error but danger as well?

Holmes wrote before the world had fully appreciated the wickedness of which civilized man is capable. He knew not the Nazi concentration camps, not the Goebbels propaganda for circulating the big lie, nor the Communist-disciplined subordination of man's interest in truth to man's interest in material progress, nor the use of domestic dissidents as auxiliaries of a foreign state, nor the speed with which in our modern technological society forces of evil purpose may overwhelm the majority of peaceful men. Holmes wrote without reading Kierkegaard and Niebuhr and without hearing of Fuchs and Eisler.

If Holmes knew what you know, would he ask the right to reconsider his premises and would he invoke as an avenue of retreat his most famous epigram, "The life of the law has not been logic; it has been experience"?

It is plain that some who have oft repeated their allegiance to Holmes's creed would do so. Consider the impressive opinion of Judge Learned Hand given in the summer of 1950 in affirming the conviction of the eleven Communist leaders tried before Judge Medina; or the decision in May 1950 of the Supreme Court of the United States upholding that provision of the Taft-Hartley Act which denies the privileges of the National Labor Relations Act to unions which have Communist leaders; or the action of the 81st Congress in September of this same year in overriding President Truman's veto of the Internal Security Act of 1950.

For one who has my other duties it would be inappropriate to make a personal comment from this platform upon those recent manifestations of our democracy. But I may without impropriety observe that it is only by rewriting Holmes's premises, recasting his criteria of judgment and adding uncanonical qualifications to his formulas that judges and legislators of this year 1950 have reached the results which the overwhelming majority of our contemporaries seem, at least in the pressure of the moment, to endorse.

We do not live in an era which looks with placid self-assurance upon nonconformity. We have not the civil courage, the confidence in other men's capacities, the consciousness of ultimate victory, to admit as full partners in our society those who will not take without reservation the oaths we set before them. This is not the place to say whether we shall be justified before the bar of history. But those who subscribe to the dissents of Holmes in the *Schwimmer* and *Macintosh* cases must recognize that in the circumstances of his day he was prepared to allow a broader liberty to dissenters, malcontents and radicals than are our statesmen in the circumstances of our day, a day in which this country has reached a new high in physical resources, in armament, in productive facilities, in employment and in liquid capital, if not in spiritual leadership.

I turn now to the final point, Mr. Justice Holmes's attitude toward what some would regard as the central belief of the true democrat — the dignity of the individual man.

It is worth emphasizing at the outset what have been the sources of that belief — for, as we shall see, they include some currents in which Holmes was never caught up. One of the main sources has been natural law; another the Judaic-Christian religious tradition; and a third the classical influence of Greece and Rome on England and her offspring.

Holmes in letters, essays and legal opinions often attacked natural law concepts as a mere attempt to dress up as eternal verities our own limited experiences and hopes. He had no use for absolutes, legal or philosophic. Man did

well to form generalizations of what was good and true
and beautiful, but the generalizations had no claim to be
ultimate standards or to be final criteria of judgment.
"The best that is known and thought in the world" was
of profound interest, but it was no copy of a Platonic set
of universal ideas good *semper ubique,* marketable as coin-
age of the heavenly realm. Man could never find gold pure
enough to fit a universal standard. For him it was enough
to learn how to mine, to refine, to use the alloyed metals
of this earth. These mundane minerals were to be tested
pragmatically. They were to be fitted into some workable
and passable currency for our daily needs — on the understanding, of course, that the system of values was purely
artificial, devised for convenience and subject to devalua-
tion or revaluation whenever experience dictated.

To the Christian or any other formal religious discipline
the mature Holmes never professed to be an adherent.
He would not have denied that there was a power bigger
than himself — he wrote that he knew he was in the
belly of the cosmos and not the cosmos in him. But he ir-
reverently referred to the Deity as the Grand Panjandrum
who had not disclosed the plan of campaign, if indeed
there is one. While he admired his father's friend Ralph
Waldo Emerson and imbibed from him and older New
England divines a sense of obligation and of Puritanical
duty, he did not share their faith in God which gave New
England its distinctive Transcendentalism.

Intellectually he was a skeptic. His ideas were not far
different from those of the early Santayana — the author
of *The Life of Reason.* And at times, as on his ninetieth
birthday, Holmes could summarize in severely physical
terms the insignificance of man's existence: "To live is to
function. That is all there is in living." But this rigorous
separation of what he knew from what he did not know

was never uttered in arrogance or pride. Indeed he disdained the impetuous defiance of our modern Prometheus, Bertrand Russell, who, as Pollock said, thought himself "a valiant fellow for throwing stones at God Almighty's windows."

Yet this intellectual skepticism was to some extent balanced by a desire to plunge himself into the full tide of emotional forces in a way that would have astonished a complete Pyrrhonist like Montaigne. There was something far deeper than an imperturbable materialism in the judge who told a Harvard graduating class that a soldier's faith was "true and adorable" even "in a cause which he little understands," in the Civil War veteran who told his former comrades in arms that "it is required of a man that he should share the passion and the action of his time at peril of being judged not to have lived," and in the American citizen who saw mere belittling innuendo in Charles Beard's portrait of the framers of the American Constitution as businessmen motivated by concern for their own investments. Holmes fully acknowledged the power of things of the spirit. He could never have enthroned as an ultimate trinity Freud, Marx and Darwin and said that the combination of their psychological, economic and biological theories explained the totality of life. For Holmes's rejection of the theological system was a rejection of all systems on the ground that life was too big, too multifarious, nay too mysterious to be comprehended. He rejected the parson for his certitude and his narrowness — but he did not delude himself with any lesser substitute of cocksureness.

Was then Holmes's attitude toward man classical in its origin? Some have persuasively argued that Holmes was an incurable romantic leading the younger generations to a wasteland where agnosticism, violence and force hold sway. But Holmes had none of the optimistic exuberance, love of the wildness of nature, or the admiration for the varieties of eccentricity which characterized his two great contemporaries in literature and philosophy, Walt Whitman and William James. The latter he regarded as a sentimental Irishman; the former's poetry is never quoted and never pulls at his vitals like Sophocles' *Philoctetes* or Dante's *Divine Comedy*.

If by the classical tradition in the Anglo-American world we mean the emphasis on the rounded man who, conscious of the ideal of excellence, disciplines himself to perform competently and unobtrusively, and without being diverted, whatever task falls to his hand, confident that every detail has significance, and that every task greatly done makes the world more meaningful to the doer, then Holmes was a classicist. For Holmes, though he did not proclaim that human goals were eternal goals, never doubted that man could rise above the particulars of a sordid existence. If he could not discover God's purposes, he could nonetheless live a purposeful life of his own designing.

For himself, Holmes, at least after his Civil War years, chose as his design what may seem an austerely solitary life — first that of a scholar and then of an appellate judge. He never participated in the struggles of the marketplace nor of the political hustings nor even, to any substantial extent, of the trial court. He did not follow with reasonable closeness the diurnal conflict of other men's existences — going so far as often to avoid reading the daily newspaper. He never sought the spotlight of public attention and contemned those who advertised their own distinction. Cloistered in the library of his home he read voluminously, mostly philosophical, historical, classical and juristic literature, interspersed with occasional French novels and current humorous books. He talked to and corresponded exclusively with the intellectual elite. His public appearances were virtually confined to four or five hundred hours a year on the bench in the former Senate Chamber in the Capitol. There he seldom spoke, but when he put one of his rare questions, it cut like a stingray to the heart of the case he was hearing. And then he went home to Eye Street to stand erect behind a tall bookkeeper's desk to write with a deft and sparkling pen opinions that "with a singing variety" epigrammatically crystallized his profound insights.

In listening to this description of Holmes you may have asked yourself whether I have shown the democracy of Holmes or his aristocracy. Quite plainly if democracy be the apotheosis of the lowest common denominator and if, to use Holmes's phraseology, every "great swell" is by definition an aristocrat, then the Holmes view of man was not democratic. But does democracy imply that the ideal man is the average man? Historically surely it does not, as Pericles would be the first and Franklin Roosevelt the latest to teach us. Democracy no less than aristocracy has always stressed the dignity or, if you please, the nobility of man. The difference between the aristocratic and the democratic philosophies is that in an aristocracy the terms dignity and nobility connote titles founded on the accident of birth or principles of invidious selection from an artificially restricted field. In a democratic society the same terms are reserved for those who have so disciplined themselves that their countenances, their conduct, their code command respect. And it is in this sense that Holmes is a supreme instance of one democratic ideal of the dignity of man.

He has not (no man born in 1841 could have) given the answers suitable to our modern technological economy, to our new world order, to the rising tide of collectivism and, above all, to our crisis of faith. But like the Winged Victory of Samothrace he is the summit of hundreds of years of civilization, the inspiration of ages yet to come without being the foundation stone of any new school. He is the final authentic representative of the period of English democracy in America — the period that spans from 1607 to World War II.

But some of you may not be quite content to give Holmes that role unless I meet head-on a point now often pressed by detractors of the Justice. Despite the grandeur of the man and the style with which he carried off his life, was Holmes a believer in any durable values, democratic or otherwise? In his refusal of allegiance to any church, in his pervasive intellectual skepticism, in his praise of the soldier's faith apart from the soldier's cause, in his emphasis on adventure and on power, would he not have been as much at home in the world of Hobbes or of Hitler as of Jefferson or of Lincoln? Was he only a glorious specimen of Nietzsche's life force, a superman who but for the accident of birth into a Brahmin, Beacon Hill family might have turned his theories and his talents to support an evil, destructive power.

One can make a superficial collation of Holmes's epigrams to fortify this sort of critical question. And there are some writers who have recently done so in theological pamphlets and bar journals. Holmes is himself not without blame for this criticism because he delighted to arouse his audience and stamp their memories with a witty or poetic phrase. He never spoke with cautious pedantic exactitude, qualifying every "bully generalization" with the express proviso that it was a mere *aperçu*, understandable only as one of a series of partial visions.

Yet we shall make a fundamental mistake if we assume that because Holmes was so happy a phrase-maker, because he was so disdainful of all absolutes, and because he refused to accept or announce a systematic approach to the universe, his philosophy can be reduced to the two principles "Whatsoever thy hand findeth to do, do it with thy might" (Essay on "Life as Joy, Duty, End") and "Let thy neighbor go in peace."

Rigorous standards for himself and tolerance of his neighbor were, to be sure, two important articles of his creed. Yet each of these derived from this more basic postulate: although absolute truth, undiminished beauty, unalloyed good are not to be found by man, the never-ending quest for the true, the good, and the beautiful is the activity most satisfying to man. Even if the quest serves no cosmic end, even if when the earth has made its last revolution round the sun not a trace of man's long journey will be left in any heaven or hell, nonetheless the search for truth and beauty and goodness seemed as desirable to Holmes as it was inevitable for him. And the final glory of the democratic life, as Holmes exemplified it and extended it, is that democracy keeps every door open to searchers for ultimate values, and demolishes every irrelevant barrier standing athwart the oncoming adventurers in ideas.

The Marshall Woods Lecture, 1950

Brandeis: The Independent Man

O N November 13, 1856, in Louisville, Kentucky, was born Louis Dembitz Brandeis, who can fairly be claimed to rank in influence upon American law second only to John Marshall. He was not the philosopher-poet that Holmes was; nor had he the range of scholarship or the purity of detachment which characterized Cardozo; and he was without the magisterial command that Hughes so magnificently embodied. Yet, even in company with those giants, Brandeis made the second long stride which gave American law a pace distinctive from, if responsive to, English jurisprudence.

John Marshall showed what judges could draw from a written constitution to support the ancient doctrines of government under law. L. D. Brandeis demonstrated, first at the bar and then on the bench, that legislative history and the legislators' avowed concern with economics, social policy, and statistical science could furnish not merely the inarticulate premises but the express grounds of judicial opinion.

From 1916 to 1939, when Brandeis served as a Justice of the Supreme Court of the United States, any visitor to the Court would have been struck by his presence. Much was attributable to his countenance, Lincolnian in its benevolent sympathy and austere beauty. Something was due to the electric shock of his white hair, unforgettably sculpted by Eleanor Platt. And then, as Brandeis talked, the soft Southern voice, so persuasive in its appeal to reason, so simple in its choice of words, so moral in its undertones, moved the auditor even more perhaps than the majestic utterances of Chief Justice Hughes, the vigorous clarity of Justice Roberts, and the urbane gentility of Justice Sutherland.

On the bench in front of Justice Brandeis, but not before any other judge, was crooked a gooseneck lamp, obviously lacking the ornate resplendence of standard judicial equipment. Its immediate purpose was severely utilitarian — for none followed more closely and with less interruption the arguments and page references of counsel at the bar. But may it not also have been a symbol to notify the stranger that although the Court had been moved into a palace of justice over Brandeis's protest, L.D.B. had a distaste for ostentation?

Were you to see the Justice in his home, there you would find no display of wealth or elegance. He himself would probably be wearing the dark blue serge suit that annually he bought by mail from Filene's Boston store. If he were in his apartment at Florence Court, the furniture would be typified by a green sofa with a long stiff back which perhaps began its career in a shipment from a Victorian store to Otis Place in Boston. On the wall was a photographic reproduction of the statue of Venus de Milo. If you were allowed to go a floor above, to his crowded study, the surrounding books were law reports from the federal and Massachusetts courts, and a collection of albums filled with clippings reporting Brandeis's cases as an advocate and his championship as "the people's lawyer" of controversies before court, commission, and Congress in the first decade and a half of the twentieth century.

Perhaps, if your intimacy with the Justice reached back
into those earlier days, and even more probably if you
shared his concern with the aims of Zionism, you might be
invited to the Justice's summer cottage at Chatham for an
hour's visit strictly clocked by Mrs. Brandeis. If possible,
there were even fewer signs of luxury there than on California Street in Washington. Some books were placed not
on shelves but in packing cases. And on the wall were
framed not famous etchings or impressionist paintings but
something far more revealing: a legal instrument — a
contract executed several decades before in which Mr.
Brandeis agreed to pay to each of his daughters an allowance of five cents each week and they in turn agreed to
polish his shoes, all on the understanding that "there are
no catchwords in this contract."

Whether you came to his home on the Cape or in the
District of Columbia, you would meet (mixed with the
famous — the senators, the wife of the President, the heads
of executive agencies) a number of both men and women
who were engaged in tasks that, though they might not be
newsworthy, had a critical importance in the civic and
cultural life of the nation: the librarian of the Labor Department; a manufacturer of tags who, before the congressional social-security legislation, had tried an unemployment compensation system in his own plant; the associate
editor of the *Encyclopedia of the Social Sciences;* the
chief economist of the Department of Agriculture; the
most original mind on the staff of the Interstate Commerce
Commission; a New York magazine writer who sought
to interest a larger public in the intricacies of governmental
bureaus; a young lawyer representing New England tex-
tile interests; a publisher of pocket books; an expositor of
the growth of savings-bank life insurance; a member of a
Jewish charitable association's board; an associate counsel

of an international intergovernmental organization; the secretary of the chairman of the Senate Committee on Finance; the president of the Seaman's Union; a young professor from the Harvard Law School; a statistician from a Wisconsin public utility commission.

The Justice would take aside visitors, one or two at a time, and ask them on what they were working and what had struck them as interesting. From the judge would come a word of encouragement to pursue the investigation of the causes of an alleged evil, or to remain in a small office in a Southeastern community, or further to consider a particular administrative or legislative problem. Sometimes the judge would broach a topic in which he thought his guest would have interest, and then would find the response unexpectedly negative. Once, for example, he spoke to me of the development of small village community life in Palestine. It took no extensive plumbing to find me completely ignorant. The Justice said nothing. But some days later I found in my morning's mail a set of pamphlets on Palestine, all rolled in a slit plain envelope with no identification beyond the familiar strong, straight handwriting of L.D.B.

It was by hand that all his correspondence and his opinions were written after he went to Washington. He gave up all stenographic assistance and never used as substitutes dictating machines or even, to any extent, a typewriter. But he did have one curiously expensive habit. In preparing an opinion as a Justice of the Court he regularly sent many rough drafts to the Court printer, and then worked from galleys as other lawyers would work from typewritten drafts. Sometimes, as in his celebrated dissent in the *O'Fallon* case, he dispatched perhaps more than a score of versions of his opinion to the printer's shop on Twelfth Street before he was satisfied with the product. A reason for this extraordinary use of printed rather than typewritten copies may have been that only when a document appeared to him as he thought it would appear to a reader was he able to judge its quality. But whatever the reason the result was as striking stylistically as it was substantively.

The process of constant revision, rearrangement of ideas, and reshuffling of paragraphs and sentences made the final opinion in each sense of the word highly "articulate." The text had an organic tightness that did not rely for its clear relationships merely on enumeration of separate sections of the text. Footnotes were arrayed with a compelling completeness of supporting authority. And the several points raised by counsel or by other judges were comprehensively answered. To a sensitive, strictly literary taste, the style might seem gaunt. But this criticism must be taken as praise, not blame, by anyone who regards as a test of prose its faithful reflection of the mental and moral standards of the author.

Thus Brandeis emphasized the special responsibility which falls upon a judge of our highest court to contribute in its deepest sense to the political growth of the American people. From the time of Chief Justice Marshall, the opinions of the Supreme Court have been a text unto the people. Read in the daily press, studied in the common school, knotted into the rope of enduring history, they may well be the largest single contribution to the philosophy of the American way of life. Conscious of this aspect of his office, Brandeis shaped his opinions not merely as judge but as teacher. No one who has digested his judicial opinions will be surprised at the tale told by one of his most distinguished law clerks, Professor Paul A. Freund of the Harvard Law School. Brandeis had been assigned a case to write for the Court. After he had analyzed the facts, derived the principles to guide the conclusion, and achieved his judgment, Brandeis was not yet content to utter the opinion. For he was still inquiring of his law clerk, "What can we do to make it more instructive?"

Unlike so many leaders in his profession, Brandeis almost never wrote memorial tributes or similar biographical essays which in form purport to sketch the character of other lawyers and judges, but which so often in substance become revelations of the aspirations and accomplishments of the author, rather than of the subject. Once, and in a manner unforgettable to anyone who has read this now difficult-to-procure record, Brandeis came close to painting the sort of double-mirror portrait of which I am speaking. I allude to the magisterial summary of the character of Louis R. Glavis which, as his counsel, Mr. Brandeis gave to the Congressional Joint Committee to Investigate the Interior Department and Forestry Service, conducting the so-called Ballinger investigation. Does Brandeis describe himself or Glavis when he tells us of the four cardinal virtues of a witness — power of observation, perfection of memory, clarity of expression, and ability to envisage the whole situation into which his testimony fits? And is there a more thoughtful defense of Brandeis's own professional career, or for that matter a more pertinent tract for the present times, than the argument offered Congress in support of the concept of loyalty exhibited by Glavis and by Ballinger's stenographer, Frederick M. Kerby?

One issue which perplexed the investigating Congressmen, the wider public, and not least Brandeis's fellow counsel in the case, was whether there rested a moral duty of disclosure upon a subordinate in the Civil Service who had discovered what he thought were departures from principle by his superior officer. In Glavis's case the subordinate believed that his chief, Secretary Ballinger, was

surrendering portions of the public domain to private rapacity. The stenographer Kerby knew from the letters he
had transcribed that Secretary Ballinger, Attorney General
Wickersham, and President Taft had misled the Congressional Committee as to the chronological order in which
documents had been prepared, and thus had altered their
import and value. What was the duty of Glavis and Kerby
under these circumstances? How far, and to whom, were
they warranted in becoming informers? Was there an
overriding obligation to individuals with whom one had
been confidentially associated? Could this conflict of attachments be resolved by a profounder understanding of
the principle of loyalty?

Whether or not we accept it as valid, the answer Brandeis fashioned states with admirable clarity one viewpoint:

The danger in America is not of insubordination, but it is of
too complacent obedience to the will of superiors. With this
great Government building up, ever creating new functions
. . . the one thing we need is men in subordinate places who
will think for themselves and who will think and act in full recognition of their obligations as part of the governing body.
. . . We want every man in the Service . . . to recognize that
he is part of the governing body, and that on him rests responsibility within the limits of his employment just as much as
upon the man on top . . . they cannot be worthy of the respect and admiration of the people unless they add to the virtue of obedience some other virtues — the virtues of manliness,
of truth, of courage, of willingness to risk positions, of the
willingness to risk criticisms, of the willingness to risk the misunderstandings that so often come when people do the heroic
thing.

These are so plainly the virtues which Mr. Brandeis himself possessed, and they are so excellent a definition of the independent man, that I shall devote the remainder of this paper first to a canvass of the leading themes with which his name is indelibly associated, and then to an appreciative critique of his personal way of life. It is not an exaggeration to say that like Franklin, Washington, Jefferson, Hamilton, Lincoln, and Holmes, Brandeis has become for many men much more than a hero in American narrative history. He has become a symbol of particular threads woven into the enduring pattern of American life. He has become the embodiment of the independent man, the inner-directed man of rational bent and moral integration.

The overriding problem of the independent man living in Brandeis's age and ours is the reconciliation of his essential spiritual nature with the powerful forces of an expanding industrial society, a society proceeding at unprecedented speed to produce novel instrumentalities, to spread geographically, to reach new levels of population, to concentrate into fewer hands vast administrative power, and to standardize both information and criteria of judgment so that they may be digested by the mass of men possessing a minimum of bite and taste.

Concern over the relationship between the individual and the mass is, of course, a topic with a longer history than the twentieth century. And even the accentuated phases of this problem which are attributable to the accelerated technological advance since the Victorian era have a bibliography of inordinate length. So Brandeis would claim no patent for his discovery of the central illness of his time. Nor would he, I am sure, suggest he deserved credit for diagnosing as one of the chief causes "the curse of bigness."

The Brandeis program can be conveniently analyzed under his treatment of public power and private power. One advantage of this procedure is that it reveals that the Brandeis opposition to bigness, while always an important criterion, was never an exclusive one, at least where what was at stake was public or governmental power.

For more than a century and a half, or since the overthrow of the yoke of what was regarded as British tyranny, American political science had been keyed to the task of preventing oppressive government. According to the schoolbook version, the devices chiefly relied upon were the federal structure of our Union, the tripartite division of the government into executive, legislative, and judicial branches, judicial review of arbitrary official action, a bill of rights, and representative government.

Our federal structure was an historical consequence of a victorious Revolutionary War consolidating the foreign, commercial, and fiscal interests of diverse colonies accustomed to a large measure of self-determination. The pressures which produced our United States Constitution established a framework which promptly excited widespread admiration. It is unnecessary to recite the degree to which parts of the then British Empire copied our Constitution, or to repeat the panegyric which we received from the most celebrated historian of liberty, Lord Acton. For him the pluralistic structure of the United States, contrasted with the unitary administration of the French Republic, represented our distinctive contribution to the principle of political freedom.

As a judge, Mr. Justice Brandeis often had occasion to show his allegiance to the federal principle. In the cases where progressive legislation of local governments was assailed, he frequently resisted the attack by resorting to the principle that our Constitution protected the right of experimentation in the insulated chambers drawn by state boundary lines. Yet it would be naïve to assert that that principle, of which Mr. Justice Holmes was an even more ardent champion, remained with either of them as inflexible dogma, especially when the coin was reversed and Congress sought to legislate in areas theretofore local. Brandeis, despite occasional votes, as in *Schechter Corporation* v. *United States*, declaring unconstitutional the National Industrial Recovery Act, was almost always the upholder of, sometimes even the instigator of, that expansion of central governmental power whose growth seems to the critical eye to have made the present United States an increasingly unitary power. This admittedly strong statement I believe can be supported by noting the role of Brandeis in fostering the furthest reaches of congressional taxing and spending power, as well as in the interpretation he gave to the commerce power and the war power, and his refusal to find more than a precatory injunction in the Tenth Amendment.

May I, as a dramatic example, state from personal knowledge his obscure though decisive role in the initiation of our federal-state unemployment compensation system? For now, after two decades, the tale has moved from the realm of gossip into the realm of history. It was in his apartment that his non-lawyer daughter, in his absence, made the highly legalistic suggestion of a new federal excise tax, modeled on the federal estate tax, with a credit to the taxpayer of amounts paid by the taxpayer to state unemployment compensation systems to be created under state law. Whatever may be said of the constitutionality of the plan — and on this point I am free from doubt, as was the majority of the Supreme Court in 1937 — and whatever may be said of the degree to which the plan preserved opportunities for local administration and for minor variations in local substantive policy, the plan effectuated a marked increase in the relative degree of national control in our federal system.

But the support which social security received was only

symptomatic of what appears to me to be the unmistakable trend of other Brandeis decisions. He always regarded as virtually absolute, aside from issues of due process, the grants to Congress of power to tax, to spend, to regulate commerce, and to declare and carry on war. To be sure, he sometimes privately urged that these national powers should be used to supply money, information, or legal backing for state laws. But whether this advice was followed or not, the political result, achieved mainly during his time on the Supreme Court, was to aggrandize the central power.

Likewise, so far as concerns adherence to the hornbook principle of "separation of powers," the impact of the decisions during the Brandeis period was hardly in the spirit of the American founding fathers. As an advocate before the Interstate Commerce Commission, as a sponsor of a bill ultimately merged in the Clayton Act to establish the Federal Trade Commission, and as a judge interpreting regulatory New Deal legislation, Brandeis is properly regarded as one of the architects of our modern system of administrative agencies, which commonly combine some subsidiary executive, legislative, and judicial powers.

So that I may not be misunderstood, let me make explicit that I am not on this score attacking Brandeis. I happen to share his viewpoint. But I recognize, as I am sure he did, that he participated in a most significant increase in public power in the direction of bigness and contrary to individual initiative. He acquiesced in the conversion of government from a largely negative role in combating force and fraud into an affirmative instrument, moving in novel ways, to establish for private persons, corporations, and industries approved patterns of minimum conduct, sometimes appealingly called "fair" conduct.

However, if the swelling of the Washington bureaucracy

owes something to a favorable wind blown from Brandeis's quarter, he was at the same time most active among those who reduced the pretensions of the Supreme Court to be a super-legislature. His strict avoidance (with one conspicuous exception in *Erie Railroad Co.* v. *Tompkins*) of unnecessary constitutional issues has become legendary. He had an admirable judicial tolerance toward legislation which in his private capacity he disliked. Witness the ironical fact that one of the dissents with which his name will always be associated was in *New State Ice Co.* v. *Liebmann*, where he voted to uphold a legislative grant of an ice monopoly of which he might not have approved as a voter.

Even in the field of civil liberties — where the celebrated letter of March 15, 1789, from Ambassador Thomas Jefferson to Congressman James Madison suggests that the Supreme Court of the United States was intended to have a more liberal veto than it had exerted over economic, commercial, or like legislation — Justice Brandeis exercised his judicial negative with restraint. Examined closely, the Brandeis opinions in this field are more often directed at improvement of judicial procedure, at the establishment of safeguards against the reception of tainted evidence, at scrutiny of the precise facts of record, and at cautious interpretation of the legislative command, than they are at invalidation of deliberate legislative choices as to repressive measures.

This was thoroughly consistent with the Justice's deep belief in responsible, representative government. He had no illusion as to his personal omniscience. His tendency was to adopt those courses which gave opportunity for legislators, or administrators, or lower courts to speak more clearly. What he strove to do was to make others examine difficult problems as carefully as he did, so that before final action they would inform the judgments for which they justly bore responsibility. Indeed this is why time and again he will be found supporting investigatory powers, disclosure statutes, and even private group action aiming at a wider dissemination of basic statistical material.

If, as I have suggested, the program in which Justice Brandeis at least acquiesced strengthened during his lifetime the forces of public power and of bigness in government, the record is quite the reverse in the field of private power.

Monopoly, and even bigness which fell short of monopoly, he consistently opposed for practical considerations which he believed experience had taught. He thought men were so inherently limited that they could not intelligently command large enterprises with mastery of detail and economy of operation. He was skeptical of vast concentration of power not because it was inevitably wicked but because he thought it tended to be slothful, unimaginative, and unresponsive to the needs of the market, the problems of the worker, and the claims of the investor. More than the likelihood of corruption, the certainty of capriciousness in large enterprise was what Brandeis feared.

With this outlook, there are many who agree — not least Mr. Justice Douglas, who, to the expressed delight of Mr. Justice Brandeis, became his successor on the Supreme Court of the United States. But it is doubtful whether on the extreme limits (as distinguished from the main trend) of this issue Brandeis can ever get on his side more than a sharply divided vote.

To a large extent, bigness in the modern world seems inevitable unless we are prepared to emulate Switzerland or a Scandinavian country. Our high standards of consumption at relatively low cost are in large part the result of mass production, as we are every day reminded by the automobile and the household gadgets which lighten the housewife's toil. Our military security at the moment rests chiefly on the products of nuclear fission coming from enterprises on a scale so mammoth that only one or two nations can undertake similar establishments.

Those who disagree with Brandeis argue that the evils he discerned are not peculiar to bigness, and are not curable by a planned program of dispersal of power. What the opponents assert is that there are two sounder methods of dealing with the dangers of which Brandeis spoke.

The first is the less important and, to the uncommitted mind, the less warranted by the evidence of experience. It is the promotion of countervailing forces operating exclusively in the economic realm. They are composed, first, of the rival giants in the same area of business; and second, of the giants in those fields of supply, labor, and consumption directly tangent to the first area.

If there can be achieved such a desired resolution of forces operating in the economic realm, then one fortunate by-product of bigness in private enterprise will be the balance which vast establishments of private power are able to exert on the even more vast domain of public power. Our generation has learned what history never before taught so clearly: that public power, even when nominally executing programs for the common man and the social interest, is not always to be trusted with total authority. Absoluteness always becomes arbitrariness. If we are to have a government constantly promoting the general welfare and not the selfish interest of a dictator or of an administrative class of civil servants, it is not sufficient to rely on verbal constitutional limitations, nor on automatic checks internal to our mighty Leviathan. Only if private forces are also of considerable moment and have the courage that comes from independent power can we avoid the capriciousness inevitable in unmitigated totalitarianism.

The second method for dealing with bigness which is advanced by those who dissent from Brandeis's view has an element of paradox, but is nonetheless, I believe, persuasive. The dissenters say, "Justice Brandeis, we agree with you that power and bigness are heavily freighted with risk. Grave dangers there are of abuse, arbitrariness, selfishness, corruption, inefficiency, loss of nerve, staleness, and dull inertia. But, sir, these are not dangers peculiar to bigness, and are not cured solely by competition. You, sir, when you planned the library at Louisville, the savings-bank insurance system in Massachusetts, the yardstick method of calculating gas rates in Boston, were convinced that the mechanism you had provided, so admirably adapted to your theories, would prove your case for small units. If you were to come back now, and again scrutinize your favored institutions, would you not agree with us that what made those enterprises so successful was not their scale but the quality of the gifted man that conceived them and for a time guided their operations? When he left they lost some of their unique quality. In all life proof abounds that he who is a good and faithful servant over a few things can usually be set over many things."

For, as Lord Radcliffe's Reith Lectures and his apt citation of the experience in India of British civil servants showed, the "problem of power" is less a question of the magnitude than of the morality of responsibility. Power and bigness are no more inherently good or bad than are water and land. All turns on the use made of them. And men in large and small undertakings alike may be trained to self-discipline. In this they may be aided by codes of professional behavior. They are even more helped to become better stewards and better men by the habitual vision of greatness in others.

Thus it is primarily because of his example of personal greatness, not because of his program and doctrine, that we stand so in debt to Brandeis. His practice was even sounder than his precept. If we reject as thoroughly impractical his notion that jobs should be cut down to man-size, and instead reluctantly conclude that to achieve peace, to reduce illness, poverty, and ignorance, and to promote the efficient use of human and natural resources, large-scale organizations with oversize jobs are inevitable in our times, Brandeis illustrated for us perhaps better than anyone else how to fill such posts.

First is his method of work. He sought out the detail and pondered it while he savored its significance. When Brandeis understood all that there was to know about the facts, he himself (at least until his last years) prepared his own statement of his findings and conclusions. I well remember a remark the Justice made to me when I first entered the public service: "The reason the public thinks so much of the Justices of the Supreme Court is that they are almost the only people in Washington who do their own work."

There are those, I am sure, who will say that this practice is well enough for a judge, removed from most of the harassments of ordinary office life, considering problems neatly packaged in bound records with defined issues, and not under strong inducement to solve forthwith urgent practical problems, but that this is a ridiculous model for the crowded executive or other man absorbed in active struggle. I suggest that the rejection of the Brandeis model often comes too fast. It is extraordinary how much even the man charged with vast administrative responsibilities can gain in discriminating judgment, in overall appraisal, in effectiveness of communication, and in that respect of his fellow workers which breeds authority, when he speaks from personal knowledge of detail. What initially may appear a sacrifice of time comes back manyfold in the form of durable increased reputation.

More than his method of work, Brandeis's *moral character* deserves prolonged contemplation. You may suppose that those emphasized words are a conventional tribute of the type customarily paid to all but the most venal men who have ever held high office. But I mean no such naïve standard compliment. Brandeis's morality, though it was the undoubted foundation of a life of unusual consistency and, in that sense, integrity, presents shortcomings as well as extraordinary depths that repay extended consideration.

One shortcoming has struck most commentators who have assayed the claim that Brandeis was in the Renaissance sense "a complete man." Of the three cardinal values, Brandeis prized highly only two — truth and goodness. Beauty received scant attention. Absence of a vibrant interest in art and poetry is perhaps not always meaningful. But here it is, I suspect, of importance, for it underlines how severely rational was the ethics to which he adhered. His moral order is economic, not poetic, in its foundations. Far from the mark are the comparison of Brandeis to the Biblical prophets and the appellation of Isaiah which he won from President Franklin D. Roosevelt. Mysticism, poetry, the prophetic vision that passeth understanding, never governed Brandeis's utterances. Indeed Brandeis was not like the Old Testament type of moralist the Jewish people has produced — for his ultimates are hardly tinged with emotion. Certainly he was not, like Spinoza, "God-intoxicated." Nor was he suffused with an indiscriminate love of all mankind. And just as he was not overwhelmed by an awareness of fraternal love or of its magic key to the solitariness that lies at the core of all men, so he was not troubled by irrational evil in the world, nor by man's innate perversity which some orthodox theologians ascribe to original sin, and which others of us regard as being a waywardness as mysterious as our sudden impulses for good.

But the most intriguing and optimistic aspect of Brandeis's moral life, the one that I believe especially repays study, is what seems to me its progressive improvement beginning in middle life. Some there are who prefer to worship heroes who sprang full-armed at birth from the head of Zeus. And for those used to rites appropriate for such primitives, Brandeis is a quite unsatisfactory model. As was the case with Abraham Lincoln, whom Brandeis so much resembled in physical appearance, certain episodes in Brandeis's youth and early maturity are so contrary to the idealism proclaimed in later life that some hostile critics have doubted his sincerity.

There are others who suppose that there was at some stage in Brandeis's life a dramatic forking of the road. Some have suggested it came with marriage to a strong wife with a deep social conscience, reared in a family consecrated by a high sense of duty. Others offer a rationale in terms of an inner response to specific outside stimulus: horror at the Homestead strike, contact with the garment workers in New York, gradual withdrawal by the Boston Brahmins of the hospitality early extended to Brandeis, a determination to become a factor in politics, the acquisition from legal practice of an "independent fortune" which made it easier for him to be an "independent man."

All of these analyses strike me as naïve substitutes for a far more common, but nonetheless wonderful and encouraging, explanation. Brandeis himself was the exemplar *par excellence* of his own doctrine that "responsibility is the great developer of man." L.D.B. was a man of constant inward growth. And let us not take from him the glory that he won, by our pretending either that he was always noble or that he became so by external pressure. He grew by trial and error. We are reminded of the dilemma presented to Senator Albert J. Beveridge while he was collecting material for his four-volume biography of Lincoln. As he proceeded with his investigation of original sources, Beveridge became so alarmed at what he regarded as discreditable episodes in Lincoln's early life that he contemplated burning his papers and abandoning the project. Then Beveridge determined that to the reflective student Lincoln was the greater man because it was by conquering himself that he had won the world.

The life of Brandeis had no such depths as the Illinois politician's from which to rise, nor did it ascend quite to Lincolnian heights of pity and love; yet it is a great, perhaps the greatest, American saga of the independent man of our times, the man who believes that ultimate questions must be referred not primarily to some official power or legal proclamation, but to an inward authority — an authority that may be religious, or humanistic, or humanitarian; an authority for which the ethical and creative aspects of the individual man are paramount considerations; an authority that promotes the unflagging search for those arrangements of life, of work, and of leisure which enlarge the capacity of man to discover truth, to achieve beauty, and to foster a fraternal fellowship.

From the *Atlantic Monthly*, 1956
Originally delivered at
Brandeis University as the
Brandeis Memorial Lecture

Augustus Noble Hand

SYMBOLICALLY we have chosen to meet in the rooms of a voluntary association rather than of a courthouse to honor the memory of Judge Augustus Noble Hand. For we assemble in response not to conventional public duty, but to deep personal desire. We seek to remind ourselves, and to inform those who come after us, of his massive character and serene wisdom. We recall him as our friend and as our teacher of a scale of durable values.

Yet we also come to honor one who through four decades was one of our most influential magistrates. And he would have asked us to stress his contribution to the law in institutional rather than individualistic terms. So let us, before turning to any biographical detail, emphasize Judge Hand's contributory role in giving first to the United States District Court for the Southern District of New York and later to the United States Court of Appeals for the Second Circuit a distinction in the profession and an authority in the schools comparable to that enjoyed by the New York Court of Appeals under the leadership of Chief Judge Cardozo, and by the Massachusetts Supreme Judicial Court under Chief Justice Shaw. Although there were among his brethren others of more striking originality, larger practical experience, more varied public service, and richer style, there was none in whose judgment litigants, lawyers, and especially his own associates had greater confidence. He supplied an extra measure of that steadiness, courtesy, patience, and dignity that are the essence of gravitas.

That A. N. Hand became a judge must have appeared inevitable to anyone who followed his career from his birth in Elizabethtown, New York, on July 26, 1869. His grandfather, Augustus C. Hand, who, in a phrase reminiscent of De Tocqueville, had written that "law is the patent of nobility and the only patent in this land," had served as Surrogate and as Justice of the New York Supreme Court. His father, Richard, and his Uncles Clifford and Samuel had become leaders of the bar respectively in Elizabethtown, New York, and Albany. His father had been appointed by Governor Hughes a Commissioner to try William Travers Jerome; and both uncles had been offered, and one had accepted, appointment to the New York Court of Appeals. At the gate leading to the home in which A. N. Hand was brought up, and where he continued to spend summers until he died, was the family law office, with its more than a century-old library of English and American reports. Nearby was the courthouse, where, when only seven years old, A. N. Hand had heard a farmer's complaint that his horse had been frightened by the negligence of a traveling circus — a trial which led the boy to write and deliver what he called "a speech and a charge."

As a lad A. N. Hand went to the local Elizabethtown schools from which he graduated at fourteen, already a competent Greek and Latin scholar. Having overworked, however, he spent two years "resting, trapping, shooting, studying French," and learning songs like "The Monitor and The Merrimac" which remained with him all his life. Then for one year he went to the Phillips Exeter Academy, where he was not only a good student but an active participant in the debates of the Golden Branch Society. He entered Harvard College in the Class of 1890, despite his Jacksonian Uncle Clifford's fear that he would end up "a damned little Federalist." As he wrote in his class report, from William James he learned that "truth, earnestness, and humility" were the sound methods of any worthy achievement. He had the good luck one year to dine at the same table as George Santayana, whom he regarded as the American Keats, and whose sonnets he memorized and added to his large repertory of English and classical poetry.

For a year following his graduation he read law in his father's office, but then on the advice of his Plattsburgh friends, Ralph and Henry Kellogg, went back to Cambridge as a member of the Harvard Law School Class of 1894. Having received no mark less than A in any law school course, Hand was elected an editor of the *Harvard Law Review*. He met Louis D. Brandeis, an alumni trustee of the publication; through his close friend, Arthur Dehon Hill, he was introduced to and spent some evenings at the home of Judge O. W. Holmes of the Massachusetts Supreme Judicial Court. But the professional men who most deeply influenced him were the extraordinarily gifted teachers who composed the Langdell faculty. He has described Samuel Williston as "the best teacher and clearest expositor"; John C. Gray "had the most general culture"; J. B. Thayer "was the most original" and his views of evidence and constitutional law "made the most important impression on the best students."

After receiving both his LL.B. and his A.M. degrees, and spending a few weeks in the office of James B. Ludlow, Hand was for two years in the office of Stearns and Curtis, until in June 1897 he became a partner in the successor firm, Curtis, Mallet-Prevost and Colt. While there, on August 5, 1899 he married Susan Train, the daughter of

Captain Train of the United States Navy. With Mrs. Hand, with their daughter Serena, and her family, he enjoyed a relationship of such comradeship, admiration, and love that even the most casual acquaintance recognized how much they meant to his happiness and balanced way of looking at life.

In September 1901, upon the death of his uncle Clifford, Augustus N. Hand succeeded him as a member of Hand, Bonney and Jones. Here he handled many important fiduciary and estate problems. However, few of these took him to court, although he did try cases at least occasionally, as, for example, in the contest over Hodnett's will, about which Judge Hand spoke in his remarks at this Association in honor of Chief Justice Hughes. The personal character of Hand's practice was evident in his reluctance to render bills adequate for the services he performed. Indeed for drawing even the most complicated will, involving literally millions of dollars, he charged only his standard fee of twenty-five dollars.

In 1914 upon the resignation of Judge Holt from the United States District Court for the Southern District of New York, President Wilson, following the suggestion of this Association's beloved member, Charles C. Burlingham, appointed Augustus N. Hand to the vacancy. Hand's brethren were Charles M. Hough, Learned Hand, and Julius Mayer.

A. N. Hand was one of the best members of that distinguished quartet because of his equable temperament, accurate apprehension of the central questions, realistic appraisal of facts, and solid background of law. He completely avoided the two dangers which he always regarded as most serious in a trial judge: conceit and arbitrariness. He particularly enjoyed the zest and variety of the motion list, which he looked upon as a challenge to a judge's native capacity and balanced judgment. In full-dress trials, as he illustrated in the espionage act cases during and after World War I, he was a model of fairness and patience, skillfully maintaining not merely decorum but the order that enables issues to emerge clearly. He was never a much-speaking judge for, as he said later, "It did not expedite matters for the judge to take over . . . a large proportion of the examination and imposed unmerited burdens." When he became Senior Judge of the District he proved an efficient administrator, whose even-handedness was acclaimed by his brethren as well as the bar.

Most of Hand's District Court opinions were not reported. But of those that have been published some are so significant that they deserve mention here. In the famous case of *Associated Press* v. *International News Service,* Judge Hand on a preliminary hearing held that a newsgatherer is entitled to prevent the use of its news by a rival, for a sufficient time to enable the daily newspapers throughout the country to receive and publish the news. Yet, characteristically, he refused to issue an injunction until there had been a full trial or a review by an appellate court. Since a majority of both the Circuit Court of Appeals and the Supreme Court accepted Judge Hand's reasoning, they directed him to proceed with the relief he proposed. In *Peterson* v. *Davidson,* Judge Hand, despite the Seventh Amendment to the United States Constitution, sent a jury case involving complicated accounts to an auditor to make a preliminary examination, to hear the evidence, and to report his findings so as to simplify the issues for the jury. This procedure was approved by the Supreme Court and has become a practice specifically authorized by the Federal Rules of Civil Procedure. *United States* v. *Western Union Telegraph Co.,* rejected the claim of the President that in time of peace he had inherent constitutional power to pre-

vent the landing of a submarine cable from a foreign country upon the shores of the United States.

When Circuit Judge Hough died in 1927, President Cool-
idge, in accordance with Hough's frequently expressed
wish, named as his successor District Judge Hand. Respond-
ing on May 28, 1927, to Justice Brandeis's congratulatory
note, Judge Hand wrote:

As for my appointment I felt flattered to have the support of
the best of the bench and bar. Beyond that I looked forward
to the pleasure of being in the same Appellate Court with
Learned. We are the only men of the family, have been like
brothers and will see the male line extinguished together. Aside
from these pleasures of the imagination, I did not care much. I
am almost abnormally without ambition and I am by no means
sure that I am not better [fitted] to administer an important
trial court, full of interest to me, than to sit in appeals. However, here I am, and I should be and am content enough.

In twenty-seven years as an appellate judge, A. N. Hand
wrote approximately eight hundred opinions. Most of them,
as one would expect in an intermediate appellate court, review evidence and deal with points of statutory construction or minor variations of orthodox legal doctrine. Yet
they reveal his qualities of workmanship and character.
Outstanding is the careful and comprehensive statement of
the facts. For from his mastery of the details of records
he became an expert in admiralty, though neither as a boy
or man had he intimate familiarity with the sea. He became
a sound patent judge, though he entirely lacked Yankee ingenuity, the habit of tinkering with gadgets, or personal
acquaintance with research laboratories. In bankruptcy and
corporate reorganization cases he had no peer, for in this
field there was special scope for his practicality, penetrating understanding of character, and aloofness from partisanship.

In all fields his opinions manifest deep concern that the relevant authorities, English as well as American, shall not merely be cited but be precisely applied. The kernel of each principal precedent is enucleated as it would be in the schools. The reader is thus rightly persuaded that the judge himself examined the earlier report and did not leave his law clerk free to splatter the opinion with citations of unanalyzed cases.

Judge Hand's intended audience was not the bench, bar, or university world in general, but the particular lawyer who was about to lose the case and the particular trial judge whose judgment was being reviewed and perhaps reversed. And it is because of their direction toward this specialized audience that Judge Hand's opinions so often deserve the adjective "thorough" — the adjective which he chose to describe that part of Justice Brandeis's work which he most admired.

The painstaking methods that Judge Hand adopted sometimes made memorable what would otherwise have been an ordinary case. An example is *Exner* v. *Sherman Power Construction Co.*, an opinion frequently reproduced in casebooks, which involves the application to a dynamiting operation of the rule in *Rylands* v. *Fletcher*.

In this paper it is impractical to list all the leading cases in which Judge Hand sat. A few may be singled out for comment. The most complicated was the decision in *In re Associated Gas & Electric Co.*, placing the final stamp of approval on the plan for reorganizing one of the world's largest public utilities. The case which attracted the widest attention in literary circles permitted the importation of James Joyce's *Ulysses*, a volume which in private correspondence Judge Hand described as a "swill pail tragedy of the human soul at a low ebb." *Baird* v. *Franklin* refused to impose liability upon the New York Stock Exchange for the loss sustained when Richard Whitney embezzled plaintiff's securities. *In re Salmon Weed & Co.* earned academic plaudits as "the best opinion on tortious repledges to be found in either the English or the American reports." *Norman* v. *Consolidated Edison Co. of N.Y.* has a most searching and discriminating analysis of the right of a stockholder to maintain suit to enjoin his corporation from paying an allegedly illegal tax. *United States* v. *Paramount Pictures, Inc.*, while modified on appeal, laid the main lines for the dissolution of the producer-exhibitor relationships in the motion picture field. *United States* v. *Sacher* covered the extremely contentious issues raised by the misconduct of counsel in the protracted Communist conspiracy trial before Judge Medina. The dissent in *York* v. *Guaranty Trust Co. of New York* presages that view of the application of the rule in *Erie R. Co.* v. *Tompkins* to local statutes of limitations which was ultimately accepted by the Supreme Court. *United States* v. *Polakoff* reveals a characteristic attitude toward wiretapping problems: "I am convinced that prohibition of the use of wire taps to detect the activities of criminals, who chose to conduct their negotiations by means of the telephone, imposes great and at times insurmountable obstacles upon the prosecuting authorities . . . Congress . . . can constitutionally permit wire-tapping."

As Judge Hand grew in judicial stature he also grew in general reputation. A majority of the judges of the New York Court of Appeals wanted him to become their associate when Chief Judge Cardozo went to Washington. But he wrote, "I declined to be considered because I didn't want to be thrown out of a job at 70 . . . I also hated to leave the old U.S.A., and Learned Hand and Swan." With those two associates he did become a member of the Council and of the Executive Committee of the American

Law Institute and was an active adviser in the Institute's restatement of torts and its codification of evidence. He served as president of the Maritime Law Association of the United States, the Havens Relief Fund, and the New York Phillips Exeter Alumni Association; as trustee of the Episcopal Theological School; and warden and vestryman of Grace Church in New York City. His was one of the most powerful voices in the affairs of Harvard University and its alumni organizations: he led the ballot for Overseers in 1936; in 1944-1945 he was president of the Harvard Alumni Association; he was President of the Harvard Law School Association of New York and vice-president of the Harvard Club of New York. Yet he remained almost unaware of how influential he had become: "I often think indeed that I am such a 'pallid bust of Pallas,' as Poe would say, that I have never influenced anyone or anything." When Columbia, Harvard, Middlebury, Pennsylvania, Williams, and Yale sought to persuade him otherwise by conferring upon him honorary doctorates, his reaction was "I . . . would never give" degrees of this kind "if I ran the world, except to scholars who wrote books on the 'sex habits of the tree toad.' "

This summary of Judge Hand's judicial work and outside activities falls far short of describing his moral impact upon an ever-widening community. We recognized in him the ancient type of our ancestor's worth. He had a simple, unpretentious pattern of daily life. Yet his dislike of any form of ostentation was not carried to the extreme of an unaesthetic egalitarianism. He wrote that "I have no opinion at all of living in a sordid way . . . If a Judge of the United States Court can have a home of dignity it is so much better for his peace and really good work . . . To have a good place for books, family and friends I believe is much better than acute barn-yard democracy." These principles Judge and Mrs. Hand carried out in their warm hospitality in the ancestral home in Elizabethtown and in their New York City apartments, first on West Ninth Street and later on East Sixty-eighth Street.

In an era when, as he said, the tendency is to regard "big output" as "the great thing," he continued faithful to the tradition of "a mellow . . . culture based on time to reflect." He never cared much for organized entertainment, although he readily joined a family circle in which each read aloud a part of a Shakespearean play. Erasmus was his favorite author. The humanist's portrait hung in the judge's chambers; and early editions formed an important part of the judge's library. Judge Hand constantly read history, particularly American Colonial and English history, for next to his own country he cherished "the ties with the mother country which," he said, "I believe will never be broken." Greek and Latin classics were on his table; he carried them on the elevated railway; at seventy-three years of age he was "reading Virgil's Aeneid" with his grandson; later he was rejoicing in Dryden's translation not only for its merit but because Mrs. Hand, through Anne Hutchinson, claimed kinship with the translator. While he applauded the attitude of his grandfather who "would not give unstable Shelley shelf-room," he stored his mind with quotations from other poets that he playfully applied to his granddaughters and others whom he especially loved.

Judge Hand's infectious good humor, his forthrightness of speech brought warmth to all his personal relations. Only a man known to be without any element of spite or self-seeking could have talked as freely as he sometimes did of members of his profession without stirring wrath. We have all heard him describe the style of one judge, whose

substantive views he admired, as "exotic, florid, fairy-airy."
Another he called a "literary sharp shooter." A third he
asserted "would get up on a charger to attack a moat." Of
a fourth he said "political microbes here stay away from
him like an iced hog."

But if Judge Hand scored his fellows' foibles, he also
underscored their virtues. He knew the worth of Miss
Libby, who was his secretary from the time he was a private lawyer until he died on October 28, 1954. His chuckle
brightened Mrs. Coleman's day in the library. Although he
told new law clerks that their task was only "digging out
material . . . and helping him think about it," before
long they found that this modest man, who because he
doubted his competence as a teacher had in 1916 refused
appointment to the Harvard Law School faculty, was in
reality giving them a more profound education than any
that a university could offer. This he did partly by making
them share his feeling of the importance of the task before them. "You had better stick to your job and not become an asteroid, coruscating but without orbit." "Join
no clubs and have no slogans." "Remember that nobody
amounts to much and keep natural and humble in all circumstances." Don't allow yourself to be "shrouded in
mist from the rising incense" of your "own meditations."
"Keep to the English tradition and don't go in for orna-
mentation or cleverness." Disregard those "Lucifers who
have had no relation" to the affairs of this world "but seem
to have minds that look down long vistas."

In a revolutionary age Judge Hand's recurrent theme
was "moderation and an attempt to appeal to everybody
to be reasonably fair and detached in his judgments and
seriously and sincerely to follow the light that is in him
. . . The talk of the average conservative about the movements of the day is distressingly ignorant and can hardly

be exceeded in intolerance or stupidity by that of the liberal who advocates everything that involves change and has the imprimatur of the 'children of the dawn.' "

This spirit of forbearance explains many of Judge Hand's votes sustaining legislative and administrative action. He believed in leaving the parties to " 'fry in their own fat' until the legislative branch sees fit to change the procedure or the administrative tribunals themselves become more circumspect." Yet Judge Hand was by no means an advocate of the abolition of the characteristic American device of judicial review of legislation. He wrote at the height of the 1937 court-packing plan, "I hope to see constitutional limitations interpreted by a court in spite of some public irritation that may be involved. We are far from England yet and I fear to lose a final hearing, especially as to personal rights, before the only bodies that have any tendency to do justice in an orderly way."

But the primal source of Judge Hand's influence was his religious faith — an aspect of man having a cover of mystery that resists full description. To Judge Hand, as to so many others, religion meant more than the avowed acceptance of one particular creed or the regular participation in one established ritual. Indeed he served simultaneously as a vestryman and warden of Grace Episcopal Church in New York City and as a trustee of the Congregational Church in Elizabethtown. His general attitude is revealed by a quotation from one of his most famous opinions, *United States* v. *Kauten*, where he wrote:

Religious belief arises from a sense of the inadequacy of reason as a means of relating the individual to his fellow-men and to his universe — a sense common to men in the most primitive and in the most highly civilized societies. It accepts the aid of logic but refuses to be limited by it. It is a belief finding expression in a conscience which categorically requires the believer to disregard elementary self-interest and to accept martyrdom in preference to transgressing its tenets.

Judge Hand's religious faith showed itself in his devotion to "Duty" as the "Stern Daughter of the Voice of God." It animated his companionship with a wife who shared his outlook. And it was the foundation of the bravery and calm confidence in divine purpose with which Judge and Mrs. Hand faced unforeseeable sorrows.

Those who watched the victory of the spirit in Judge Hand gained new insight and new courage. They became convinced that beyond the clash of interests and the compromise of competing claims there can be found standards of rectitude and generosity, and that in the search for these standards and in the steadfast adherence to them lies the triumph of man. To quote the words that the poet Archibald MacLeish wrote in his honor, Judge Hand taught us that

> We are neither weak nor few.
> As long as one man does what one can do—
> As long as one man in the sun alone
> Walks between the silence and the stone
> And honors manhood in his flesh, his bone,
> We are not yet too weak, nor yet too few,

When at the end of this meeting we depart through the doors of this house, we will reflect how often in this very neighborhood walked our friend of broad frame and broader vision, of strong step, and stout heart. We see him coming out of the Lexington Avenue subway, his briefcase bulging with records from his chambers in Foley Square. A little late for its opening hour he is headed toward the session of the Council of the American Law Institute in the courtroom on the fifth floor of this building. We recall him arriving at the Harvard Club across the street to dine in the Mahogany Room as the guest of a score of law clerks who thought of him as a second father. We see him Saturday at lunch time turning round the corner into Forty-third Street to meet friends at the Century Association, to talk of letters, or music, or art, or education. We watch him on his way to the Grand Central Station to take the sleeper for Westport in the Adirondacks. We know that once he has returned to the country home of his boyhood, he will exercise a jurisdiction more varied, more intimate, more surely incontestable, than any known to the United States Code; for in Elizabethtown his authority rests not upon Presidential commission, but upon the reverence accorded to one who by merit and by birth, by achievement and by affection, is the community's first citizen.

And as we recall him passing along the street to one or another of his destinations, we always see him moving steadily forward, undeflected by the pushing crowds, and indifferent to the effect upon them of his impressive manner. Impervious to strife and strain, conflict and controversy, resolutely he pursues the path on which he first set forth when this republic was half its present age.

You may join him if you will. But he will not press for your company. He does not promise you rewards, either now, or at the journey's end; nor even assure you that in his pocket is the map to lead you safely there. All he will say is that he himself has received help from those who went before, and that this help he would gladly share with you, if you would like it. And while this is all you are told, you may come to believe that, though Augustus Noble Hand knew it not himself, he had found the road that leads to the Abiding City.

An address delivered to the
Association of the Bar of the
City of New York and the New
York County Lawyers' Association, 1955

Learned Hand

FEW judges have been so acclaimed during their lives as Judge Learned Hand, who died on August 18, 1961, in his ninetieth year. Two years before, the court in which he had sat held a special session to commemorate his unprecedented half-century of service on the federal bench. Lay and professional journals in countless articles rightly referred to him as the greatest contemporary judge in the English-speaking world. Everywhere he was recognized as the heir of Holmes's triple crown as jurist, philosopher, and poet of liberty.

Much of Judge Hand's reputation was derived from the skill and artistry with which he performed court tasks that others would have treated as routine. Some of it was traceable to the felicity with which he spoke on ceremonial occasions; his speech lent "a lustre and more great opinion, a larger dare to our great enterprise." But what counted most was that his vision, unrestricted by boundaries of partisanship, provinciality, or narrow mores, had an inclusive wisdom, a Shakespearean understanding of what men are like. He shared their melancholy and their robust joy. Like Montaigne, he knew that, though a man sits upon the top of the world, yet sits he upon his tail.

Judge Hand's strength traced its sources to the most distinguished legal family in northern New York. His father was for a short time judge of the state Court of Appeals, and his uncles, grandfather, and more remote ancestors held places of eminence at the bar and on the bench. His training at Harvard College coincided with and benefited from the golden age of its philosophy department. At the Harvard Law School he studied under masters, whom he praised in memorable words, now carved on the walls of Austin Hall and originally spoken as part of the 1958 Holmes lectures, delivered to the largest throng ever assembled to hear a law-school speaker.

At thirty-seven years of age, Learned Hand was appointed by President Taft to the United States District Court for the Southern District of New York. He averred that his acceptance involved no sacrifice, for he had not been a large moneymaker at the bar. No doubt, potential clients regarded him as too brilliant to be a counsel of sound judgment. And, as Holmes indicated, it is judgment, or, more strictly, a reputation for it, for which men pay.

When he sat alone in the trial court, Judge Hand often touched the superlative. The *Corn Products* case may serve as an example. A generation in advance of the Supreme Court, he grasped the relevance of the Sherman Act to the second industrial revolution. Judge Hand's injunction against the postmaster's exclusion of *The Masses* from the mails, though reversed on appeal, is seen, in retrospect, as the precursor of the federal courts' present protection of freedom of the press.

With a jury, Learned Hand was not always a sufficiently silent judge. Yet he could speak to laymen with such simple persuasiveness in civil-liberties cases that his charges were regarded as textbook models. They foreshadowed his most renowned address, given in Central Park to newly naturalized citizens.

Hand waited fifteen years before promotion to the Court

of Appeals. One reason may have been that, imprudently, in 1912 he had accepted the bootless nomination of the Progressive Party for Chief Judge of the State of New York. He had responded to affection for Theodore Roosevelt, despite the reckless Colonel's misstatement that it was Judge Hand who led him to advocate the recall of federal judges.

By the late 1930's, when L. Hand, Swan, and A. N. Hand had become, as it were, its "first team," the Second Circuit had acquired a professional reputation comparable to that of the New York Court of Appeals under Chief Judge Cardozo. For Judge Learned Hand, the companionship of his brethren was, aside from his deep ties with a charming, sympathetic wife and three beautiful and attractive daughters, the central satisfaction of his life. He cherished the friendship of Judge Swan, the distinguished former Yale dean, whose purity, learning, and experience balanced Hand's own almost feminine intuition and quickness. His "Cousin Gus" had been a friend since childhood. As boys, "Gus" and "B" (the surviving indication that he had been christened Billings) had roamed the countryside of Elizabethtown, New York, where Grandfather Augustus and Uncle Richard, in turn, had been leading lawyers of the county. Together the youngsters had cross-examined Civil War veterans, learned their slang, and memorized their songs, which later Learned Hand was to record for the Library of Congress.

One day B said, "Gus, we have jawed about everything except religion." The devout yet ever sensible older cousin replied: "I've never thought that would be useful." Indeed, when in his eighty-ninth year, Judge Hand, and Mrs. Hand, read aloud the Gospels, he was still troubled by the number of miracles; although, as his speeches show, he was much moved by the personality of Jesus and by his message of compassion. In the Hand family, from the days of their youth, it was oft repeated that Gus had better judgment than B — a view shared by Justice Robert H. Jackson, who wittily advised the bench and bar: "Quote B; but follow Gus."

Sitting with Judges Swan and Augustus N. Hand, and their subsequently appointed colleagues, who revered their chief, or, as he later became, their "Old Chief," Judge Learned Hand wrote more than two thousand opinions. Many dealt with what from other pens would have been dull accident cases, published as a shapeless mass. But the Hand touch has marked them with principles possessing generative power. Thus, a doctrine originating in the common law of torts sometimes was transplanted by Hand in an admiralty cause and gained a new posterity. In regard to unfair competition, he wrote with such comprehension of the marts of trade, of competitive needs, and of the limits of fair play that a casebook on equitable relief could have been compiled from his judgments alone.

To criminal law he brought a mind informed by experience, deepened by erudition, and sensitized by awareness of the history of the struggle for liberty. He did not need to be reminded that "Power and Appetite are the two sides of Commodity." Hobbes, Rousseau, and Whitehead had taught him that civilizations are held together in part by persuasion, but also, in no small part, by coercion. Those who by their own lawless violence resisted the legitimate violence of the Great Beast Leviathan received from him short shrift. When a plainly guilty man had had a fair trial, Hand was not quick to discover error. Even when he cared little for a particular prohibition or penalty, he did not evade the law's mandate. Yet he was no friend of barbaric police or ruthless prosecutors. The squalid huckster whose constitutional rights had been abused had no better guardian.

More than any other lower-court judge, he was the architect of our present structure of antitrust law. Entrusted by a special act of Congress with the *Aluminum* case, for which a quorum could not be found in the Supreme Court, he faced a record so prodigious that *Life* magazine amused its readers by photographing the judge flanked by the dozens of printed volumes. Yet he cut through the jungle a path which has been to all his successors the clearest route for decision of cases charging monopolization. In *Associated Press* are *aperçus* not yet fully explored. The judge's imaginative reach forecasts an emerging "rule of law" for private associations. It suggests ways by which limitations may be placed upon clusters of combined strength, procedural fairness may be assured, power be divided, and adverse interests be marshaled. The opinion stretches the "rule of law" from the public sector where it originated to the private sector which it seeks to subdue.

Judge Hand's interpretation of statutes reflected his long concern with the ultimates of political theory. Since his student days, he had pushed the inquiry into whether there is a "common will." His answer was that law represents a compromise achieved by competing interests. If the compromise was made in the strictly political forum of the legislature, the statute embodying the agreement is merely to be interpreted, not altered one jot, by the judge. For him to substitute his supposed sagacity or sympathy is an arbitrary, despotic intrusion.

Some in the Supreme Court and in the law schools saw in Hand's admonitions too great a reluctance to construe statutes in the light of a tradition of common-law liberties and a prospect of social progress. They condemned him for "*il gran refuto*" — for his unwillingness to use the keys of power and direction they regarded as characteristic of high authority. But Judge Hand made it clear that he had no commission or competence for the office of guardian in a Platonic or in a welfare state.

He saw no reason to believe that judges know best, or, indeed, that there is any theoretical best to be known. How he would have chuckled in agreement with Bacon: "We are much beholden to Machiavelli and others that wrote 'what men do, and not what they ought to do.' " Much as he admired his friend Lord Radcliffe, Judge Hand did not subscribe to the revival of natural law concepts so appealingly developed in *The Law and Its Compass*. If the legislature votes to go to the everlasting bonfire, let the voters, not the judges, stand athwart the primrose path!

Hand never held unconstitutional an entire act of Congress. His *Schechter* opinion invalidated the labor, but would have saved the fair-trade-practice, provisions in the NRA codes. If his 1958 Holmes lectures on the Bill of Rights are to be taken at one of their Janus-faced values, Hand would not have declared state law unconstitutional unless it impinged on national power. But on that occasion Hand was speaking with the nonresponsibility enjoyed, and enjoyed to the full, by academic lecturers. A retired judge's telling the young of the follies of power and the futility of judges is one form of sharing experience. He who sits where marching orders must be enforced or canceled is not free to be a mere "captain of a huckleberry party."

When Judge Hand faced one of the most awesome responsibilities that ever rested upon an American judge, the appeal of the eleven Communists in *Dennis*, he did not evade responsibility. He knew that, ever since he had construed a mere statute in *The Masses*, he was regarded as an authentic glossator of the First Amendment. His letter to Holmes, dated June 22, 1918, published in connection with Laski's comment thereon dated July 5, 1918, showed that there was a time when he drew almost no boundaries to free speech. More than this, because Hand was *facile princeps* among American judges, because he was the successor in public imagination of Holmes as the apostle of liberty, because none doubted Hand's integrity, detachment, and long vision, his voice carried a reverberating echo. If he voted to set aside the convictions, five on the Supreme Court might follow. If he voted to affirm, five would follow him in both result and reasoning.

With unmatched persuasive power, Judge Hand sustained the convictions. With scrupulousness and simplicity, he analyzed the case law. He found Holmes's "clear and present danger" test wanting, and he substituted as an approach "the gravity of the evil discounted by its improbability." From the premise that no government can tolerate revolution, he concluded that the Constitution does not preclude Congress from punishing preliminary steps, even if they be only in the form of advocacy of action.

The majority of the Supreme Court, of the bar, and of the public have agreed with Judge Hand. He made the choice which was not merely vindicated by contemporary opinion but was consistent with his deepest conviction of the subordinate role of the judiciary as only the disinterested interpreter of the stated will of the dominant forces in society. Not a few critics say this puts too low the creative, ethical, and spiritual possibilities of the judge. It minimizes his constitutional role of appealing to the sober second thought of the community. It reduces to "seven green withes" the constitutional bonds restraining the legislative Samson. And it converts what the framers erected as a prohibition into a mere adjuration.

But Judge Hand would have answered that a constitution which only a court can save can no longer be saved. Judges, he believed, were not only weak in numbers and in influence but often too far removed in origin, experience, and outlook from the emerging forces in society to overrule them on grave matters. He would have denied that he had any augmented authority derived from the esteem enjoyed by great judges, of whom he was so conspicuous an example. Such place as he had, he professed to believe, followed from the disinterested limitations he and his fellows recognized, not from the affirmative aspirations he and they had realized. He spoke of giving to each litigant his due under the rules of the game. But did he wrestle hard enough with the Angel to be sure of what lies beyond the rules and fills some with a confidence that that is not law which is only law?

In preparing opinions, the judge almost never dictated, and assuredly never copied the text of any law clerk. He sat with his legs upon the desk, a drawing board spread across his knees. On yellow sheets he scribbled, crossed out, and interwove well-nigh undecipherable symbols. As he said, he "thought with his fingers." No room is there for Ben Jonson's oft-quoted criticism of Shakespeare: "in his writing . . . he never blotted out line. . . . Would he had blotted a thousand."

Judge Hand's final product was trimmed of all excess. Yet the published form was a faithful mirror of his manner of speech. Latin tags were part of his normal system of thought. Literary allusiveness reflected the overflowing pressure of his constant reading. And the odd turn he sometimes gave a compressed phrase was the revelation of his personality, not the contrivance of an artificial man. Is not his style reminiscent of John Donne's? Both use a poetic gift to pierce patterns dulled by habituation. A

Hand opinion is comparable to a sonnet: a distillation of thought, prepared within limits strictly defined by convention, but emanating an afflatus beyond the established boundaries.

Hand's most important activities away from the courthouse were at Harvard and the American Law Institute. Twice he was an Overseer. In the tercentenary year he was chosen president of the Harvard Alumni Association, it being the universal view that he was Harvard's most eloquent living spokesman, the William James of his generation.

The ALI officially recognized him as founder, vice president, member of the Council, adviser on many restatements, and its frequent choice as principal speaker. But the unofficial side was even more sparkling. With Senator George Wharton Pepper he sang Gilbert and Sullivan. He told the Council that the only fellow handsome enough to succeed Senator Pepper as president was Harrison Tweed. He played penny-ante poker at Northeast Harbor with the advisers on the torts restatement. He recited with the full flavor of the original Irish, Yiddish, and Italian accents the story of the New Jersey political meeting held at attention by repeated invocations of the verse from Goldsmith's *The Deserted Village:*

> Ill fares the land, to hast'ning ills a prey,
> Where wealth accumulates, and men decay.

Sometimes Learned Hand could be fierce in battle at the Council table. But even the neophyte soon perceived that this most royal warrior, while valiant, was never spiteful, mean, or petty. And what a triumph it was for any professor or junior judge to have the great Hand admit, as he so readily did when there was occasion, "a hit, a palpable hit."

Off in a corner at a Law Institute session, a former Hand law clerk would recall, from his year of glory, a tale or two to amuse the judge's friends. Do you remember the year the court had to pass upon the patent for a Kiddie Kar? The judge put himself astride the toy and rode around the Post Office Building, calling on one after another of his brethren. What do you think of the photographs of Judge Hand in *The Jump Book* and at the exhibition of *The Family of Man* at the Museum of Modern Art? Were you in Washington when the judge scandalized the graybeards by proposing that in the Model Penal Code sex offenders, except where there was involved violence or seduction of minors, should be left to canons of taste and morals? Do you recall how Learned Hand wouldn't let his law clerks give the Harvard Law School a painting of him, and how he finally agreed to a bust by Eleanor Platt, "who made Brandeis look like Loki." Then, when the sculpture was finished, the judge said it was too grand for any place but a bowling alley. Finally his son-in-law, Norris Darrell, had the imagination to get Gardner Cox to visit him at his home. Gardner Cox, sharing the judge's own sense of fun, caught him in, or provoked him into, a puckish mood, a mood quite as characteristic as the more commonly seen self-scrutiny and ever-deepening doubt of a Hamlet.

Judge Hand was a regular attendant at the Century Association, which took such pride in him that it struck a medallion in his honor. There, at the Monday Club, which met on Tuesday evenings, and at a dozen other places he proved that, unlike Holmes, he was the hero of his own crowd, as well as of the intellectuals and of the artists. They would have backed "B" against any American or Englishman, living or dead, for omniscience and raillery. Sometimes they may have found him not too far from T. S.

Eliot's description of Paul Valéry: "Intelligence to the highest degree, and a type of intelligence which excludes the possibility of faith, implies profound melancholy." But when he appeared depressed, Learned Hand would rally his friends by proclaiming that he most resembled one of his own female relatives who asserted that she did not remember the morning when she had risen from bed glad to be alive, to which her vigorous, vital husband replied: "And I don't remember the night, darling, when you weren't glad to go to bed!"

How could it have befallen that this paragon was never tendered appointment to the Supreme Court of the United States? Luck, says Justice Frankfurter. Political distrust, say the diehards who crushed the Progressive wing of the Republican Party. Geographical accident, say those who recall that Hughes, Stone, and Cardozo, all from New York, sat in Washington when Hand was ripe for appointment. When two of them had gone, F.D.R., mindful of his specious argument at the time of the court-packing bill, felt compelled to conclude that "B has just the right intellectual age; can't you do anything about his chronological age?" That was an insurmountable question. Yet some felt that, while Learned Hand outwardly accepted his situation with calm, "the trophy of Miltiades would not let him sleep."

But those who most loved the judge believed he had been governed by a kind fate. For, though he easily bore battle when the contestants respected joy in work and his faith in the Jobbists' creed, he suffered more than most when participants and onlookers descended to personal abuse and indecent exposure of private confidences. The judge cared far too deeply not only for truth but for a value even higher, love for the errant spirit of man. No man, nor woman either, can show a scar he willingly inflicted. He himself had lived too near the edge of despair. He had looked into the pit, and nearly reeled.

But if Learned Hand knew of men's sadness and of their need for pity, so also he knew and shared their zest for life, their enjoyment of pleasure, their search for the superlative. There is no man or woman who in his happiest hour would not have wanted Learned Hand in his company.

There he walks out of the frame in which Gardner Cox portrayed him. He wears that suit he had made in England with the cuffs unbuttoned and rolled back. See that smart gray vest! Hear him sing with such bravura! Observe the twinkle under those bushy brows! He has unashamedly announced that his destination is the Abbaye de Thélème, and that there he plans to file an affidavit of loyalty to its motto, *"Fay ce que vouldras."* But the words he has chosen have been, as always, most subtly selected upon the assumption that you, too, have more than a bowing acquaintance with the masters of the past. What he has denominated pleasure freely chosen indubitably signifies what others call man's highest duty: To cherish the spirit radiant from every man; To pursue unflinchingly the quest for truth; To hold aloft the pennant of honor.

From the *Atlantic Monthly*, 1961

Judgments on the Judges

PROFESSOR MASON's analysis* of the last four decades of Supreme Court history will add much to even a lawyer's knowledge of constitutional law. In his new book he undertakes an analysis of more than biographical scope. And though the initial chapters add little that is new, the chief-justiceships after the Taft period are illumined by fresh materials.

His first cogent comments are on Justice Hughes, whom he depicts not as the master of his craft, but as the master of craftiness. He endorses Justice Stone's view that in difficult constitutional cases Hughes "didn't care what was said, as long as the opinion seemed plausible on its face, if not compared with any other." "Determination to hold fast the appearance of stability even while shifting decisions is the key to Charles Evans Hughes' constitutional jurisprudence." And Mason accepts an anonymous scholar's judgment that "a synthetic halo is being fitted upon the head of the most politically calculating of men." To John W. Davis is attributed the statement that "from the point of view of personal character I would put [Chief Justice] White ahead of Hughes." And Mason twice draws attention to the occasion

* *The Supreme Court from Taft to Warren* by Alpheus Thomas Mason.

when only a lad in college, Hughes, for money, wrote themes for his fellow students.

A more generous commentator might have struck the balance differently. Hughes might have been credited with a deep understanding of the role law accords to tradition and myth, nay even to fiction, in making power palatable and revolution effective. The Chief's handling of Roberts might have been noted as an example of the art of leadership in a group of self-willed men. His care in preserving his own records of his early derelictions might have seemed proof of his essential humility and his understanding of moral growth. His accomplishments as a magistrate might have been so arranged as to place him in the select company of John Marshall and Lemuel Shaw.

Mason values Stone for his sophisticated awareness of the judge's power of choice and his duty of self-restraint. Mason calls him "one of the great creative judges of our time" and quotes Taft as authority for "the ease with which he expresses himself."

Most lawyers would agree that Stone ranks high in any list of judges. But they might question whether Stone was as creative as Holmes or Brandeis. Was not Stone's clerk Louis Luskey the author of the celebrated fourth footnote in the *Carolene Products* case which distinguishes between the Court's duty to presume the constitutionality of economic legislation, and the Court's obligation to suspect legislation curtailing freedom of communication or restricting the franchise? And is it not fatuous, in the light of what many law clerks have whispered to the contrary, to repeat that Stone was a facile writer of opinions? For one who has had unrestricted access, as Mason had, to Stone's papers to claim for Stone a pre-eminence equal to the giants of the law does no service to Stone's memory. He deserves to be recalled as a judge of considerable learning, free from partisan taint, solid in his judgment, and wise in discerning the deepest currents of his society. Men instinctively and rightly trusted his good sense and fairness. But he was no more a genius than he was a great chief. He was the true center — not the leader in ideas or in organization.

In the present court Justices Black and Douglas appeal most to Mason. He accepts their view of the preferred status of claims of freedom of speech, press, assembly and petition. Justice Jackson, at least in his earlier phases, also commands Mason's admiration. Indeed, who can resist the charm and wit of Robert H. Jackson's style? And who can deny that in many ways he is the outstanding man of the last quarter century of the Court's history — the one who grew in character and in insight as he grew in learning and in experience?

Toward Justice Frankfurter Mason displays an attitude which may be nourished by contacts not fully disclosed on the record. Mason contrasts those philosophical generalities of *Professor* Frankfurter which recognize the political role of the Supreme Court with those opinions of *Justice* Frankfurter which avoid issues by declaring them suitable for decision only by strictly political bodies. Without quoting John Mason Brown's *bon mot* that "Justice Frankfurter is the Joseph Conrad of the law," Mason is plainly annoyed by what T. R. Powell used to call "the felixity of his style," and what Mason terms "Frankfurter's fastidious pronouncements."

A completely detached critic might say that Mason had some justification for the points he scores. But would he not give at least equal emphasis to those gifts Felix Frankfurter has brought to the conference of his colleagues and the interpretation of the Constitution of this country? What judge has approached his knowledge of American history and institutions? In the seventeen decades of our national existence has any lawyer had a wider or deeper familiarity with the principles of liberty as practiced in the English-speaking world? Has he not shown skeptics that mastery of procedure and resourcefulness in technique can be combined with sensitiveness to emerging claims and hospitality to new ideas in every field of human learning? And who would deny that whatever errors he may have made, Justice Frankfurter has a mind of profoundly moral cast, testing each proposal against a pattern of high principle?

From the New York *Herald Tribune,* 1958

II

The Compass of the Law

Constitutionalism:
Limitation and Affirmation

WHEN F. W. Maitland lectured on *The Constitutional History of England* he postponed until his concluding chapter his definition of constitutional law, and this apparent inversion of the normal order is a precedent peculiarly appropriate for our discussion of constitutionalism. For although the dictionaries trace the evolution of the term from its first appearance in English on the eve of the Glorious Revolution, and men can thus readily agree upon what it meant in a specific place at a particular past time, the interpretation of its precise current connotations has little objective warrant and reflects largely a subjective political philosophy. So this paper attempts to understand what modern constitutionalism is by considering why the doctrine is so widely acclaimed by the lay public, how far the praise accorded it is questioned by those of unusual insight and candor in the academic and legal professions, what are the basic elements found in virtually all states universally recognized as constitutional, and to what extent these elements serve not merely as limitations upon arbitrary power but also as the source of an affirmative creed of political values.

To the layman constitutionalism never stood in higher esteem than now. The cruelties of the Nazi and Soviet totalitarian regimes have given horrible illustrations of Lord Acton's aphorism "Power tends to corrupt, and absolute power corrupts absolutely" and have focused popular concern upon the need of some avowed limitations upon political authority. This concern finds its natural expression in a renewed declaration of faith in the Western doctrine of constitutionalism — a doctrine so historically conditioned as to be more resistant to perverted explanations than the older, more abstract terms "liberty," "freedom," and "democracy." For constitutionalism draws its main tenets from a clearly marked line of intellectual development to which outstanding contributors were the Stoic founders of natural law, the religious teachers of the dignity of man and of his duty to "render unto Caesar the things which are Caesar's and unto God the things that are God's," the mediaeval contestants seeking to establish or maintain immunities, privileges and licenses, eighteenth-century philosophers with whose names we associate theories of "social contract" and "separation of powers," and the leaders of the English and American (and, to a lesser degree, the French) Revolutions. With due allowance for chauvinistic exaggeration, one might almost say that the doctrine reached not perfection but maturity in Philadelphia in 1789. At any rate, that particular embodiment of the principles of constitutionalism, as Lord Radcliffe reminded us in the Reith Lectures, "was one of the most important events in modern history."

The political conceptions of the Founding Fathers and the instruments they devised for their realization, spread throughout the world, particularly in English-speaking countries, in Western Europe and, in form at least, in Latin America. And the pace of apparent if not real influence has been recently accelerated. Since the end of World War II the United States Constitution has been among the important influences shaping organic charters adopted in fifty different nations.

In this country loyalty to the Constitution has become

what in *An American Dilemma* Gunnar Myrdal quite correctly described as part of "the American creed." All observers recognize the practical role the United States Constitution played in uniting under one symbol men of diverse racial, religious, and cultural backgrounds, and in facilitating the expansion of a small settlement of colonial peoples into first a continental and then a world power. Indeed, the American Constitution is almost the classic case to prove Whitehead's proposition that "The art of free society consists first in the maintenance of the symbolic code," for "when we examine how a society bends its individual members to function in conformity with its needs, we discover that one important operative agency is our vast system of inherited symbolism."

Yet although conceding constitutionalism's record of practical accomplishment and its continued symbolic value, some of our most penetrating professional thinkers are disturbed lest we put too high our value of its present worth as compared with other possible approaches to the never-ending attempt to accommodate the rival claims of authority and the individual.

For the moment we may lay aside criticisms founded on the failure of constitutionalism in ordinary times effectively to cover all its claimed area, and in extraordinary times fully to maintain all its asserted barriers. Such criticisms, no matter how well buttressed by facts, have only a secondary importance. No doctrine of politics or indeed of human behavior, no code, legal, moral, or religious, grasps all it seeks to reach, or commands perfect obedience under stress. And while it is important in assessing a doctrine of politics or law to know how far it is a rule adhered to in practice, the questions which the learned raise as to the value of constitutionalism probe much deeper. Their challenge is based not on a narrow statistical chart of constitutionalism's day-to-day performance of its promise, but on the broader analysis these critics make of the structure of modern society, the problem of power, and their view of the insignificance of legal institutions compared with popular habits in maintaining the standards of a society.

Of doubts as to constitutionalism's value today the most radical is the view that its assumptions reflect and its remedies are addressed to a world that no longer exists. Constitutionalism, according to this approach, presupposes an unplanned society where the economic and social as well as the political system is highly individualistic. It coincides with the existence of small-scale capitalism. It takes for granted that most men are either self-employed or employed by enterprises that are within the measure of their understanding. It assumes that men live in communities where they mingle freely with their neighbors, exchanging views with workers from varied occupations, and assessing not merely their character but their competence. Not only are the economic, social, and political dimensions comprehensible by the average man, but the conflicts of interest are at least obscured and minimized, if not eliminated, by the common life, the constant scope afforded for discussion and the exercise of reason, and the consensual selection of leaders intimately appraised. In such an atmosphere of apparent freedom, initiative, and enterprise the state alone seems powerful, and it alone is to be feared and checked.

Regardless of the accuracy of this Arcadian picture of the eighteenth century, it is, as we are reminded by E. H. Carr's lectures on *The New Society*, assuredly no portrait of our world. Whatever country may be our residence, we live in a mass democracy founded on a refined technology and administered by a managerial class controlling vast organizations. For prudential and pietistic reasons we may talk as though men retained a high degree of independence, were intimate enough with their neighbors and with the graver issues of the day to have a common understanding, and were accustomed to solve their differences by rationally selecting representatives who in turn choose the wisest policies for the nation. But as Schumpeter asks in his *History of Economic Analysis*, is not this picture of the "freely voting rational citizen, conscious of his (long run) interests, and the representative who acts in obedience to them, the government that expresses these volitions . . . the perfect example of a fairy tale"?

Our society is one in which men work in highly specialized occupations, many of them located in a different community from the one where they live, so that they hardly know either community well. Their opinions are formed largely from their vocational associations and from what they derive from the strident and reiterated appeals of mass media of communication. The political world becomes a realm governed not by natural reason but by immediate pressures. And a large part of each man's concern is with utilizing these pressures to achieve new material advantages for himself and to hold in check the adverse forces. The state now emerges as the mechanism through which he and his associates in interest will gain victory and not agreement.

Under the view just stated constitutionalism sinks into a minor role in political theory. The vital issues revolve upon objects and techniques characterizing the struggle to acquire, not to restrain or mold, power. In this study of the clash of interests, constitutionalism represents a sub-topic — the limits that the victor imposes upon himself not because he is required to do so, for by hypothesis he has command of the field, but because he is sentimentally attached to a tradition of moderation or because he is prudently planning precedents for a future day when another may conquer him. So regarded, constitutionalism becomes little more than acceptance of the Melian argument to the Athenians. It is adherence to the counsel of expediency attributed to Thucydides: "Of all the manifestations of power, restraint impresses men most."

A kindred deprecatory view comes from those who, without relying particularly on the changes in the economic and social background, assert that our political theory and hence our political life suffer from the historically false notion that power tends to be evil and should be curbed. No one has put the argument more persuasively than Lord Radcliffe in the slender but superb volume of lectures upon *The Problem of Power*, an as yet unacknowledged masterpiece of political science. Some quotations, taken out of order but not out of context, will summarize his theory. He recognizes that at least in all English-speaking countries there is a "wry native tradition that all men abuse power and are the worse for having it." "One attitude is to be afraid of power . . . Mistrust is the dominant note . . . expressed by such constitutional devices as those of the American Constitution. Power is placed under restraint; it is deliberately shared out so that it cannot all be grasped in the same hand." But "power is good or evil according to the vision it serves." And in English life sources of that vision are not the rules of law but the traditions of the people and the insight of its noblest men. "Great words such as constitutional rights, liberty and the rule of law seem to change their meaning even while one looks at them." "There is a tradition of life in these [British] islands that both ennobles and restrains authority. Only it lives in the spirit, and has no special form to express it." "The best in us wants to be ruled by the best that others can reveal to us. The best is the real commonwealth."

Whatever else may be said of these utterances of a Lord

of Appeal in Ordinary, they do not echo the hymns to constitutionalism regularly intoned at festival rites by laymen or by the run-of-the-calendar lawyers. Lord Radcliffe, it is true, does pay tribute to "the tradition that there are a citizen's rights standing between him and despotic power . . . rights . . . in the main, won in the courts of law." Yet he makes this deserved acknowledgment not because power is evil, or law is its antidote, but because legal tradition is part of our culture, our culture is part of our vision, and our problem of power is a problem of vision, "not the vision of governors alone, nor the vision of governed alone but a vision that is somehow common to them both, though not discerned with equal range of sight."

Not fundamentally different, although more specifically challenging to American lawyers and to judges, is the skeptical attitude toward constitutionalism and to the cognate subject of judicial review proclaimed by the most distinguished living judge of the United States Courts. Judge Learned Hand's addresses, collected in *The Spirit of Liberty*, reiterate the theme that constitutional prohibitions are not law and do not depend primarily upon institutions, judicial or otherwise, but reflect "a mood, an attitude towards life, deep rooted in any enduring society." He concludes that "a society so riven that the spirit of moderation is gone, no court *can* save; that a society where that spirit flourishes no court *need* save."

There is nothing unusual in the first half of this last quotation. Not even the most optimistic supporter of constitutionalism has supposed that it could be saved if the only ones prepared to defend it were judges acting without support from the habits and prejudices of the people. But the second half should give us pause. The assertion is that the courts and, one might fairly add, the constitution as a legal instrument play so subsidiary a role that society would get along as well without them. We must not suppose that this extreme statement was made carelessly or merely provocatively. Judge Hand is giving utterance to a widely held positivist position that the Constitution and other forms of law are to be regarded primarily as historical compromises among competing interests, that they embody almost nothing in the way of durable principle and have little to contribute to modifying the moral climate of the community and that those who interpret them have only the subsidiary task of discerning the meaning of the compromisers. For judges to search for any more ultimate value or to furnish any more comprehensive guidance to society is to violate the basic postulates of democracy, to go beyond the jurisdiction granted to courts, and to assume a role for which men on the bench are not suited because of the limits of their background, their social and professional allegiances, and their incapacity to manage large issues within the forensic framework.

The foregoing contrast between the attitudes of the applauding unsophisticated layman and the critical informed professional is admittedly exaggerated. But the recital of these diverse opinions will remind us not to be too facile in attempting to determine what is the essence and value of constitutionalism.

Surely little hangs on whether in a particular state the doctrines have been codified. It is true, as has already been said, that in the United States the codification of 1789 became a symbol of unity, its words making possible a much greater range of emotion and perception, helping people comprehend the incomprehensible, and fulfilling Tom Paine's boast that with us "The Law Is King." But we must not be so provincial or naive as to regard this as of primary importance. One of the most constitutional of states, the United Kingdom, has no single record of its constitution;

one of the least constitutional of states, the U.S.S.R., has a document dated 1936, not yet effective in altering the tone of the government.

What then is the root nature of constitutionalism?

Many would assert that its fundamental quality is "the division of power." This is assuredly a respectable view, supported, for example, by Professor C. J. Friedrich's *Constitutional Government and Democracy*. It quite rightly reminds us that constitutionalism has as its antonym "absolutism," or "tyranny," or, in modern parlance, "totalitarianism." Also it summons to our recollection the mediaeval distinction between the King's *gubernaculum* and his *jurisdictio*, the attempts since the seventeenth century to keep separate legislative, executive, and judicial power, and the constantly expanding practice of federalism, so recently reviewed at the Columbia University Bicentennial Conference.

We may readily agree that structural arrangements restraining the concentration of power are essential to a constitutional state. But we should be quite provincial if we supposed that one particular pattern was clearly the best. In the United Kingdom we all know that the chief executive and legislative powers rest in the same hands — a Cabinet drawn from the Parliament; in France there is hardly any application of the federal principle. Can we say more than that the multiplication of centers of governmental power prevents one centralized authority from stifling growth, and allows more opportunity for new or different ideas to be given a chance for development and trial? The separation of powers prevents one arbitrary will from ruling a people. It gives time for the presentation of opposing considerations, and the strength to insist on them. It permits the development and trial of new ideas. It underlines our belief that, in politics as elsewhere in life, antinomies are eternal

and polarity is of the essence of truth. It represents our con-
fession that today we are all pluralists. And from these premises, it accepts as a counsel of prudence the principle that
there should be legal limits not only to any particular organ
of the state but to all organs of the state looked at collectively. It is for this reason that Professor C. H. McIlwain in
Constitutionalism Ancient and Modern writes that "constitutionalism has one essential quality: It is a legal limitation
on government; it is the antithesis of arbitrary rule; its opposite is despotic government, the government of will instead of law."

Does this mean that we should take as the core of constitutionalism the application of "the rule of law" — a phrase
against which, let us not forget, we were warned by Lord
Radcliffe, even though it seems closely akin to the overall
title of this conference, "Government Under Law." The
idea of governors acting under the law was expressed as far
back as Aristotle. Yet perhaps Professor McIlwain is right
in saying that the Greek notion was that the state made the
laws, while constitutionalism presumes that the law makes
the state. At any rate, in Anglo-American legal history the
most quoted statement of the principle comes from Bracton's *De Legibus et Consuetudinibus Angliae* — "The King
ought to be under no man, but under God and the law, for
the law makes the King." Yet Bracton meant that governments are under a fixed set of principles of divine origin, a
view which only a minority of us would be prepared to
support.

What then does the phrase mean to most of us? Not that
there is a corpus of principles derived from a natural law or
a theory of social justice which governs the substance of
positive law. We know too well that there is no such corpus
to settle the major questions of foreign affairs, of the rates
of taxation, of the objects of expenditure, of the regulation

of enterprise. Nor does the phrase imply that there is a definable corpus which regulates the due procedure of the government. The same types of matters are handled quite differently in different constitutional states: in one state by courts, and in another by executives; in one after hearing, in another summarily; in one by accusatory methods with severe limitations upon the prosecution, in another by investigatory methods founded upon full disclosure. Indeed all that one seems able to spell out of the rule-of-law concept, when looked at universally, is first, that the state recognizes a presumption that an individual has the right to have his person or property free from interference by any officer of the government unless that officer can justify his interference by reference to a general law, and second, that the state provides some machinery for the vindication of that right before an independent tribunal in all cases where a crime is charged, and sometimes in other cases involving serious interferences with persons or their property.

To go beyond this is to indulge in readily disproved fictions. The presumption that a person can be restrained only by general laws is overborne in time of crisis. Without leaving our own national boundaries, we know that in war the writ of habeas corpus has been explicitly suspended by the President and implicitly by the courts through failure to provide relief to citizens detained in guarded reservations on account of their color. Nay, no less a believer in constitutionalism than Justice Holmes expressed the Supreme Court's view that in a purely domestic situation a governor could imprison a labor union official for two and a half months. "When it comes to a decision by the head of the State upon a matter involving its life, the ordinary rights of individuals must yield to what he deems the necessities of the moment."

Moreover, aside from penal, tax, and property matters,

most regulatory laws, although drafted in general terms, in fact vest unreviewable discretion in officials. In most countries this is true of the admission and deportation of some or all aliens. It is often true of the appointment and dismissal of persons from the public service. And, in practice, close to unlimited discretion exists in the conferring of many financial benefits, grants of property, and license privileges.

Despite these and many other illustrations that will occur to any sophisticated person, it is not meaningless to assert that constitutionalism includes as a primary element the application of the rule of law to an ever-increasing area. The constitutional state has a progressive tendency to enlarge the jurisdiction of independent courts before which an individual can challenge the fairness of the procedure underlying official action. Once the rule of law is accepted as governing the main procedural impacts of the criminal law, its principles may, by the force of public opinion, be accepted as binding in additional fields where the state exercises coercive power. Such extensions have, in fact, almost always covered disciplinary actions in the armed forces, some aspects of the treatment of aliens, and the more drastic types of regulation of private economic action. The contest over the extension of the rule of law is even now being debated in connection with the dismissal of public servants and interrogations conducted in administrative or legislative hearings.

As important as legal procedures are political procedures in maintaining a constitutional state. It may be conceded that the critics are correct in pointing out that we no longer live in a world governed by the individual rational voter or the type of independent representative depicted in Burke's November 3, 1774, Speech to the Electors of Bristol. But if it be true that political power now responds chiefly to organized pressures, it has become even more vital to emphasize that a constitutional state provides that there shall be orderly, regular processes of election of officers and amendment of the fundamental laws. Professor Lon Fuller's observations in *The Law in Quest of Itself* put the point admirably: "It is only in a democratic and constitutionally organized state that ideas have a chance to make their influence felt. By preserving a fluidity in the power structures of society, by making possible the liquidation of unsuccessful governments, democracy creates a field in which ideas may effectively compete with one another for the possession of men's minds." Conventional arrangements for terminating existing administrations and installing successors with different ideas are essential to constitutionalism, in a monarchy as well as in a republic. For such conventions give significance to the principle that victory in the free state is founded not upon coercion, but persuasion. Thus paradoxically the merit of a constitutional regime rests upon its promotion of constant peaceful revolution. In this sense, there is much wisdom in the apparently extreme aphorism of Jefferson that "every constitution . . . naturally expires at the end of 19 years."

Neither the division of power, the recognition of the rule of law, nor the maintenance of political machinery for making a government responsive to current conflicts of ideas and interests, reaches what most laymen would regard as the most characteristic element of the doctrine of constitutionalism as it spread from nation to nation in the last two centuries. To the layman constitutionalism's emphasis upon freedom of movement, freedom of belief, freedom of communication, and freedom of association would seem the kernel of the doctrine. These freedoms are directly connected with the recognition that the individual is the ultimate seat of authority. They emphasize the principle that the end to be served by organized government is the cultivation of spiritual and creative values in the individual. They are the values guarded by rules of law and devices of politics.

There is abundant truth in this approach. But the difficulty is that we professionals know that no matter how hospitable to these freedoms a constitutional state may be, no one of them represents an absolute right. All liberties are the result of a social process. Charles Morgan gave us as his perceptive image of freedom the room which would not exist without the walls. We know that each day constitutional liberties are weighed against considerations of order, stability, security. Often we see that even in the most clearly constitutional state the balance is cast against the claims of freedom. Their practical place in the life of a particular people or in that people's state can only be portrayed casuistically, just as they can only be, in Jacques Maritain's words, "realized institutionally." How then can we say that upon such evanescent shadows rests the existence of a constitutional state?

Although no answer will be completely satisfactory, may it not be said that the vital distinction between a tyranny and a constitutional state is that the latter recognizes these freedoms as ends not means, promotes procedures to further these freedoms, and always gives these freedoms a high, perhaps a preferred, place in framing all policy decisions.

But it may now reasonably be asked if the essentials of constitutionalism are as vague and vagrant as this paper suggests, does it not follow that Judge Hand was substantially correct — all depends upon the mood and habits of a people; courts amount to little; and the doctrines of constitutionalism constitute not law but the sort of myth which has as its chief worth the encouragement of a continuity of customary habits and a spirit of moderation.

Before we jump to embrace this self-deprecatory skeptical seer, let us ask ourselves why it is that no constitutional state seems ever to have existed without independent courts, and that those states that have reached the highest levels of constitutionalism have the deepest respect for courts. May it not be that, as this paper illustrates, constitutionalism cannot be either meaningfully defined in, or maintained by, abstract absolutes? It cannot even be preserved merely by the retention of the conventions of the past or the practice of reasonable compromise. What is required is the careful analysis of concrete issues arising in current controversies, the weighing of conflicting claims, the expression of preferences based upon practical reasoning. For these requirements courts are the best instrument so far devised. In performing these tasks their role far transcends the search for, or the formulation of, rules purportedly emanating from a written compact, or the statute book, or the common law. The courts, especially in constitutional cases, are teachers to the citizenry. In every country where there is an independent judiciary, not only in countries where courts have power to disregard statutes violative of the local constitution, the judges mold the people's view of durable principles of government.

Indeed, the instruction given to the public by the judges is indispensable for the existence of a pervasive spirit of constitutionalism. For, as is pointed out in Professor Arthur L. Goodhart's Hamlyn Lectures on *English Law and the Moral Law*, constitutional law does not rest on the ordinary type of Austinian sanctions. It rests upon the reverence people show and the obedience they give to rules which they regard as obligatory. And such reverence and obedience flow in no small part from an awareness of basic principles concretely illustrated in court decisions and constantly explained in opinions circulating among a wide audience.

We turn now to consider the oft-repeated contention that both in popular estimation and in legal character the chief role of constitutionalism is negative — a system for the division, limitation, and restraint of power to prevent its abuse — and that, being negative, the doctrine is, if not outworn, at least subordinate in a world where modern technology, military and economic conditions, and the prevailing desire to translate the claims of private interests into legal rights all contemplate not a less powerful but a more powerful state.

There are times in history when constitutionalism has appeared to be largely a negative doctrine. Emphasis on the negative was natural in a society where the barons sought to check the king, or the church sought to be free of the royal power. It was likewise natural in the succeeding period when bourgeois capitalists purported to operate in a laissez-faire economy and to wish state action confined to the suppression of force and fraud.

But constitutionalism has always been more than a prescription against Acton's disease. It is not addressed solely to curbing "the strong man's craving for power," nor does it entirely ignore "the poor man's craving for food." Constitutionalism has not so far departed from Cicero's "conception of a universal justice which ought to animate all human legislation and pervade all acts of human authority," to quote E. S. Corwin's *Liberty Against Government*. Nor is it hostile to the deeper religious vision of what Professor Tillich in *The Protestant Era* calls "the principle of love" and what others might call the political principle of fraternity.

Neither analytically nor historically, nor in the light of present day social and economic conditions, is there any reason to take a view that constitutionalism implies exclusively constitutional limitations and never constitutional affirmations. If constitutionalism is defined, as I believe it should be, as the institutionalization of the principle that the state's goal is the increase in opportunities for the development of the individual as the seat of ultimate spiritual, political, and creative authority, and if the four essential means used by constitutionalism are first, a division of power upon pluralistic principles; second, an expanding rule of law; third, political devices allowing peaceful revolutions in the state's machinery responsive to alterations in the structure and power of interests and ideas in society; and fourth, continued emphasis upon practical measures for achieving the liberties of movement, belief, communication and association, then there is as much room for affirmative as for negative aspects of constitutionalism.

Indeed, unbiased history would reveal that the object and means of constitutionalism have always required the active intervention and procedural assistance of the state. This is true of the writ of habeas corpus. It is illustrated by almost the whole of criminal procedure from the requirement that the defendant be informed of the charge to the guarantee that he will be able to compel the attendance of witnesses on his own behalf. This is equally true of the so-called private law of property, contracts and torts where rights regarded by us as basic to a free society exist only as a result of remedies supplied by the state and its courts. It is often true of the right of association — for most business enterprises act under state charter and most trade unions could not have grown without state action preserving them from employer interference.

Nowhere indeed has the affirmative aspect of constitutionalism been more stressed than in the United States. John Marshall deserves to be remembered as much for *McCulloch* v. *Maryland* as *Marbury* v. *Madison*. And though the two sides of his contribution have not been equally emphasized at all times, neither theme has for long been obscured, as we are reminded in Professor E. S. Corwin's paper on *The Constitution as Instrument and as Symbol*, delivered at the Harvard Tercentenary symposium on *Authority and the Individual*. Nor is this a purely parochial attitude. Witness the recent proposals at the United Nations for a Declaration of Essential Human Rights and the debates in every land when a written constitution is under consideration. Only those whose views reflect a particular economic creed or social bias regard constitutional liberty as being always a problem of freedom from state intervention and never a problem of freedom through state action. Lord Radcliffe speaks for many of our profession when he writes that "liberty looked upon as the right to find and to try to realize the best that is in oneself is not something to which power is necessarily hostile: more, such liberty may even need the active intervention of authority to make it possible."

In estimating the value of constitutionalism today it therefore becomes relevant to ask how far we are concerned with affirmative procedures which encourage freedom of movement, which stimulate men in forming their own judgments, which enable them effectively to communicate their opinions, and which foster associations free of state domination.

In these directions no government has made many significant forward steps in recent years. Fear of foreign foes has caused sharp retreats. The tendency in new procedures has been to regard all else as subordinate to the physical security of the nation. The postwar generation has lacked the self-confidence and adventuresomeness proclaimed by the older belief that liberty is our best security.

But the quintessence of constitutionalism's virtue is that retreats from liberty make us not merely remorseful, but also determined to establish better methods for safeguarding the interests of the individual as well as the state. On the local scene we observe the constant stream of proposals for establishing standards for legislative committees, for improving the methods of checking the loyalty of government employees, for moderating exclusionary immigration rules, for assuring free access to mass media of communication, and for more favorable treatment under the law of taxation and of business corporations for those who contribute to voluntary associations. Similar tendencies in other countries reveal that a chief virtue of constitutionalism is that it makes men believe that they are the masters of the state; it keeps fresh their hope that they may achieve freedom through the political order. Like Prometheus, constitutionalism does not merely defy whatever powers there may be; it brings an alphabet for the more specific formulation of our aspirations and a set of tools with which to build ladders to scale the ramparts of destiny.

Before concluding, let me confess how gravely troubled I am at the inadequacies of this presentation. Full well I recognize how far it recites platitudes and reviews them sententiously, almost bathetically. To say something new, interesting, and true about any fundamental value system is a privilege granted only to genius. A man of pedestrian mind, unable to find new insights, and too immodest to be content with reciting ritual, may injure the cause he purports to serve. His cautious analysis of the record of performance, of qualified successes and apparent failures, drops to the lowest level of truth, and diverts men from contemplating the deeper meanings revealed to those who sense an indescribable yet ever influential climate of opinion. He fails to recognize the realities experienced by the "company of those who are continually conscious of the weight of all this unintelligible world," as Basil Willey terms it in *The Eighteenth Century Background*. His narrow criticism overlooks what Wordsworth called "the vital power of social ties endeared by custom." His barren phrases, lacking the familiar accents of a simpler faith, never convey the beauty of the well-remembered creed.

Concerned to avoid the cant which characterizes so much worship of the Constitution, we may forget that only through reverence can one build or maintain a system of immaterial values. Let us, the legatees of the Western heritage, not destroy by corrosive cynicism the structure through which we have realized our liberties. Let us forgive more readily the simple, sincere overstatement of constitutionalism's value than the subtle, timorous understatement. For faith has virtue in politics and in law as in religion and in personal relationships. It summons men to the performance of their best. It makes them conscious that citizenship in a constitutional state brings communion with a great tradition — the tradition that the state is a spiritual as well as a territorial, historical, and economic partnership and that its spiritual end is to nourish the dignity and creativity of individual men.

An address delivered as part
of a symposium on
Government Under Law,
Harvard University, 1955

The Bill of Rights

No commentator on the United States Constitution has a better title to be heard than Judge Learned Hand. When he delivered the Holmes Lectures in his eighty-seventh year, he was universally acknowledged as the greatest living judge in the English-speaking world, and was greeted by an overflow audience unmatched in law-school history.

Part of his reputation sprang from the distinction with which he served in the Federal courts during an unprecedented tenure, from 1909 to 1961. No lower-court judge was so often cited by name in opinions of the Supreme Court of the United States or in academic publications. None in so few strokes could etch the growth of a legal principle, or reveal, without massive, pretentious quotation, its cultural and philosophical import. Justice Holmes had written that he would have welcomed him as a colleague; and the press spoke of him as the Tenth Justice of the Supreme Court.

The character of Judge Hand was perfectly mirrored in his theories of jurisprudence. Subscribing to Montaigne's skepticism *"Que sais-je?"* he had never discovered any immutable principles of natural justice, and doubted if any existed. Nor if he found them would he as judge have been prepared to import them into the system of positive law which he was commissioned to apply. He saw the law, certainly in its enacted form, and often in its common law forms, as principally a reflection of compromises among competing interests. No doubt he would have agreed that law owed much to tradition, to reason, to ideals; yet in the end he would have accepted the Hobbesian declaration that "Power and Appetite are the two sides of Commodity."

Judge Hand's view of the judge was austere, even Austinian. He regarded it as his chief obligation to be a disinterested interpreter of other men's wills. He was to remain detached, not merely from immediate partisanship, but also from any ultimate passion for reform. Such abstinence he regarded as the only condition upon which appointed judges could properly be tolerated in a democracy. For judges to offer themselves as Platonic guardians would wrongly lead the laity to expect of judges more than they could perform, and would impair such limited authority as they might properly enjoy.

Holding these jurisprudential views, Hand readily accepted the constitutional-law doctrines of his law-school professor James Bradley Thayer, who taught that it would discourage the citizenry from bearing its fair share of political responsibility if courts, except in the plainest cases, exercised a jurisdiction to invalidate a legislative choice. Indeed, in 1908, the year before he became a District Judge, Learned Hand wrote in the *Harvard Law Review* that the Supreme Court's use of the "due process" clause to invalidate legislation governing hours of work was a "usurpation" and that where a statute is not "obviously oppressive and absurd," but is "fairly within the field of rational discussion and interest" the Constitution gives no authority to the Supreme Court to set aside the legislative judgment.

Half a century later in these Holmes Lectures, Judge Hand elaborates the same views. He asserts that the only reason that the Supreme Court has any veto is because if the

Constitution were not to fail it became necessary to add to
the text a power in the Court to act as arbiter among competing governmental authorities. But this necessity does
not, and the first ten amendments and the Fourteenth
Amendment do not, furnish any basis for any judicial declaration of unconstitutionality once the Court has determined that a matter lies within the boundary of a particular
governmental authority, be it Congress, or President, or
state. The Court is not authorized to reweigh what a competent authority has weighed.

The power which the Court has exercised under the "due
process" clauses to annul "arbitrary," "unreasonable," or
"discriminatory" laws, Judge Hand declares, does not lend
itself "to any definition that will explain when the Court
will assume the role of a third legislative chamber . . . I
have never been able to understand on what basis it does or
can rest except as a *coup de main.*" Judge Hand not only
denies that courts have a legitimate power to annul unreasonable laws, he believes that for them to exercise such
power promotes political appointments to the bench, encourages dissenting opinions revealing to the laity how
much of the law is debatable, and, contrary to democratic
principles, vests ultimate power in a small unrepresenta-
tively selected group of persons.

Despite his erudition, beauty of expression, and poignant
invocation of traditional ideals, Judge Hand's thesis has not
yet been supported by a single eminent judge or professor.
And, paradoxically, he himself was unwilling to have
United States Senators cite these lectures as proof that the
segregation cases represented judicial usurpation. Nonetheless, as McGeorge Bundy, then Dean of Harvard's Faculty
of Arts and Sciences, affirmed in his review in the *Yale Law
Journal*, these lectures are destined "to become a permanent
part of our constitutional commentary" — chiefly, I sug-

gest, because they ask questions which cannot be avoided
and which can no more be conclusively answered to everyone's satisfaction than can any other cardinal problem of
political philosophy.

The first question that these lectures ask is whether at the
time it was adopted the Constitution expressly or impliedly
empowered the Court to invalidate action taken by one of
the departments within its authority. This is perhaps the
easiest inquiry because it is less philosophical than historical.
And here I must report that the Judge seems demonstrably
in error. The overwhelming view of qualified scholars is
that, despite what Judge Hand asserts, the eighteenth-
century consensus was that the Constitution did give the
Court a power to invalidate action which transcended the
substantive limitations of the document. A convenient summary of the authorities is in Hart and Wechsler, *The Federal Courts and the Federal System*. A more direct response
to Judge Hand's assertion was given in *Toward Neutral
Principles of Constitutional Law*, the 1959 Holmes Lecture
delivered by Professor Herbert Wechsler. Moreover, even
if there were better historical grounds for charging the
Court with a usurpation, "successful assertion has sealed its
title," as Judge Hand himself conceded in 1908. "*Quand
tout le monde a tort, tout le monde a raison*." Finally, whatever may have been the intention of the eighteenth-century
framers, the victors in the Civil War who drafted the Thir-
teenth, Fourteenth, and Fifteenth Amendments and the
states which adopted those amendments incontrovertibly
intended some federal judicial review of the substance of
state legislation.

But to admit that, by original agreement, by subsequent
assent, or by appropriate amendment the Court has a judicial veto over the substance of certain legislation, does not
settle the question whether the standards set forth in the Bill

of Rights are sufficiently specific for judicial enforcement.

Let us concede — for the concession is inevitable — that the phrase "due process" has never achieved, even in the field of civil liberties, a precise meaning. No twentieth-century Justice of the Supreme Court has acted on the principle that it is limited to departures from procedural regularity. None has acted on the principle that it is limited to precluding state governments as well as the national government from denying rights specifically set forth in the Constitution.

Yet to concede this does not require us to conclude that, in determining whether a law violates due process, the Supreme Court acts entirely at large. What the Court has sought are standards of value which are expressed or implied by the Constitution, which the Court believes are supported by a preponderant, current, and relatively durable public opinion, and which are susceptible of more than a purely subjective assessment. In refusing to accept this approach, Judge Hand takes the position that "values and sacrifices are incommensurables," that the Constitution sets no tables of value, and that the choice made by a legislature must be respected unless the Court is to exercise political powers of a purely legislative character. To me, at least, it seems that Judge Hand ignores essential aspects of American history in assuming that the Constitution does not imply the enforcement of a system of ulterior values with respect to personal liberties. While not set forth in a table of atomic weights, these values and their relative priority are universally recognized as the hallmarks of our society and not an expression of the mere capricious will of individual judges.

> But value dwells not in particular will;
> It holds his estimate and dignity

> As well wherein 'tis precious of itself
> As in the prizer.

And, despite all the controversy which particular decisions may arouse, there is far more agreement than dispute as to the technique by which to determine whether a particular law has violated the values recognized by the Constitution. On this topic no one has written with greater illumination than Professor Paul A. Freund, particularly in his chapter on "Standards for Civil Liberties" in his masterly volume on *The Supreme Court of the United States, Its Business, Purposes and Performance.*

There remains, however, the question whether it is in the interest of democratic government for a bench of judges to exercise a judicial veto over the substance of legislation.

Certainly Professor Thayer's teaching that judicial vetoes undermine civic and legislative responsibility is not a self-evident proposition. On the contrary, the legal presentation of the dominant facts, the forensic canvas of all relevant legal, historical, economic, and social considerations, and, above all else, the carefully articulated opinions of judges have nourished public understanding of political issues, increased the care with which laws and ordinances are enacted, and enhanced the role of political theory in political decision. There is hardly a schoolboy whose civic education does not stand in debt to Marshall, Holmes, Brandeis, and other judicial expositors of the Constitution.

Nor is it true that respect for law is undermined by dissent. Law is a means of social control, which, while it reflects present power and traditional patterns, is also always open to reconsideration in the light of disinterested reason and durable principle. The strength of the law is not in its mystery, but in its capacity to withstand social criticism and intellectual combat. It is the embodiment of the Maxim of

Heraclitus that "Strife is the source of all things." Obedience to its commands increases insofar as their enforcement rests upon persuasion as well as coercion.

However, we are asked by Judge Hand to realize how far the doctrine of judicial review of legislation will lead to political appointments of judges and to political attacks upon the judicial system. The risk is real. Whoever exercises political power is and ought to be subject to popular criticism, intense, emotional, partisan, and often irrational.

But consider the risks which rejection of the doctrine would entail. Without judicial enforcement, written constitutional declarations of civil liberties are apt to be mere admonitions. Absent an institutionalized framework for their vindication they will have no greater force than the parson's injunction. To be sure, there are countries where the institutionalized framework is supplied by a parliamentary chamber, or a council of revision, or a vigilant press. But our tradition has always emphasized the role of courts in preserving fundamental rights.

Furthermore, in our American experience a fundamental tenet has been that the greatest safeguard for liberty has been the maintenance of multiple centers of power, a built-in series of checks and balances. Under our ever-growing Constitution there has been a prodigious increase in both executive and legislative powers. Today the President has a dominant role in the initiation of domestic and foreign policy. The power of the military establishment, now so clearly intertwined with scientific, technological, and production processes, is unprecedented. A congeries of administrative agencies exercise daily control of myriad activities. The Congress, by virtue of an expanded reading of its powers to tax and to regulate commerce, is master of the whole economic life of the nation, including finance, transport, trade, business, labor, agriculture, and social security. It is against these developments that we should consider the power of the Supreme Court to invalidate legislative and executive action which violates the substantive guarantees of the Constitution. How small, relatively speaking, is that power we are reminded by the perceptive introduction to Eugene V. Rostow's *The Sovereign Prerogative: The Supreme Court and The Quest For Law*. To reduce this relatively small role of the Supreme Court would be greatly to increase the possibilities of executive, legislative, or military tyranny, and could hardly promote the kind of democracy in which the Founding Fathers and Judge Hand were interested.

Nor need we fear that in its exercise of power the Supreme Court will for long act contrary to a durable public opinion. I pass with no more than brief mention the power of Congress to increase the number of justices of the Supreme Court, and its power to regulate the original jurisdiction of the inferior federal courts, and the appellate jurisdiction of all federal courts. What is more significant is that history teaches that the Supreme Court's veto tends not to be so absolute as it is in theory. Whenever Congress has been determined to legislate on a particular subject, it has ultimately prevailed. The judicial veto is in fact a mere suspensive veto, so far as it concerns national laws. Regarding local legislation the situation is different. Yet if the Court's decisions on local law produced a strong national reaction, other routes than a Constitutional amendment are available to override the judicial veto. What Congress could do under Section 5 of the Fourteenth Amendment has never been adequately tested. But we do know that widespread protests by state court chief justices and by members of Congress considering legislation restricting the jurisdiction of federal courts have promoted cautious reconsideration of precedents by the Supreme Court.

To summarize, may we not say that while Judge Hand has asked what are undeniably the right and the difficult questions, he has given answers which minimize the practical political ways of maintaining liberty in America, and which reflect to too large an extent his professional view as a high priest in the temple of the law. He is chiefly concerned to keep out of the law avowedly political choices lest at every stage of decision, not merely in constitutional but also in routine cases between the government and the citizen and between private parties, judges come to regard themselves as free of any restraint except to follow their private notions of justice. Such absence of restraint he rightly regards as arbitrary despotism. Nor will any studious observer of the current judicial scene say that Judge Hand's fears are groundless. Judges who daily exercise constitutional power exercise more latitude in cases of statutory construction and of common-law rules than do judges whose experience lies in more conventional professional paths. And yet completely to follow Judge Hand's teachings and to take his strict canons of judicial review would open, at the present stage of our history, possibilities of political tyranny of far greater dimensions than anything within the scope of judicial caprice.

Unless I am much mistaken, the people of the United States have consciously chosen to adhere to the institution of judicial review because they enjoy a larger measure of democracy within its framework than they would without it. And so long as there are judges with the skepticism, tolerance, and humility of Judge Hand to remind us how cautiously judges should proceed, this popular delegation to the judiciary is not likely to be revoked.

Introduction (with deletions) to Atheneum edition of
The Bill of Rights by Learned Hand, 1963

The Open Window and the Open Door

AN INQUIRY INTO FREEDOM OF ASSOCIATION

CALIFORNIA is deservedly known throughout the land as being first in many ways: in the warmth of its hospitality, in the number of clear and sunny days, in the quantity of students engaged in higher learning, in the quality of its educational opportunities, and, certainly, not least, in the variety and vigor of the groups into which people combine to express their political, economic, religious, social and humanitarian ideas. This rich diversity of group movements, the manifold problems they raise and the curative legislative proposals they evoke make California an especially appropriate place to deliver a lecture inquiring into the nature and limits of freedom of association.

And if this be the appropriate place for such an inquiry, now is even more clearly the appropriate time to wrestle with the conflict between the claims of society as a whole, and the claims of partial, parochial or partisan groups. For as the recent sessions of deliberative bodies in Sacramento, Washington and Lake Success indicate, it is a topic at the forefront of current local, national and international debate. It lies at the root of controversies that require immediate decision by lawyers, by legislators, by leaders of public opinion.

I need not begin by reminding this learned audience that, unlike the draftsmen of the constitutions of postwar France, postwar Japan, prewar Russia, and more than thirty other countries, the Fathers of our Constitution did not insert into our eighteenth-century Bill of Rights a declaration in favor of freedom of association. They were not deceived by the verbal kinship of the phrases freedom of speech, freedom of assembly, and freedom of association. They observed that the triad represented an ascending order of complexity. Or, to use the legal catchword of the day, they represent successively closer approaches to a "clear and present danger." For, in common usage the term "association" implies a body of persons who have assembled not on an *ad hoc*, but on a more or less permanent, basis and who are likely to seek to advance their common purposes not merely by debate but often in the long run by overt action.

That the problem of freedom of association is peculiarly complicated finds ready illustration in events of the last year. In March, President Truman directed heads of government departments when hiring or firing an employee to consider whether he had a sympathetic association not only with the Communist party but with any group deemed by the Attorney General to be subversive. Yet a few months later, representatives appointed by the President to attend an International Labour Conference held in Geneva, Switzerland, successfully pressed for the adoption of an international resolution declaring that freedom of association should be accepted as a universal principle for *all* employers and workers. In June, Congress enacted the Taft-Hartley Act. It opens with a reaffirmation of the Wagner Act's declaration that workers are entitled to "full freedom of association," yet it denies an association of workers the right to bring its cases before the National Labor Relations Board if one of its officers is a Communist, or if it fails to file with the Secretary of Labor prescribed information regarding its organization and finances.

Lest you suppose these at least superficial contradictions are eccentricities of the Washington scene, let me turn for a moment to the work of the Commission on Human Rights. You will recall that this is a subordinate agency of the Economic and Social Council of the United Nations. It was established obedient to the Charter of the United Nations adopted in California. And it is seeking with the aid of government and nongovernmental organizations to draft an International Bill of Rights. Now strangely enough those who are coming forward with proposals couched in the broadest language take action which is in conflict with the apparent meaning of their words. Take, for example, the American Federation of Labor which urges that there must be "freedom of association . . . for those who oppose no less than those who support a ruling party or a regime." Yet only a few weeks ago the California State Federation of Labor refused to seat a delegate at its annual convention on its finding that he was a Communist. Or consider the dilemma in which the leaders of the Labour Party in England have found themselves. In their role as spokesmen for the government of the United Kingdom they favor freedom of association. In their role as party officers they must obey a party resolution expelling any member who joins the Society of Anglo-Soviet Friendship.

Surely this apparent gulf between these recent unlimited professions of abstract principle and the specific decision of concrete cases reveals a situation which invites scrutiny. Therefore, I propose to examine with you the history of the idea of freedom of association, the values which are at stake, and the possible evolution of the concept. In this examination I shall at the outset make three assumptions.

First, I shall assume that you, though learned in the law, would not want me to pitch my discussion solely in terms of legal technicalities and precedents. You will realize that the problem of freedom of association cuts underneath the visible law to the core of our political science and our philosophy. Moreover, so far, there are few court cases which include an explicit ruling on "freedom of association" *eo nomine*. The phrase, to be sure, crept into at least three opinions of the Supreme Court of the United States. But in none of them was it part of the *ratio decidendi*. And usually, up to the present time, the courts have been able to avoid an explicit ruling upon the issue by resort to other and more familiar concepts. This was true, for example in the distinguished opinions of your Chief Justice in *Communist Party* v. *Peek* and of Mr. Justice Traynor in *Danskin* v. *San Diego Unified Sch. Dist.* And I had a similar opportunity to avoid ruling upon freedom of association in *Galardi* v. *Hague* where I decided that a captain in charge of the United States Navy Yard in Boston had the right to discharge a machinist whom he believed to be a Communist. I rested my ruling on the narrow ground that a naval officer can discharge for any reason, good or bad, a person whose original appointment was made for a reason which may have been good or bad, but which was not in any event based on Civil Service rules or on contract.

Second, I shall assume that, even if we regard the problem of freedom of association with eyes of political scientists and not of lawyers, we shall agree that whenever society may justifiably forbid one man to take certain action, it may likewise justifiably forbid one thousand men to do the same act in concert. Multiplication of offenders does not give immunity. Hence in this talk I need not consider the right of men to form associations for what are literally treasonable or criminal purposes, including, for example, espionage or acting in defiance of law as the unregistered agent of any foreign power. I am not unaware that this assumption may exclude a territory of extent as yet unknown. But, regardless of what party or group may be thus excluded, I am prepared to stand on the point that the doctrine of freedom of association has never been thought to extend to an alliance for crime. Anyone who, knowing its purposes, joins a combination for crime is a criminal.

Third, I shall assume that you, like myself, agree with the remarks of Dean Dickinson in his admirable and as yet unpublished address given June 10, 1947, before the Lawyers Club of San Francisco, that it is legally justifiable and politically wise for our government to exclude from its political departments and its armed services any man who has a *proved* allegiance to a foreign temporal sovereign, regardless of what sovereign it be. We lawyers know that in private matters an agent can not act for two principals on subjects where their interests are antagonistic. So in public matters a man can not serve two nations in fields where their interest may be opposed.

Having limited my topic in the three ways I have just indicated, I now propose to consider the right of groups of men to organize in our society. I shall start from the teaching of the greatest of English historians, F. W. Maitland, and shall stress the family resemblance between all types of voluntary associations, those which exercise power in its grosser political and economic forms and others which rely on the subtle pressures of sentiment and intellectual curiosity: unions and universities, clubs and churches, reform movements and scientific societies.

This is, admittedly, an inclusive approach not characteristic of the best lawyers and judges in their daily practice. In our professional work we warily move from case to case. We know the merits of separate diagnosis and prescription. And we pride ourselves on our professional contribution to social stability through sensible, concrete, *ad hoc* adjustments rather than through logical and universal patterns.

That there is a time for such particularism, I agree. Such would be the case if we were holding court and had to render a judicial decision on the strict legal right of the President or of Congress, or of a labor union to exclude from office some person deemed to be undesirable. But now seek to invoke your interest not in the small side eddies of judicial decision, but in the broad currents of political theory.

And in such a philosophical inquiry I have more than one reason for inviting you now to take a generalized view. One of the greatest thinkers of our time, the Cambridge philosopher Professor Alfred North Whitehead, has told us that in almost all intellectual fields progress comes from the fruitful generalization. And this aphorism has a special application to the social sciences because of the large risk which comes from the personal prejudice of every observer in those contentious fields. If he looks only at the organization which he already loves or hates, the observer merely has his prejudice reinforced. He may, on the contrary, have his emotion diluted and his vision deepened if he will try to see resemblances and comparisons. Indeed, is that not the way we moderns came to write constitutions and formulate the concept of liberty itself? What is a constitution but a generalization drawn from many codes? And is not the difference between the way we moderns understand liberty and the way Chaucer did, attributable in part to the fact that he used the word liberty in the particularized sense of the right of a bondsman to be released from captivity, while we generalize it as representing the sum total of that and many other emancipations and franchises.

If we take the generalized view that I have proposed, the first point which commands our attention is the obvious hostility of Americans of the eighteenth century to the broad principle of the freedom of men to form whatever political and economic associations they pleased.

The Fathers of the American Constitution plainly did not believe in such a wide freedom. In the tenth paper in the Federalist series Madison denounced the "dangerous vice" of "faction." "By a faction," he wrote, "I understand a number of citizens, whether amounting to a majority or minority of the whole, who are united and actuated by some common impulse of passion, or of interest, adverse to the rights of other citizens, or to the permanent and aggregate interests of the community." And the same attitude was restated in memorable form nine years later, on September 17, 1796, by George Washington in the *Farewell Address* which had as one of its main themes a declaration against the forming of combinations. In this hostility Americans were representing not some quirk of provincialism, but the generally accepted democratic view of their time, as is illustrated in France, for example, by the passage of the well-known Loi Le Chapelier of 1791 prohibiting the creation of occupational associations, and in England by the judicial outlawing of combinations of workingmen.

In the United States three roots for this hostility deserve mention. First, as the Declaration of Independence recites, the experience of the American colonists with royal cliques and royal monopolies had left an indelible mark. Powerful private associations had become symbols of interference with individual liberty. Second, the United States, like other nations of the world, had a relatively weak government one hundred and fifty years ago—weak in the force it could bring to bear not only externally but internally. We are apt to forget that even the practice of a standing paid well-staffed domestic police force is only just one hundred years old. In 1800 the larger cities of the Atlantic seaboard had merely a night watch; the other cities often depended on posses. And when in 1844 the New York State

Legislature made the first provision for a consolidated day-and-night police, the City of New York began with a regular police force of 16 men! In such circumstances the nation and the state looked at every private combination as a potential rival and a challenge to its authority. Third, the Founders of our Republic were heirs, and to a large extent conscious heirs, of a tradition more than two thousand years old which up to then had sharply separated the rights of the individual from the rights of the group. Of this tradition I must give a brief parenthetical review because it forms no small part of the intellectual climate of our day as it did of theirs.

The tradition of individual liberty of which the Framers were legatees was woven from five principal strands—strands supplied by the Athenians of the Periclean Age, the Stoic lawyers of Ancient Rome, the religious leaders of the Christian Church, the English lawyers of Tudor and Stuart days, and the philosophers of the seventeenth and eighteenth centuries. While each of these sources has contributed to the creation of our faith in the dignity of the individual man and in his right to freedom of expression, almost all of them have opposed unlimited freedom of association and have looked with misgivings upon the claim of men to form groups not specifically licensed by the state.

Thus Thucydides, to whom we owe our report that Pericles advocated "discussion" and "the knowledge which comes from discussion" and preached that "liberty is the secret of happiness, and courage is the secret of liberty," inveighed against political clubs and associations "for such associations are not entered into for the public good in conformity with the prescribed laws, but for selfish aggrandizement contrary to the established laws." And in this warning Thucydides spoke as a typical Greek.

Taking their cue from the Greeks, the Stoic lawyers and their successors who codified the Corpus Juris Civilis of Justinian never recognized the right of men to form associations without official authority. And the mediaeval glossators interpreted Roman law principles to condemn all unlicensed corporations, even those which had been formed by university students and teachers. Even in the period of the post-glossators, after the teachings of Innocent IV and of Bartolus had been absorbed, the only organizations which were permissible were those formed for religious and charitable purposes, mining organizations, farming partnerships, trade guilds and other purely domestic associations which were not offensive to the *jus civile*. Thus there was no right to form a combination with men outside the local area of government. It was thought that the *jus gentium*, or as we should say principles of international law, forbade "civitates" who already owed allegiance to one sovereign to form an independent federation. In Bartolus's day that conclusion was directed at the far-flung Papal and Imperial parties, the Guelphs and the Ghibellines. Some of you may be reflecting on a contemporary parallel.

The very limited amount of freedom of association which mediaeval theorists recognized was not, surprisingly enough, much extended in the period of the Reformation when it might have been supposed that diversity of religious affiliations in the same territory would require substantial modification of earlier doctrines. In the respective areas where they were a minority the Jesuits and the Dutch Protestants, each, of course, from a different standpoint, successfully established the right of each man to belong to two separate communities, the one civil, the other religious. This right was founded on the doctrine that the state and church are each, as they said, perfect societies. Such a doctrine was formulated in terms of, was intended to be applied to, and was in fact restricted to the right to belong to the two types of association known as state and church. The doctrine never grew to include the unfettered right of men to join other associations or the right of other associations to exist without specific governmental sanction.

The view of the ancient, the mediaeval, and the Reformation thinkers that, with few and peculiar exceptions, associations had no claim to exist unless officially authorized, was also held by the English lawyers and philosophers who were best known to those who molded our governing charter.

Thus English lawyers from Tudor times were familiar with an interpretation which the Court of Star Chamber had added to the common law of conspiracy. That court applied the broad rule that it was against the common law of England for an unlicensed body of men to combine for any purpose which the judges regarded as against public policy even if those purposes were not criminal or even tortious. That is, the law of conspiracy implied the proposition that what is permitted to one man is not necessarily permitted to one thousand men.

A similar restrictive rule won the approval of philosophers. Thus, Hobbes in *The Leviathan* had written that "all uniting of strength by private men, is if for evill intent unjust; if for intent unknown, dangerous to the Publique." Similar expressions could be quoted from philosophers as different as Rousseau and Burke.

These currents of opinion flowing from English teachings as well as from the Greeks, the Romans, the Mediaevalists and the religious controversialists, played, as I have already said, a decisive part in forming the intellectual climate of the eighteenth century in America. They contributed to a once widely held American article of faith that grave danger to the public interest is presented by the existence of powerful private political or economic associations.

But the hostile attitude which characterized the Founding Fathers has gradually changed as our nation experienced the full force of modern technology, transportation, and communication.

The attitude of the community toward business organizations was among the first aspects of our society to respond with significant changes. Originally, as we all recall, it required a special legislative act to create a corporation. Thus there could be no association that had limited liability unless the state gave its specific license. But by the end of the nineteenth century it was customary for a state to have on its statute books a general incorporation law, the terms of which could readily be met by almost any group of men engaged in commerce or industry. And so liberty of business association became the rule, except where there was restraint of trade.

Labor achieved a similar emancipation less through statutory than through judicial development. The right of workingmen to form their own associations without a special license from the state was declared in 1842 in a memorable opinion by Chief Justice Shaw. And this right was soon widely recognized, as Chief Justice Taft stated in *American Steel Foundries* v. *Tri-City Central Trades Council*.

Accompanying these economic developments there was a widespread increase in secret social organizations. Thus the Masonic organizations — which had existed in England at least since 1717 and which were familiar in Franklin's day — became more important in the United States in the nineteenth century. And, following the lead of the Masons, the Independent Order of Odd Fellows was introduced into the United States in 1819. Thereafter, secret societies proliferated in abundance. Indeed "between 1890 and 1901 no less than 490 different fraternal organizations were founded."

These diverse developments made acute foreign observers aware even before we ourselves recognized the drift, that we were becoming more favorable than our ancestors to freedom of organization. In his famous book, *Democracy in America*, published between 1835 and 1840, the Frenchman De Tocqueville devoted a whole chapter to what seemed to him to be the good "use which the Americans make of public associations in civil life." And a like favorable attitude was displayed by the German-born Columbia professor, Francis Lieber, who sought to teach the tens of thousands of readers of his books that all civil liberty in America depended upon what he called "institutional liberty." By the time that James Bryce came to write his *American Commonwealth* and Gunnar Myrdal, his *An American Dilemma*, freedom of association was considered a deeply rooted characteristic of American society.

What were the values offered by freedom of association that appealed so to these discerning foreign observers? Why did they regard that freedom as characteristic of a modern democracy? And why did the American Law Institute include in its 1945 Statement of Essential Human Rights a declaration favorable to "Freedom To Form Associations"?

First, associations and groups give men a chance to realize their potential qualities as human beings. Man, as Aristotle told us, is essentially a political animal — political not in the sense that he must vote or hold office, but in the sense that he needs group activity to fulfill himself. In a world that would otherwise emphasize the solitariness which is at the core of every man, association brings the joy of companionship. And under the pleasant form of fellowship it encourages each man to assume a leadership that he finds it difficult to achieve directly in states and cities of the vast dimensions of modern times. Far from being swallowed up by the association, his activity within its bounds gives him a chance to grow in moral stature.

Second, these voluntary associations are the indispensable instruments of the progress of civilization. We so regularly and so properly emphasize that the individual and not the group is the unit of spiritual significance and therefore the repository of ultimate religious and philosophical value, that we tend to minimize the role of the group as the decisive unit of intellectual advance. And yet the history of ideas, in short, the history of man's progress is largely the history of group action. The first great Greek thinkers were members of an Academy. President Conant of Harvard reminds us that the critical point in the rate of scientific advance was reached in the seventeenth century with the founding of scientific societies. These groups were the precursors of the great university and industrial laboratories and even of the teams of scientists led by Mr. Conant himself and by Mr. Bush in World War II.

Indeed the function of coteries and groups has counted for much even in literature and the arts, as was magnificently illustrated in the Italian Renaissance and in the Impressionist and Symbolist movements of France at the start of this century. The members of these groups do more than stimulate one another. Though we seldom realize it, members of the group act cooperatively, one building on the work of another. Listen to what the poet Valéry has written about originality in his own métier: "It takes two to invent anything. The one makes up combinations; the other one chooses, recognizes what he wishes and what is important to him in the mass of things which the former has imparted to him. What we call genius is much less the work of the first one than the readiness of the second one to grasp the value of what has been laid before him and to choose it."

A more subtle social contribution of these associations is their effect in guarding against the dangers of a powerful centralized government. The Founding Fathers, though they lived in an age when there was no immediate prospect of a strong central government, were aware of the risks inherent in such Leviathans. They supposed, as did Lord Acton a century later, that the constitution which they drafted eliminated the dangers of central despotism and belligerence not merely by a formal arrangement of checks and balances but by the fundamental division of power between the nation and the states. The Fathers were sound in their objective, but they were overly optimistic in the means on which they counted to achieve their goal. The reliance they placed on territorial federalism has been of an ever-diminishing importance since the Civil War. If we were today faced with a militant threat of totalitarianism few would look exclusively to the state governments to rescue us from tyranny or despotism or a war of aggrandizement. The vigilance to see the danger and the power to arouse effective opposition must both be found at least in part in other groups of vitality and cohesion.

But we may be told that groups strong enough to hold the state in check are themselves a menace because they cultivate a double loyalty in our people. Is it not appropriate to reply that the very meaning and purpose of a federal democracy as opposed to a totalitarian state is that the citizens shall be bound, and the state shall be held in check, by multiple though secondary loyalties? Liberty recognizes that its cause owes its principal advances to, and will be best preserved by, men who have always denied the omnicompetence of any one terrestrial power.

While you may concede that groups give many of their members opportunities for self-development, for intellectual adventure and for counterbalancing the power of the modern state, you may contend that there remains the risk that such groups will oppress those who remain outside their inner circles. In short, you may argue that the liberty of the few is purchased at the expense of the many.

If we had only the political and legal techniques which were known to the Court of the Areopagus or the Court of Star Chamber or the Court of John Marshall, the danger that groups presented to those not in their inner circles would be a real danger. But in modern times we have learned that in handling bodies corporate the state has other choices than either to suppress them or to allow them to thrive unchecked. We are now familiar with a hundred regulatory devices which require organized groups to do their business in public, to conform to specified standards of external and internal conduct, and to make their terms of admission and exclusion consistent with the purposes for which the groups were formed. You will recall as recent vivid instances the requirement of the New York Legislature that the Ku Klux Klan should make public its list of officers and members, its rules and its financial accounts; the similar obligations of disclosure imposed upon many labor unions first by some state legislatures and this year by Congress; the Supreme Court's decree that the Associated Press must open its membership to newspapers prepared to conform to objective standards; and the same tribunal's determination that a statutory collective bargaining status should be accorded to a labor union only if it admitted workers regardless of the color of their skin.

From these examples can we not divine the future of the principle of freedom of association? Will not the symbols of its future evolution be the open window and the open door? Through the window not only the government but indeed any merely curious outsider may see the character of the organization. Through that door may enter any one who subscribes in good faith to the announced purposes of the organization and who seeks to maintain its hospitality. And through that door those who so desire may freely leave.

I agree that what I see as symbols of the future are not characteristic of the prevailing thought in many quarters today. Some there are who would have associations treated as private preserves immune from scrutiny and supervision. They want their activities, finances, systems of election and contracts hidden behind a curtain. To them I would repeat the maxim of one of the greatest historians of liberty, Lord Acton: "Everything secret degenerates; nothing is safe that does not show how it can bear discussion and publicity."

A few there are who want the right to enter every association, even those whose principles they deny. The answer is that for them the principle of freedom of association means the right to form their own dissenting group. The open door is open only to those who meet relevant standards of admission.

Still others there are — and some in high place — who are not content with a program that allows every majority and every minority — except the criminal and treasonable — a right to form their own associations, and that exacts as the only obligation a duty to submit to public scrutiny and public supervision. These critics want, in addition, the power to suppress completely any group, whose members do not believe in all the implications of civil liberty according to the democratic creed. There is a certain plausibility in that argument, for it is based on a kind of sporting notion that before you can play you must accept the rules of the game. And yet I venture to believe that the argument is unsound.

I first note that the argument proves too much. It would, for example, end religious toleration. It would revive John Locke's absurd argument that we should deny religious toleration to Catholics on the ground that were they "an overwhelming majority" they would deny to others the rights they themselves sought.

Next, I observe that the argument proceeds on the assumption that the state can effectively suppress a group for holding opinions or engaging in conduct for which the individuals can not be tried under the criminal law of the land. I doubt whether the assumption ever has been or can be proved to be correct. Particular groups may, of course, be disbanded. But by hypothesis, the members remain free individually to entertain, to express and to effectuate the same ideas. And in such a situation the normal consequence is that the individuals will form new but secret combinations, about whose character the authorities are ignorant. That was the history of the attempts directly to suppress left-wing labor groups at the end of World War I. And it seems almost inevitable that suppression of groups which are subversive but not criminal will always work in that manner and will be less effective than governmental scrutiny and supervision of these same groups.

Finally, if an exception of the sort suggested were made to the general principle of freedom of association some of its chief advantages would be lost. For the heart of the principle of freedom of association is our confidence that by the stimulus of fellowship men will not only realize their full potentialities but will bring to the surface and to fulfillment the new adventurous ideas which the mass has not yet discerned but on which their future progress may be built.

Freedom of association like the other basic freedoms looks at all conflicts of opinion and of doctrine *sub specie aeternitatis*. And it is ever mindful of the profound wisdom of Heraclitus's gnome, "That which opposes, fits. From different tones comes the finest tune."

The Morrison Foundation Lecture,
delivered before the State Bar of California, 1947,
and subsequently published in the *California Law Review*

The Communist Party and the Law

THIS is a time of trial for Americans. For some few it has been a period of public probing of what they personally believed and with whom they associated. For all it has been and is a time of trial in the religious sense — the occasion for self-scrutiny and for the choice of ground on which to take a final stand.

From the outset of our history the American has declared that his is the open mind. Now he is called upon to look at what has been uncovered by a series of dramatic federal trials involving Communist activities in the United States and by the even more informative 1946 Canadian investigation, and to ask himself just where he stands on the future status of the Communist Party of America and on its relation to the perennial problems of allegiance, loyalty, security, and liberty.

In one sense none of these issues is new. During the more than thirty years since the Russian Revolution there have been sporadic legal efforts to checkmate the growth and spread of Communism within our land. From the days of the First World War, state authorities sought to bring the movement within the cover of legislation usually designed to reach other forms of political danger such as anarchy, syndicalism, or even slave rebellion. Simultaneously in these three decades Congress has been moving step by step to close the net by successive enactments specifically aimed, though in circuitous language, at the Communist Party. In 1918 Congressional concern reached only aliens seeking the privileges of immigration and naturalization. In 1939 it covered persons holding public office. In 1940 it led to novel additions to the criminal law. In 1947 it included labor leaders. In 1950 it embraced every member of the party, all who mailed its literature, and all who came under its dominance.

Though each of these advances in minatory legislation evoked wide attention, there was little in the way of fresh domestic evidence to consider until the Canadian investigation, the recent trials, and the reports of the President's Loyalty Board created in 1947. Up to then the alert American could reasonably contend that in the period since the 1920's there had been laid before him few facts which were both new and adequately authenticated. That plea is no longer available to him. And if he is to be true to himself, he must now candidly and courageously check the drift of his arguments in the light of the disclosed dangers.

For a generation we have been warned that the Communists are not a legitimate political party. The thrust of this charge has not been directed at the Communists' ultimate economic, political, or religious goals. In short, it is not a condemnation of radicalism as such. It has been an indictment of the immediate means they use to reach what they regard as utopia. Perjury, espionage, sabotage, and violence stand at the head of the list. And those specifications are rounded out by the catchall condemnatory phrase "unconstitutional methods."

A frequent reply has been that this indictment confused fulmination and prophecy with fact and plan. Defenders of the party admitted that its manifestoes were filled with revolutionary rhetoric but asked where was the evidence that in any concrete instance the party's members and supporters had been the first to cross the lines of conduct permitted under law. Radical might be their belief but righteous was their behavior.

This defense has been, or so it seems to me, in at least two vital points adequately disproved.

From many witnesses we have the most circumstantially buttressed testimony that the American Communist Party as an organization has acted as the belt for the transmission from this country to the U.S.S.R. of documents held in trust for the United States. Without directly or by implication expressing any opinion upon the guilt of Alger Hiss or William Remington or any individual whose case is still under judicial consideration, every fairminded person must concede that Chambers, Wadleigh, Bentley, Fuchs, and Gold — to cite only the most prominent — have used the apparatus of the American Communist Party to "defraud the United States" by depriving it of its secrets, not to mention, in some cases, the honest services of its employees. These have not been casual unrelated transactions. They have been part of a system which, though it certainly was not known to every member of the Communist Party, was more than a miscellaneous collection of isolated episodes of misguided zeal.

In addition to the pattern of espionage, we find beyond cavil a pattern of planned perjury. Here it is of the highest importance to make a sharp distinction. No one mindful of the history of political and religious liberty would charge with perjury a sincere heretic on the mere basis of his heterodoxy. Honest conflict on fundamental values must be tolerated unless we are to betray the heritage of Western liberty. Even in those cases where we suspect that a revolutionary is not only misguided but insincere in his rejection of orthodoxy, we should hesitate to charge him with fraud.

In matters of religious and political belief the best — some might say the only satisfactory — proof of insincerity must come from a man's own explicit admission.

But in the case of the Communists the problem is not whether they sincerely believe their gospel. It is whether they respect their legal duty truthfully to answer relevant questions put to them by duly constituted authorities. Browder, Chambers, Bentley, and numerous witnesses in the long trial before Judge Medina have given abundant examples of the Communists' tactic of telling what they knew were material falsehoods under oath to public officials authorized to issue passports, address interrogations, or make other lawful inquiries. Again, we need not say — and I for one do not suppose — that every member of the Communist Party agreed to follow a superior's direction to commit perjury whenever it was in the party's interest. Yet the record shows that the use of perjury was a frequent and approved tactic of party members and followed directly upon the express teachings of their literature. Thus the only inference which seems to me reasonable is that the use of perjury is a means which the party has officially accepted.

Now I come to what is a much more debatable problem. Does the Communist Party in America seek the overthrow of our government by force and violence? The critical nature of this issue is obvious. If this is one of the means used by the party, it is the most dangerous imaginable. It would present a peril far transcending a pattern of espionage and a pattern of perjury. Moreover, this is the specific means which Congress has selected for emphasis in the statutes to which I previously referred. And it is the charge which Judge Medina's jury considered and found proven.

There is evidence that the 60,000 American Communists are an army indoctrinated with the belief that at an appropriate day they must seize the power of the state, habituated to conspiratorial (if lawful) practices of meeting secretly and disguising their thoughts in "Aesopian language," disciplined to respond to the orders of a foreign hostile government, and articulated into a world organization which has already been engaged in military battle with American forces.

Let us not dispute the evidence. It is more important to decide whether such evidence is enough to satisfy the standards of liberty to which we have pledged "our lives, our fortunes and our sacred honor." Is articulation into a hostile power's organism the equivalent of armament upon our own shores? Have the Communists in America taken *le premier pas qui coûte* as surely as the would-be murderer has when he takes his gun from the shelf and enters his would-be victim's home? The greatest of living American jurists, Judge Learned Hand, has given an affirmative answer. Considering "the gravity of the 'evil' discounted by its improbability," he has concluded that a democracy faithful to the canons of freedom has the legal right to convict the leaders of the Communist Party of advocating the overthrow of the government of the United States by force and violence.

Yet the answer does not satisfy all fair-minded critics. Some of them turn to the earlier opinions on free speech of Judge Hand himself, of Justice Holmes, of Justice Brandeis, and of the majority of the Supreme Court in the Herndon case decided in the 1930's and the Schneiderman and Bridges cases decided in the 1940's. From those sources they derive the teaching that neither political speech nor political organization is punishable as a crime unless the surrounding circumstances show that there is a strong probability that such speech or organization will cause violence within the United States before there is either repentance, or change of heart as a result of discussion, or alteration of the surrounding circumstances, or resort to legal remedies less drastic than the criminal law. If this be the test, then these critics say it was not met by the evidence of the conduct of the American Communist Party at least in the 1940's.

This fundamental disagreement is likely to find its echo in our highest tribunal. Moreover, there are policy reasons why we should hesitate to outlaw the Communist Party for purely political crimes.

Unlike the problems of perjury and espionage, the problem of alleged incitement to political violence is one of the most difficult issues for courts, for juries, and for executive authorities to handle dispassionately.

Moreover, those who contend that the Communist Party of America is a disciplined battalion ready to use force are apt to rely for proof on the asserted loyalty of the American Communists to the U.S.S.R. and its interests. Despite the force of the contention that our domestic Communists have a divided loyalty and have been up to now slavishly responsive to the nod of a government that shows us marked hostility, there is grave danger in deciding that an American is a criminal because he has a sympathetic attachment to a foreign power currently unfriendly toward the United States and is in organizations affiliated with that power. To be sure, in time of war there is a risk that such a devotee may become our enemy. Yet the magnitude of the risk should be tested by our experience during the Second World War with those Nisei and first-generation Japanese-Americans who were in racial and political clubs with strong Japanese ties.

It is not then solely for legal reasons that I leave aside the charge regarding incitement to violence and confine myself to the evidence of espionage and perjury. On that evidence alone, can we escape the conclusion that those who control the Communist Party and use it as their instrument have sought and still seek to achieve political ends by means that are unlawful under the ordinary criminal law of the land? If Robin Hood and Little John, having the laudable political platform of a more equitable division of the world's goods than society now provides, organize a group of men who agree to rob and do rob Peter of his cloak in order to keep Paul warm, Robin Hood and Little John are indictable not merely for common-law robbery, but also (if Peter and Paul are in federal territory) for conspiracy under a federal statute enacted two generations ago. The purpose is laudable but the means are criminal. By parity of reasoning, if those who control the Communist Party agree to commit perjury before federal agencies and to deprive the federal government of its secrets or of the faithful service of its employees, they are personally guilty under the federal conspiracy statute of 1909.

Of course, men who joined Robin Hood's band on the theory that it was a debating society or a club for the preservation of fish and game did not by such action become guilty of abetting robbery or joining a conspiracy. By hypothesis they were innocent of their fellows' plan to do wrong. And they could not properly be convicted of crime for their original action. However, if, after the courts had convicted a dozen of the top men in Robin Hood's company and the trials had exposed the unlawful means used by the band, one who knew of these facts continued to adhere to the organization by membership, or by financial support or other material assistance, it would be difficult to resist the inference that he had conspired in connection with any subsequent similar robberies perpetrated by the band.

Would there be any difference in the status of those who chose to remain members in or give material assistance to the Communist Party after it became apparent to them that those in control of that party regularly furthered its purposes by criminal means? Logically I see no difference. But before the doctrine is applied the government of the United States should set forth in clear terms a statement, buttressed by incontrovertible examples, of the grounds on which it has concluded that those directing the Communist Party have with regularity used means that are unlawful under federal statutes. The government should then state that anyone who thereafter remains a member of or gives material support to the party will be subject to prosecution as a co-conspirator.

Such an announcement (without immunizing those who had already committed perjury or espionage) would segregate those who had been duped in the past from others who gave continued conscious adherence. Even after this segregation, a discriminating prosecutor before initiating a presentment would no doubt carefully inquire as to the moral culpability of any potential defendant. Some who knowingly give material support to wrongdoers are more properly regarded as victims of folly or of economic circumstances than as abettors of crime.

The program that I have suggested offers these advantages.

It places the Communist Party within the context of the normal substantive criminal rules. This to a large extent forestalls any criticism that we are stretching our law to condemn our political opponents. And it does much to quiet the debate which has accompanied the special legislation of the last decade.

It assures the application to suspected Communists of the familiar procedure of the common law. This implies all the safeguards of the Bill of Rights and the protection inherent in open examination and cross-examination.

In recognizing that Communism in America has been not a mere heresy but a criminal conspiracy and in proceeding accordingly, we return to our traditional American doctrine that heresy itself is lawful. If there is no resort to unlawful means, an individual or group may entertain any religious or political doctrine, no matter how radical. When we did not sharply distinguish between the objectionable goals of the Communist Party and the criminal means, support appeared for the notion that the liberties of speech and organization are available only to those who themselves believe so mightily in freedom that they would be prepared, were they in power, to accord freedom to their opponents. Here was a revival in modern dress of the indefensible proposal by John Locke to deny toleration to Catholics. And if the notion had been permanently incorporated in our political thought, it would have undermined the very bases of our Constitution. We shall be better off to return to the formula that belief is free, behavior alone is regulated.

Another important advantage of the proposed program is that it strengthens the moral fiber both of innocent past associates of the Communist Party and of the rest of us. The person who previously associated with the party and has remained innocent of individual participation in espionage and perjury is encouraged to break his dangerous ties. He is told that he will be prosecuted only if he adheres in the future. The rest of us are reminded of our spiritual obligation as well as our civic duty to join in the condemnation of what is incontrovertibly wicked. To use espionage and perjury or any other criminal means in order to achieve even a praiseworthy end cannot be defended unless we are prepared to accept the most subversive of all theories — that the end justifies the means.

The most significant by-product of the proposed program remains to be considered. For a decade we have been wrestling with what is loosely called the loyalty problem. We have set up special licensing systems to test the loyalty of government employees, union leaders, university teachers, lawyers, broadcasters, and other special classes. These systems seem to me to have confused our proper concern with four different matters: the lawful conduct of the individual, his allegiance, his loyalty, and the safety of the state.

To isolate the Communist Party as a criminal conspiracy is the first step in straightening out our thinking. Membership in or support of that party or any successor so long as it regularly uses unlawful means warrants penal sanctions no matter who the offender is or what may be his occupation. It is irrelevant that he is an alien or a citizen, a professor or a labor leader, a government clerk or a motion picture actor. It is the right and duty of the state to punish him. To hand his entire case over to an administrative agency or a private employer trivializes the offense, places in the wrong hands the problem of ascertaining guilt, and establishes inadequate sanctions.

Our country has, and always has had, in time of peace as in time of war, the right to the allegiance of all our citizens and all who seek our protection. The free man is a descendant of the Saxon "ledig" and from him takes the obligation of "allegiance." Like him, he has the duties, first, of giving and of swearing obedience to the laws and, second, of rejecting the political authority of, any foreign prince or potentate. But a man is not false in his duty of allegiance and is not unattached to the principles of our Constitution because he has an abiding interest in the culture or ideals of a foreign land or in philosophical, religious, political, or economic views not shared by a majority of Americans. Indeed the peculiar strength of our national fabric has come from an unprecedented diversity of strands.

Loyalty is a moral, not primarily a legal, relationship. It is a free-will offering to authority not because it is powerful, but because it is worthy. This is not to deny that there are areas in which the state for its own safety should inquire with painstaking care into the loyalty and other moral qualifications of persons placed in trust. In those particular posts either in or out of the government service where there are secrets which must be kept secure, it is the proper concern of the government to see that only men of responsibility and reliability are trusted. Where such offices are in question, the inquiry may justifiably extend into the uttermost corners of a candidate's career, beliefs, and associations. For safety is the first law of every state.

Yet positions which have this type of security risk are also often positions which can best be filled by men of original creative power. Here we frequently deal with that type of man who tends to be unconventional in many aspects of life, not merely in his own specialized area. And if what we seek is the maximum gain to the state, we must be sure that we weigh from its point of view the advantage of attracting that man and his ilk against the risk that he and his kind will, by indiscretion or worse, betray the state. Balancing such interests is a task of utmost delicacy. The best performances in appraising employees have been rendered by those agencies, such as the Atomic Energy Commission, which have approached the problem of security as a specialized managerial problem. The lesson is that persons familiar with the requirements and risks of a particular assignment are the best fitted to consider whether a given individual should be offered, or retained in, employment.

Certainly there is no retraction of the promise of American life in the adoption of a sound managerial system for scrutinizing public and private employees engaged in security jobs in sensitive areas. Here, as in the forthright condemnation of the Communist Party's use of criminal means, the American remains true to what he has always professed. Has not the believer in our constitutional system always said that it was not only possible but desirable to deal with domestic dangers within the framework of the ordinary law? Has he not repeated that liberty historically and pragmatically has always placed its primary emphasis on procedure? For is not the difference between despotism and freedom a difference in means — a distinction not between benevolence and malice but between arbitrariness and due process?

From the *Atlantic Monthly*, 1951

Majority Rule and Minority Rights

THE thesis of Professor Commager's learned, temperate and wise book* on the place of judicial review in a democracy is worth stating in some detail. He begins by reminding us that from the outset of our national history two fundamental principles have governed American politics: one, that our government rests upon the consent of the governed; the other, that there are certain inalienable rights which are exempt from governmental control. The first of these principles was embodied in the mechanism of constitutional conventions controlled by majority vote; the second, in constitutional bills of rights setting forth immunities. Taken together these principles necessarily imply that the majority of the persons living at any particular time have the right to determine the rules which shall prevail in society except upon certain matters, such as the right of free speech, which are beyond the proper scope of any government or any majority at any time. However, these principles do not mean (in fact they are contrary to the notion) that certain special subjects (which do not fall within the narrow category of immune and inalienable rights) may be regulated if, but only if, more than an ordinary majority supports the regulation. That notion designed to give to a

* *Majority Rule and Minority Rights.* By Henry Steele Commager. The Oxford University Press, New York, 1943.

minority a right of veto on certain special subjects had sometimes been put forward by conservative statesmen like Alexander Hamilton and publicists like Walter Lippmann. Yet it is a theory fundamentally contrary to the democratic faith we profess. As Thomas Jefferson observed, "our Creator made the earth for the use of the living and not of the dead . . . a preceding generation cannot bind a succeeding one by its laws or contracts; these deriving their obligation from the will of the existing majority, and that majority being removed by death, another comes in its place with a will equally free to make its own laws and contracts." In short, a true democracy does not admit that there is requisite for certain types of laws, say regulation of property or labor, some assent beyond that of an ordinary majority.

But a true democracy does admit that under its reign as well as under other types of government there are inalienable rights beyond the proper powers of government. In America a critical issue always has been who shall determine whether the action, particularly the legislative action, of the government goes beyond its proper powers and regulates inalienable rights. John Marshall's consistent answer was that the determination was in the last resort to be made by the judiciary.

The answer given by Thomas Jefferson was less clear. On one occasion, (though Professor Commager does not choose to emphasize this point) Jefferson was of the same view. He wrote Madison under date of March 15, 1789, that he wanted a declaration or bill of rights in the Constitution because of "the legal check which it puts into the hands of the judiciary." But, confessedly, Jefferson usually wanted the power lodged elsewhere than with the judges. In the case of the Alien and Sedition Laws, he favored having each state legislature by nullification and the President by inaction as a prosecutor and by action as a pardoner determine that acts of Congress went beyond its proper powers. In the end, however, Jefferson adopted the position that Congress itself was the only judge of whether its action was beyond its own powers, "the legislature alone is the exclusive expounder of the sense of the Constitution." Judges are not to be entrusted with the decision because they are independent of popular control and do not represent the majority will of the day.

As we all know, Marshall's and not Jefferson's final view has prevailed. While Professor Commager recognizes that "we cannot overturn now the institution of judicial review, even if we would," he asks us to look at the record to see whether it indicates that in practice the Marshall view has proven itself sound. Judges are said to be more learned and more disinterested than legislators. But in those cases where the issue of the constitutionality of an Act of Congress has arisen, such as direct income taxes or the shipment of products of child labor or abrogation of gold clauses, Professor Commager suggests that it is doubtful whether judges have demonstrated a superior knowledge or reflected a unique quality of dispassionate and detached judgment. Most of the cases in which the judiciary has declared national legislation invalid have been subsequently overturned by constitutional amendment or by a reversal of judicial decisions. And those cases in which the courts have temporarily delayed the fulfillment of the national legislative will reveal almost no instance where the delay protected freedom of speech, press, assembly or petition or aided the underprivileged — the Negro, the alien, women, children, workers, or tenant farmers. The record would seem to indicate that the chief safeguard of our national liberties has been not the courts, but the Congress, a body which is essentially conservative in tone, which reflects the constant compromises of competing pressure groups and which is drawn from a people who in 150 years have not had a single lawless revolution and have developed admirable political sobriety and tolerance.

But, asks Professor Commager, is there a difference in the record of, or the justification for, judicial decisions invalidating state as distinguished from national legislation. Here Professor Commager disarmingly (and, in view of uses to which the Supreme Court has put the "commerce clause," I submit somewhat naïvely) proposes to limit his inquiry to state legislation invalidated not on the ground of its repugnance to the harmonies of the federal system, but invalidated solely on the grounds of its invasion of the inalienable rights of man. The record here, our author admits, is somewhat more to the credit of the judges. They have struck down censorship laws, flag-salute laws, anti-Communist laws, anti-picketing laws, ordinances regulating distribution of handbills, and like regulations noxious to most believers in democracy. And in the last decade it has become the fashion to applaud this judicial nullification of state legislative acts which curtail civil liberties as distinguished from state legislative acts regulating economic questions. Those who approve the distinction advance this argument: where it is charged that a state law restricts political processes or political freedoms, the charge necessarily implies that the legislature has already so altered democratic methods, or has so stifled the expression of popular opinion, that the legislature is no longer representative and hence it would not be democratic to leave solely to the legislature the final arbitrament of the constitutionality of the law. With this excuse Professor Commager is not satisfied for several reasons: few of the noxious state laws are clear violations of specific constitutional provisions; the distinction between civil-liberties laws and other laws is artificial and misleading; legislation apparently violating civil liberties is usually inspired by a sincere but misguided desire to preserve them; judicial review of civil-liberties legislation tends to substitute in the popular mind legal for political considerations and to create a popular opinion that a law is all right as long as it is constitutional; and, most important, when the correction of legislative mistakes comes from the judiciary, the people lose the political experience and the moral education and stimulus that come from fighting the question out on the hustings and correcting their own errors. These arguments are in some part original. But in larger part they admittedly stem from James Bradley Thayer and from the Felix Frankfurter who wrote *Law and Politics* and the opinions in the flag-salute cases (though not the Felix Frankfurter who concurred in *Thornhill* v. *Alabama*, or who in his lectures on *Mr. Justice Holmes and the Supreme Court* approved of judicial nullifiction of laws curtailing civil liberties). They are arguments which make it plain that Professor Commager, believing that "men need no masters — not even judges," wants issues of civil liberties like other issues left to majority rule.

There are in the foregoing thesis elements of truth which most moderate people now accept. Judges who have voted against the constitutionality of national legislation have not usually been vindicated by the passage of time. And any judge who is called on today to consider the constitutionality of a legislative act would do well to take into account that historical fact, as well as the legal presumption that the legislature acted within its constitutional limits.

But it would, I venture to suggest, be a mistake to go so far as Professor Commager does in supposing either that judicial review as we have known it is undemocratic, or that it has hampered this nation in educating our population "for continuous and active citizenship."

Let us look first at his charge that judicial review is undemocratic because judges are appointed, not elected, and are allowed to serve so long as they behave well instead of only for so long as they follow the dictates of the majority of the populace. Imbedded in this charge is the premise that there can be democratic representation only if the representatives are elected for short terms, and the further premise that the legislature since it is elective for a short term is a perfect mirror of society. But can these premises be defended? I pass by the points that in most states restrictions on suffrage, gerrymanders, lack of proportional representation, and adoption of various electoral devices give a false equation between the people and the legislature. I come to the serious difficulty that the better the individual legislator the less likely he is to be a mere echo of his constituents. Like Burke in his famous short speech at the conclusion of the Poll at Bristol in November 1774, he may properly conclude that the voters have selected him not to record their views but to express his views. And even if the legislator does not take this high ground, he knows that on the vast majority of bills which come before him the majority of his constituents usually have either no view whatsoever, or at best a view which is not based upon experience, profound reason, firm conviction, or even abiding prejudice. In short, by necessity the legislature represents rather than reflects the people. Once this is recognized it is not a far cry to say that the judiciary also represents the people. It is true that the people do not elect and cannot retire a federal judge. But it may not be presumptuous to suggest that the majority of the people are as satisfied with their judges as with their congressmen. And surprisingly enough, the institution of judicial review seems to be liked by the majority of people perhaps because they have been educated by old-fashioned history books and, if I may say so without undue flattery, not by the perceptive teaching of a Commager.

This at any rate appeared to be the situation in the Supreme Court crisis of 1937. Thus it might plausibly be concluded that the majority of persons want the next to the last word on constitutionality to be expressed by judges.

If that is the popular view, it is not necessarily undemocratic. Judicial review is not, as Professor Commager would imply, a device for refusing to give the majority its will unless the majority is so large that it can put through a constitutional amendment requiring three-quarters of the states and two-thirds of the Congress. From American history it can be persuasively argued that judicial review is a mere device to appeal from Philip drunk to Philip sober. The Supreme Court has, I believe, never, unless the Child Labor Tax case be taken as an exception, refused to uphold the constitutionality of a measure which in substantially the same form has twice secured the adherence of a majority of Congress. And frequently, as in the Fair Labor Standards Act, the Bituminous Coal Conservation Act, the amendments to the Agricultural Adjustment Act, and the acts regulating municipal and farm bankruptcies, the Supreme Court has bowed to what may be deemed the sober second thought of the community. In practice, the Court has perhaps been primarily an educational force rather than an absolute restraint. And no estimate of the role of the Court can overlook the contribution which judicial opinions have made to political thinking. It is no accident that in almost every college course in government or economics or American political philosophy opinions of justices of the Supreme Court are studied not merely as legal authorities, not merely as expressions of the limitations imposed upon the state, but as rounded treatments of particular topics. The judicial forum with all its weaknesses does have undeniable elements of strength. Familiarity breeds respect for the sort of knowledge which can be acquired only from the examination of the cross-examination of witnesses, from the arguments of opposing counsel and from the study of economic and statistical data now commonly offered in constitutional cases. For this reason an average voter might say that he would be glad to hear not only his congressman's view but the views of nine judges on issues of constitutionality. If it be understood that in the end not judges, not legislators, not executives, but 51 per cent of those now living, have the final right to determine our form of government, it is at least arguable that the preservation of judicial review is not necessarily undemocratic.

From the *Harvard Law Review*, 1944

Nuremberg—A Fair Trial?

DANGEROUS PRECEDENT

THE Nuremberg War Trial has a strong claim to be considered the most significant as well as the most debatable event since the conclusion of hostilities. To those who support the trial it promises the first effective recognition of a world law for the punishment of malefactors who start wars or conduct them in bestial fashion. To the adverse critics the trial appears in many aspects a negation of principles which they regard as the heart of any system of justice under law.

This sharp division of opinion has not been fully aired largely because it relates to an issue of foreign policy upon which this nation has already acted and on which debate may seem useless or, worse, merely to impair this country's prestige and power abroad. Moreover, to the casual newspaper reader the long-range implications of the trial are not obvious. He sees most clearly that there are in the dock a score of widely known men who plainly deserve punishment. And he is pleased to note that four victorious nations, who have not been unanimous on all postwar questions, have, by a miracle of administrative skill, united in a proceeding that is overcoming the obstacles of varied languages, professional habits, and legal traditions. But the more profound observer is aware that the foundations of the Nuremberg trial may mark a watershed of modern law.

Before I come to the discussion of the legal and political questions involved, let me make it clear that nothing I may say about the Nuremberg trial should be construed as a suggestion that the individual Nuremberg defendants or others who have done grievous wrongs should be set at liberty. In my opinion there are valid reasons why several thousand Germans, including many defendants at Nuremberg, should either by death or by imprisonment, be permanently removed from civilized society. If prevention, deterrence, retribution, nay even vengeance, are ever adequate motives for punitive action, then punitive action is justified against a substantial number of Germans. But the question is: Upon what theory may that action properly be taken?

The starting point is the indictment of October 18, 1945, charging some twenty individuals and various organizations, in four counts, with conspiracy, crimes against peace, war crimes, and crimes against humanity. Let me examine the offenses that are called in Count 3 of the indictment "war crimes," in the strict sense.

It is sometimes said that there is no international law of war crimes. But most jurists would agree that there is at least an abbreviated list of war crimes upon which the nations of the world have agreed. Thus in Articles 46 and 47 of the Hague Convention of 1907 the United States and many other countries accepted the rules that in an occupied territory of a hostile state "family honour and rights, the lives of persons, and private property, as well as religious conviction and practice, must be respected. Private property cannot be confiscated. Pillage is formally forbidden." And consistently the Supreme Court of the United States has recognized that rules of this character are part of our law. In short, there can be no doubt of the legal right of this nation prior to the signing of a peace treaty to use a military tribunal for the purpose of trying and punishing a German if, as Count 3 charges, in occupied territory he murdered a Polish civilian, or tortured a Czech, or raped a French-woman, or robbed a Belgian. Moreover, there is no doubt of the military tribunal's parallel right to try and to punish a German if he has murdered, tortured, or maltreated a prisoner of war.

In connection with war crimes of this sort there is only one question of law worth discussing here: Is it a defense to a soldier or civilian defendant that he acted under the order of a superior?

The defense of superior orders is, upon the authorities, an open question. Without going into details, it may be said that superior orders have never been recognized as a complete defense by German, Russian, or French law, and that they have not been so recognized by civilian courts in the United States or the British Commonwealth of Nations, but they tend to be taken as a complete excuse by Anglo-American military manuals. In this state of the authorities, if the International Military Tribunal in connection with a charge of a war crime refuses to recognize superior orders as a defense, it will not be making a retroactive determination or applying an *ex post facto* law. It will be merely settling an open question of law as every court frequently does.

The refusal to recognize the superior-order defense not only is not repugnant to the *ex post facto* principle, but is consonant with our ideas of justice. Basically, we cannot admit that military efficiency is the paramount consideration. And we cannot even admit that individual self-preservation is the highest value. This is not a new question. Just as it is settled that X is guilty of murder if, in order that he and Y, who are adrift on a raft, may not die of starvation, he kills their companion, Z; so a German soldier is guilty of murder if, in order that he may not be shot for disobedience and his wife tortured in a concentration camp, he shoots a Catholic priest. This is hard doctrine, but the law cannot recognize as an absolute excuse for a killing that the killer was acting under compulsion — for such a recognition not only would leave the structure of society at the mercy of criminals of sufficient ruthlessness, but also would place the cornerstone of justice on the quicksand of self-interest.

Of course, there always remains the fundamental separateness of the problem of guilt and the problem of treatment. And no one would expect a tribunal to mete out its severest penalty to a defendant who yielded to wrongdoing only out of fear of loss of his life or his family's.

In addition to "war crimes," the indictment, in Count 4, charges the defendants with "crimes against humanity." This count embraces the murder, torture, and persecution of minority groups, such as Jews, inside Germany both before and after the outbreak of the war. It is alleged in paragraph X of the indictment that these wrongs "constituted violations of international conventions, of internal penal laws, of the general principles of criminal law as derived from the criminal law of all civilized nations and were involved in and part of a systematic course of conduct."

I shall pass for the time being the last phrase just quoted, for that is merely a way of saying that the Nazis persecuted the minority German groups to harden the German will for aggression and to develop an issue that would divide other countries. In other words, the legal validity of that phrase rests upon the same considerations as the validity of the charge of "crimes against the peace."

I consider first the legal validity of the other phrases upon which is premised the charge that murdering, torturing, and persecuting German Jews and other non-Nazis from 1933 to 1939 as well as from 1939 to 1945 are crimes.

And before I say anything of the legal question, let me make it abundantly clear that as a human being I regard these murders, tortures, and persecutions as being morally quite as repugnant and loathsome as the murders, tortures, and persecutions of the civilian and military personnel of American and Allied nations.

In paragraph X of the indictment, reference is first made to "international conventions." There is no citation of any particular international convention which in explicit words forbids a state or its inhabitants to murder its own citizens, in time either of war or of peace. I know of no such convention. And I, therefore, conclude that when the draftsman of the indictment used the phrase "international conventions" he was using the words loosely and almost analogously with the other phrase, "general principles of criminal law as derived from the criminal law of all civilized nations." He means to say that there exists, to cover the most atrocious conduct, a broad principle of universal international criminal law which is according to the law of most penal codes and public sentiment in most places, and for violations of which an offender may be tried by any new court that one or more of the world powers may create.

If that were the only basis for the trial and punishment of those who murdered or tortured German citizens, it would be a basis that would not satisfy most lawyers. It would resemble the universally condemned Nazi law of June 28, 1935, which provided: "Any person who commits an act which the law declares to be punishable or which is deserving of penalty according to the fundamental conceptions of the penal law and sound popular feeling, shall be punished." It would fly straight in the face of the most fundamental rules of criminal justice — that criminal laws shall not be *ex post facto* and that there shall be *nullum crimen et nulla poena sine lege* — no crime and no penalty without an antecedent law.

The feeling against a law evolved after the commission of an offense is deeply rooted. Demosthenes and Cicero knew the evil of retroactive laws: philosophers as diverse as Hobbes and Locke declared their hostility to it; and virtually every constitutional government has some prohibition of *ex post facto* legislation, often in the very words of Magna Carta, or Article I of the United States Constitution, or Article 8 of the French Declaration of Rights. The antagonism to *ex post facto* laws is not based on a lawyer's prejudice encased in a Latin maxim. It rests on the political truth that if a law can be created after an offense, then power is to that extent absolute and arbitrary. To allow retroactive legislation is to disparage the principle of constitutional limitation. It is to abandon what is usually regarded as one of the essential values at the core of our democratic faith.

But, fortunately, so far as concerns murders of German minorities, the indictment was not required to invent new law. The indictment specifically mentions "internal penal laws." And these laws are enough in view of the way the question would arise in a criminal proceeding.

Under universally accepted principles of law, an occupying belligerent power may and indeed often does establish its own tribunals to administer the domestic law of the occupied country for the inhabitants. Thus if Adolph killed Berthold before the American Army occupied Munich, it would be normal for the United States government to set up a military tribunal to try and to punish Adolph.

But suppose Adolph raised as a defense the contention that he was acting pursuant to orders from superiors which were the law of Germany. If that defense were raised, and if we assume (contrary to what some German jurists tell us) that in Germany there were on the statute books pertinent exculpatory laws, nonetheless under well-known principles of German law, going back to the Middle Ages and differing from current Anglo-American theories, the superior order could be disregarded by a court applying German law on the ground that it was so repugnant to "natural law" as to be void. That is, perhaps a German tribunal or one applying German law can disregard an obviously outrageous statute or executive order as offensive to natural law just as the Supreme Court of the United States can disregard a statute or executive order as offensive to the United States Constitution.

But further suppose that Adolph raised as a defense the point that the wrong was so old as to be barred by some statute of limitations. If there is such a statute in Germany, the limitation may be set aside without involving any violation of the *ex post facto* principle. As our own Supreme Court has pointed out, to set aside a statute of limitation is not to create a new offense.

I turn now to Count 2 of the indictment, which charges "crimes against peace." This is the count that has attracted greatest interest. It alleges that the defendants participated "in the planning, preparation, initiation and waging of wars of aggression, which were also wars in violation of international treaties, agreements and assurances."

This charge is attacked in many quarters on the ground it rests on *ex post facto* law. The reply has been that in the last generation there has accumulated a mounting body of international sentiment which indicates that wars of aggression are wrong and that a killing by a person acting on behalf of an aggressor power is not an excusable homicide. Reference is made not only to the Briand-Kellogg Pact of August 27, 1928, but to deliberations of the League of Nations in 1924 and subsequent years — all of which are said to show an increasing awareness of a new standard of conduct. Specific treaties outlawing wars of aggression are cited. And, having regard to the manner by which all early criminal law evolves and the manner by which international law grows, it is claimed that now it is unlawful to wage an aggressive war and it is criminal to aid in preparing for such a war, whether by political, military, financial, or industrial means.

One difficulty with that reply is that the body of growing custom to which reference is made is custom directed at sovereign states, not at individuals. There is no convention or treaty which places obligations explicitly upon an individual not to aid in waging an aggressive war. Thus, from the point of view of the individual, the charge of a "crime against peace" appears in one aspect like a retroactive law. At the time he acted, almost all informed jurists would have told him that individuals who engaged in aggressive war were not in the legal sense criminals.

Another difficulty is the possible bias of the Tribunal in connection with Count 2. Unlike the crimes in Counts 3 and 4, Count 2 charges a political crime. The crime which is asserted is tried not before a dispassionate neutral bench, but before the very persons alleged to be victims. There is not even one neutral sitting beside them.

And what is most serious is that there is doubt as to the sincerity of our belief that all wars of aggression are crimes. A question may be raised whether the United Nations are prepared to submit to scrutiny the attack of Russia on Poland, or on Finland, or the American encouragement to the Russians to break their treaty with Japan. Every one of these actions may have been proper, but we hardly admit that they are subject to international judgment.

These considerations make the second count of the Nuremberg indictment look to be of uncertain foundation and uncertain limits. To some the count may appear as nothing more than the ancient rule that the vanquished are at the mercy of the victor. To others it may appear as the mere declaration of an always latent doctrine that the leaders of a nation are subject to outside judgment as to their motives in waging war.

The other feature of the Nuremberg indictment is Count 1, charging a "conspiracy." Paragraph III of the indictment alleges that the "conspiracy embraced the commission of Crimes against Peace; . . . it came to embrace the commission of War Crimes . . . and Crimes against Humanity."

In international as well as in national law there may be for almost any crime what the older lawyers would have called principal offenders and accessories. If Adolph is determined to kill Sam, and talks the matter over with Berthold, Carl, and Dietrich, and Berthold agrees to borrow the money to buy a pistol, and Carl agrees to make a holster for the pistol, and all of them proceed as planned and then Adolph gives the pistol and holster to Dietrich, who goes out alone and actually shoots Sam without excuse, then, of course, Adolph, Berthold, Carl, and Dietrich are all guilty of murder. They should not be allowed to escape with the plea Macbeth offered for Banquo's murder, "Thou canst not say I did it."

If the conspiracy charge in Count 1 meant no more than that those are guilty who plan a murder and with knowledge finance and equip the murderer, no one would quarrel with the count. But it would appear that Count 1 means to establish some additional separate substantive offense of conspiracy. That is, it asserts that there is in international law a wrong which consists in acting together for an unlawful end, and that he who joins in that action is liable not only for what he planned, or participated in, or could reasonably have foreseen would happen, but is liable for what every one of his fellows did in the course of the conspiracy. Almost as broad a doctrine of conspiracy exists in municipal law.

But what is the basis for asserting so broad a substantive crime exists in international law? Where is the treaty, the custom, the academic learning on which it is based? Is this not a type of "crime" which was first described and defined either in London or in Nuremberg sometime in the year 1945?

Aside from the fact that the notion is new, is it not fundamentally unjust? The crime of conspiracy was originally developed by the Court of Star Chamber on the theory that any unlicensed joint action of private persons was a threat to the public, and so if the action was in any part unlawful it was all unlawful. The analogies of the municipal law of conspiracy therefore seem out of place in considering for international purposes the effect of joint political action. After all, in a government or other large social community there exists among the top officials, civilian and military, together with their financial and industrial collaborators, a kind of over-all working arrangement which may always be looked upon, if its invidious connotation be disregarded, as a "conspiracy." That is, government implies "breathing together." And is everyone who, knowing the purposes of the party in power, participates in government or joins with officials to be held for every act of the government?

To take a case which is perhaps not so obvious, is everyone who joins a political party, even one with some illegal purposes, to be held liable to the world for the action that every member takes, even if that action is not declared in the party platform and was not known to or consented to by the person charged as a wrongdoer? To put upon any individual such responsibility for action of the group seems literally to step back in history to a point before the prophet Ezekiel and to reject the more recent religious and democratic teachings that guilt is personal.

Turning now from the legal basis of the indictment, I propose briefly to consider whether, quite apart from legal technicalities, the procedure of an international military tribunal on the Nuremberg pattern is a politically acceptable way of dealing with the offenders in the dock and those others whom we may legitimately feel should be punished.

The chief arguments usually given for this quasijudicial trial are that it gives the culprits a chance to say anything that can be said on their behalf, that it gives both the world today and the world tomorrow a chance to see the justice of the Allied cause and the wickedness of the Nazis, and that it sets a firm foundation for a future world order wherein individuals will know that if they embark on schemes of aggression or murder or torture or persecution they will be severely dealt with by the world.

The first argument has some merit. The defendants, after hearing and seeing the evidence against them, will have an opportunity without torture and with the aid of counsel to make statements on their own behalf. For us and for them this opportunity will make the proceeding more convincing. Yet the defendants will not have the right to make the type of presentation that at least English-speaking persons have thought the indispensable concomitant of a fair trial. No one expects that Ribbentrop will be allowed to summon Molotov to disprove the charge that in invading Poland, Germany started an aggressive war. No one anticipates that the defense, if it has the evidence, will be given as long a time to present its evidence as the prosecution takes. And there is nothing more foreign to those proceedings than either the presumption that the defendants are innocent until proved guilty or the doctrine that any adverse public comment on the defendants before the verdict is prejudicial to their receiving a fair trial. The basic approach is that these men should not have a chance to go free. And that being so, they ought not to be tried in a court of law.

As to the second point, one objection is purely pragmatic. There is a reasonable doubt whether this kind of trial, despite the voluminous and accessible record it makes, persuades anyone. It brings out new evidence, but does it change men's minds? Most reporters say that the Germans are neither interested in nor persuaded by these proceedings, which they regard as partisan. They regard the proceedings not as marking a rebirth of law in Central Europe but as a political judgment on their former leaders. The same attitude may prevail in future because of the departure from accepted legal standards.

A more profound objection to the second point is that to regard a trial as a propaganda device is to debase justice. To be sure, most trials do and should incidentally educate the public. Yet any judge knows that if he, or counsel, or the parties regard a trial primarily as a public demonstration, or even as a general inquest, then there enter considerations which would otherwise be regarded as improper. In a political inquiry and even more in the spread of propaganda, the appeal is likely to be to the unreflecting thought and the deep-seated emotions of the crowd, untrammeled by any fixed standards. The objective is to create outside the courtroom a desired state of affairs. In a trial the appeal is to the disinterested judgment of reasonable men guided by established precepts. The objective is to make inside the courtroom a sound disposition of a pending case according to settled principles.

The argument that these trials set a firm foundation for a

future world legal structure is perhaps debatable. The spectacle of individual liability for a world wrong may lead to future treaties and agreements specifying individual liability. If this were the outcome and if, for example, with respect to wars of aggression, war crimes, and use of atomic energy the nations should agree upon world rules establishing individual liability, then this would be a great gain. But it is by no means clear that this trial will further any such program.

At the moment, the world is most impressed by the undeniable dignity and efficiency of the proceedings and by the horrible events recited in the testimony. But, upon reflection, the informed public may be disturbed by the repudiation of widely accepted concepts of legal justice. It may see too great a resemblance between this proceeding and others which we ourselves have condemned. If in the end there is a generally accepted view that Nuremberg was an example of high politics masquerading as law, then the trial instead of promoting may retard the coming of the day of world law.

Quite apart from the effect of the Nuremberg trial upon the particular defendants involved, there is the disturbing effect of the trial upon domestic justice here and abroad. "We but teach bloody instructions, which, being taught, return to plague the inventor." Our acceptance of the notions of *ex post facto* law and group guilt blunt much of our criticism of Nazi law. Indeed our complaisance may mark the beginning of an age of reaction in constitutionalism in particular and of law in general. Have we forgotten that law is not power, but restraint on power?

If the Nuremberg trial of the leading Nazis should never have been undertaken, it does not follow that we should not have punished these men. It would have been consistent with our philosophy and our law to have disposed of such of the defendants as were in the ordinary sense murderers by individual, routine, undramatic military trials. This was the course proposed in the speeches of the Archbishop of York, Viscount Cecil, Lord Wright, and others in the great debate of March 20, 1945, in the House of Lords. In such trials the evidence and the legal issues would have a stark simplicity and the lesson would be inescapable.

For those who were not chargeable with ordinary crimes but only with political crimes such as planning an aggressive war, would it not have been better to proceed by an executive determination — that is, a proscription directed at certain named individuals? The form of the determination need not have been absolute on its face. It might have been a summary order reciting the offense and allowing the named persons to show cause why they should not be punished, thus giving them a chance to show any mistake of identification or gross mistake of fact.

There are precedents for such executive determination in the cases of Napoleon and of the Boxer rebels. Such a disposition would avoid the inevitably misleading characteristics of the present proceedings, such as a charge presented in the form of an "indictment," the participation of celebrated civil judges and the legal formalities of rulings on evidence and on law. It is these characteristics which may make the Nuremberg trial such a potential danger to law everywhere. Moreover, if it were generally felt that we ought not to take a man's life without the form of a trial, then the executive determination could be limited to imprisonment. The example of Napoleon shows that our consciences would have no reason to be disturbed about the removal from society and the permanent detention of irresponsible men who are a threat to the peace of the world.

To be sure, such an executive determination is *ex post*

facto. Indeed, it is a bill of attainder. To be sure, it is also an exhibition of power and not of restraint. But its very merit is its naked and unassumed character. It confesses itself to be not legal justice but political. The truthful facing of the character of our action would make it more certain that the case would not become a precedent in domestic law.

As Lord Digby said in 1641 regarding the Strafford bill of attainder, "There is in Parliament a double Power of Life and Death by Bill, a Judicial Power, and a legislative; the measure of the one, is what's legally just; of the other, what is Prudentially and Politickly fit for the good and preservation of the whole. But these two, under favour, are not to be confounded in Judgment: We must not piece up want of legality with matter of convenience, nor the defailance of prudential fitness with a pretence of Legal Justice."

This emphasis on procedural regularity is not legalistic or, as it is sometimes now said, conceptualistic. If there is one axiom that emerges clearly from the history of constitutionalism and from the study of any bill of rights or any charter of freedom, it is that procedural safeguards are the very substance of the liberties we cherish. Not only the specific guarantees with respect to criminal trials, but the general promise of "due process of law," have always been phrased and interpreted primarily in their procedural aspect. Indeed it hardly lies in the mouth of any supporter of the Nuremberg proceedings to disparage such procedural considerations; for may it not be said that the reason that the authors of those proceedings cast them in the form of a trial was to persuade the public that the customary safeguards and liberties were preserved?

It is against this deceptive appearance, big with evil consequences for law everywhere, that as a matter of civil courage all of us, judges as well as lawyers and laymen, however silent we ordinarily are, ought to speak out. It is for their silence on such matters that we justly criticize the Germans. And it is the test of our sincere belief in justice under law never to allow it to be confused with what are merely our interest, our ingenuity, and our power.

From the *Atlantic Monthly*, April 1946

Nuremberg in Retrospect

İₙ the April *Atlantic Monthly* I raised doubts as to certain
aspects of the then uncompleted Nuremberg trial. Since
that time I have had a chance to profit from comments of
Mr. Justice Jackson, Professor Sheldon Glueck, Professor
Max Radin, Professor Lon Fuller, an anonymous contribu-
tor to the July 1946 *Law Quarterly Review,* and other writers; I have also read reports of the trial and have studied a
summary of the judgment. This further investigation has
led me to resolve some of my earlier doubts, and I hope that
if I state my own change of views I may contribute to the
thinking of others who are concerned about the great questions raised by this trial.

The doubt which seemed to critics of the Nuremberg
trial most fundamental was whether the defendants could
properly be held to answer a charge that they had engaged
in "the crime of aggressive war." Was there any such substantive offense?

Many who replied affirmatively contended that "the
crime of aggressive war" was no different from the specific
war crimes (such as killing a captured enemy civilian) that
had been defined in the Hague Convention of 1907. That is,
they argued that waging an aggressive war was a crime that
had been outlawed by a specific treaty or treaties; and that
individuals who engaged in such conduct, like individuals

who engaged in the slaughter of captured civilians, were tri-
able by any tribunal established for the occasion by a warring power, and were punishable by any penalty prescribed
for the occasion by that power.

That argument seems to me unsound. It does not seem to
me that an examination of the prewar treaties, conference
proposals, diplomatic correspondence, and juristic writings
shows that there was a specific international covenant that
individuals who waged an aggressive war were criminals in
the same sense that there was a specific international covenant that individuals who killed captured civilians were
criminals.

But it is not sufficient to stop with that purely analytical
approach. There remains this inquiry: Is it just to declare,
after hostilities have begun, that planners of an aggressive
war are criminal?

Those who believe that it is, make a twofold contention.
First, they say that when these defendants planned this war
both they and everyone else would have admitted that the
planning of aggressive war was a violation of standards
which, whether or not they had been formulated like the
Hague Conventions, were universally accepted by the international community in treaties and otherwise; and that
no one should be surprised to see such deliberate violations
stamped as criminal. Second, they say that international
criminal law in its present almost primitive state is similar to
early domestic criminal law, and therefore requires not only
the application of enacted law and of judicial precedent,
but also the retroactive declaration of new law.

At first I was shocked by those contentions. I was prepared to assent to the statement that the defendants deliberately violated standards which had been widely accepted.
But I hesitated to concede that any state or group of states
should have the power retroactively to affix the additional

label "criminal" to conduct which, when it occurred, was commonly regarded only as a violation of accepted standards and of treaties. It seemed to me that to allow such retrospective labeling opened the door to an arbitrary selection of offenses and an arbitrary selection of offenders. It struck at the roots of constitutional limitations on power and contradicted the teachings of the philosophers of liberty. Moreover, while I was prepared to assent to the proposition that some topics in international law could be, and had been, developed by judicial tribunals declaring the law retroactively, I was not aware that the particular branch of international law which dealt with individual crimes had ever been thought to be susceptible of retroactive codification by judges or by states.

On further reflection I have come to the view that the points stated in the last paragraph are not conclusive. I am now persuaded that in the formative period of international law it is just for a representative group of powers retroactively to label as criminal, conduct which, when it occurred, was universally regarded as a serious violation of generally accepted international standards and treaties. To put it in a single sentence, the reasons of my change are that the failure of the international community to attach the criminal label to such universally condemned conduct would be more likely to promote arbitrary and discriminatory action by public authorities and to undermine confidence in the proposition that international agreements are made to be kept, than the failure of the international community to abide by the maxim that no act can be punished as a crime unless there was in advance of the act a specific criminal law.

It is a choice of evils. And I do not claim that my present belief can be proved to be correct. Essentially it is what the philosophers would call a value judgment based on these considerations. If the powers had not agreed upon a rational formula for indicting those who planned World War II, it is highly probable that either some state or some unauthorized individuals would arbitrarily and perhaps even ruthlessly have undertaken the punishment of capriciously chosen Nazi chieftains. If the treaties against aggression which had been negotiated prior to World War II were treated as mere statements of intention, then postwar treaties against aggression, no matter how precisely drafted, would have been regarded as imperfect obligations.

But, regardless of its provability, the scale of values which now seems to me sound puts repugnance to retroactive legislation in a less important place than repugnance to leaving unpunished serious violations of standards universally recognized by the international community and embodied in treaties and like international obligations. To guard against misapprehension, I should reiterate that the scale applies only to grave departures from standards that have been widely and formally accepted, and only when the conduct arises in the international field where and while the organs of the international community are so undeveloped and are so intermittent in their functioning that it is impractical to expect the declaration of criminality to be made in advance of the conduct.

Thus it now seems to me to have been "just," and probably under some civilized systems of law even "legal," to have charged the defendants with the crime of aggressive war. But, in candor, I must add that I am not satisfied that it was "legal" under American law. I can best express my reservation by example. Suppose that Hess had been brought to the United States and had been here charged with, tried on, and convicted of only the crime of aggressive war by a military tribunal created by the President with or without the cooperation of other nations; and suppose that, having been sentenced to jail in the United States, he, like Yama-shita, had sought a writ of habeas corpus from a United States judge. Would he not have had a right to be released on the ground that he was held in violation of the *ex post facto* clause of Article I, Section 9, of the United States Constitution? That is, does not the United States Constitution put at the very front of its scale of values a ban on retroactive criminal laws?

Before turning to the next topic, I should note parenthetically that some persons who shared my original view, that before the Nuremberg trial there was no substantive "crime of aggressive war," say that even after the Nuremberg trial they do not know what the crime is, because the victorious powers and their court have not defined the crime of which the defendants were adjudged guilty. To them the verdict implies no more than the proposition that the victors are empowered to punish the vanquished. They say that there is no definition as to when a war is "aggressive" and that there is no rule laid down for distinguishing between the organizers and the participants in such an aggressive war.

To this the answers are that the definition of "aggressive," like other legal terms, will acquire content by exemplification; and the full meaning will become clear only after sufficient cases have been brought before and adjudicated by competent tribunals. It may be difficult at some future time to determine whether a particular war is an aggressive war, but there was no difficulty in deciding that the Nazi war was an aggressive war, since it would be generally conceded that the term "aggressive war" at its least includes a war like the Nazi war, which is begun by an attack by those who do not themselves believe that they are in danger of immediate attack by others. And although it may be difficult to say how far down the line of command responsibility goes, responsibility certainly extends at least to those who, knowing there is no danger, both plan and direct the unwarranted attack.

These answers would have been more evident if it had not been for the almost absurd citations of Grotius and other jurists made by some supporters of the Nuremberg proceedings. These supporters often seem to argue that Grotius said (which, of course, he did not) that those who kill in the course of a war commit a legal crime unless the war is a just war; and that where a war is unjust, those who engage in it and kill their fellow men are murderers. Grotius's definitions of just and unjust wars refer primarily not to mundane but to divine justice. And he did not describe — few sensible people would describe — as a murderer the common soldier required to kill his enemy in the course of an unjust war. Neither Grotius nor the powers who drafted the Nuremberg charter nor the judges or prosecutors who participated at Nuremberg have termed criminal those men who merely fought in a war not of their making.

Having shown why I now believe "the crime of aggressive war" is properly regarded as a substantive offense, I turn to the next doubt which has disturbed me: that is, whether that crime should have been tried before a tribunal composed exclusively of judges of the four major victorious powers. Was it a proper forum?

No one who has read the recent decision of the Supreme Court of the United States in the *Yamashita* case will find difficulty in concluding that it was according to law to try the defendants in a military rather than a civil tribunal and to try them before judges who were drawn exclusively from the victorious powers. But that conclusion leaves unanswered certain other questions.

While, so far as I am aware, it was legally unobjectionable to have the defendants tried by an English judge or a

French judge or an American judge, or any combination of them, can we fairly say it was unobjectionable to have the defendants tried by a Russian judge on the *particular* charge of aggressive war which was presented? Did not the charge refer to an aggressive attack on Poland? And (while deeply sensible of the later horrible sufferings the Russians underwent from an unprovoked attack by Germany on Russia itself) can we say that the Russians (who in advance were apprised of the proposed German attack on Poland and who participated in the division of the spoils resulting from that attack) were suitable persons to participate in judgment upon the charge that the Germans aggressively attacked Poland? This is not an issue (as it is sometimes supposed to be) whether it is just to prosecute one group of criminals (Germans) and not another (Russians). It is the simpler issue whether an apparent confederate is to sit in judgment on an alleged criminal.

While it was not legally necessary to have invited neutrals and even distinguished anti-Nazi Germans to sit in judgment at the trial, would it not have been politically wiser to have done so, since the type of issues raised by a charge of the crime of aggressive war, unlike the issues raised by a charge of strict war crimes, are so susceptible of national bias? Would not a tribunal which included some judges free of any connection with the victims of the aggressive attack have furnished a sounder precedent?

To these questions the usual, but not entirely satisfactory, answers are that the authors of the Nuremberg procedure believed that distinguished neutrals would not accept appointment, and that the Russians would not have sat with neutrals.

Two other political, rather than legal, questions remain. First, was it desirable to include this charge in the Nurem-

berg indictment when there were enough other charges of a
more orthodox character upon which the defendants were
being tried and were likely to be hanged? Second, was it
better to have these defendants tried before a military court
or to have them disposed of by a more summary executive
procedure?

If the defendants had been tried solely on the grounds
that they had engaged in war crimes in the strict sense and
in crimes against humanity, the practical result for the men
in the dock at Nuremberg would (with the single exception
of Hess) have been precisely the same as it actually turned
out to be. Hess is the only defendant who was convicted of
the crime of aggressive war and the crime of conspiracy but
was not convicted of other crimes as well.

Moreover, if the defendants had been tried solely on the
grounds that they had engaged in war crimes in the strict
sense and in crimes against humanity, there would from the
outset have been a far greater degree of unanimity of professional opinion in support of the Nuremberg trial.

There were, however, countervailing considerations,
which could well be thought more significant. If the defendants were charged only with the strict war crimes and not
with the crime of aggressive war, it would have deeply
offended the public sense of justice, for the public regarded
the planning of the war as the greatest of crimes. To the
general public it would have seemed grossly inappropriate
to punish Göring only for killing a few named individuals,
and not for starting a war in which millions were killed.

Furthermore, if the powers had not included in the Nuremberg indictment a charge that the defendants had committed the crime of aggressive war, not only would they
have missed the opportunity to establish the doctrine that
there is a world law against aggressive war, but their very

silence and timidity would have weakened the force now, and perhaps for all time of such declarations as had heretofore been made that aggressive war was outlawed.

There remains for discussion the problem whether it would have been politically wiser to have dealt with the Nuremberg defendants by a proceeding that was not judicial but frankly executive.

Before the Nuremberg trial began, those who, like myself, originally opposed a judicial proceeding stressed the following points, among others. There was a grave danger that the trial itself could not be conducted in an orderly way. The memories of the disturbances of the Laval treason trial and the Washington sedition trial were fresh in men's minds. There seemed no likelihood that the trial would be so arranged that the defendants would be given adequate opportunity to produce evidence and to examine and cross-examine witnesses. There was skepticism as to whether any defendant had a chance to be acquitted, particularly since it appeared that the tribunal might start with a presumption of guilt rather than a presumption of innocence. And it was feared that the tribunal would focus on the propaganda aspects of the trial and would be unduly concerned with the effect of the trial upon the public opinion of the outside world. Cumulatively, these considerations made many commentators doubtful whether the court could act as a court should act. And — though this was less important — it made these commentators fear that the trial, instead of persuading the Germans of today or tomorrow that our side was just, would persuade them that we were hypocrites disguising vengeance under the façade of legality.

To avoid such dangers, these critics suggested that the victorious powers should frankly state that for reasons which would be announced to the world, and which would include a recital of the wrongs the defendants had perpetrated and the menace they still presented, the powers proposed to deny them further liberty and, if necessary, to take their lives. Before such announcement was put into effect, the persons named for punishment would have an adequate opportunity to present any evidence they had that they had been erroneously named or charged with wrongdoing. It was believed that a course so drastic and so plainly premised on an exceptional situation would never be thought, as a trial might be thought, suitable for incorporation in the permanent fabric of domestic systems of justice.

Now that the trial has been held, many of these forebodings are shown to have been wide of the mark. Judged as a court trial, the Nuremberg proceedings were a model of forensic fairness. Lord Justice Lawrence and his associates acted with dignity and firmness and with eyes directed only to such matters as judges ought to consider.

Moreover, the very length of the trial has shown that those who originally favored a summary proceeding had overestimated the knowledge which the Allies had in advance of the trial. A year ago they did not have the specific information necessary promptly to prepare a reliable recital of who were the chief offenders and what were their offenses. Indeed, if it had not been for the trial and the diligent efforts of a staff of able lawyers and investigators, acting promptly and in response to the necessities of legal technique, the important documents in which the defendants convicted themselves might never have been uncovered. Thus the trial gave the victorious powers the adequate record which they required for proper disposition of the defendants and simultaneously gave historians much of the data which the world will require for proper evaluation of the causes and events of World War II.

But the outstanding accomplishment of the trial, which could never have been achieved by any more summary executive action, is that it has crystallized the concept that there already is inherent in the international community a machinery both of the expression of international criminal law and for its enforcement. The great powers of the world have agreed that it is in accordance with justice for a group of nations to establish on an *ad hoc* basis a tribunal first, to review the state of world opinion on conduct in order to determine whether that conduct, when it occurred, was so universally condemned as an international wrong that it can be called a "crime"; and second, to apply that determination to individuals.

No doubt such an *ad hoc* method is not so satisfactory as a covenant made by all the powers in advance of wrongful conduct — a covenant describing such conduct, fixing the tribunal which shall try offenders and fixing the penalty which shall be imposed. But until the world is prepared to follow the more satisfactory method, it has every reason to be profoundly grateful to Mr. Justice Jackson and his associates, who, in the face of enormous practical difficulties and widespread theoretical criticisms, persisted until they demonstrated the justice of the *ad hoc* method adopted at Nuremberg.

From the *Atlantic Monthly*, December 1946

The Law and Its Compass

VASARI tells us that when Boniface VIII asked Giotto for a sample of his work, the Florentine painter sent him a freehand drawing of a circle. Only the master can with apparent artlessness perfectly portray the basic simplicities.

With like mastery, Lord Radcliffe had addressed himself in these lectures,* given in 1960 on the Julius Rosenthal Foundation at Northwestern University, to the fundamental perplexities of the law today. He, like so many lesser men, has noted the ever-increasing role of legislative enactment and of administrative determination and has wondered how far they have reduced the lawyer to the minor place of traffic policeman. Together with others, in and out of our profession, he has been both horrified and challenged by the way the Nazi, Soviet, and other totalitarian regimes have purported to proclaim as law regulations drained of all ethical and religious content. And he has faced the question whether the Austinian command theory, the historicism of Savigny, the positivism for which Holmes spoke so eloquently, the social engineering doctrines as enunciated by Pound and practiced by the welfare state, and the realism of Ehrlich or Jerome Frank, have offered the frame of reference which gives law its ultimate claim upon our allegiance.

The three lectures are set forth in an order which com-

* *The Law and Its Compass.* By Lord Radcliffe. Northwestern University Press, Evanston, 1960.

pels our logical admiration. For, sentence by sentence, illustration after illustration, the lectures are articulated in a scheme that reveals how skilled Radcliffe is as a practitioner of our profession. We do not need the description on the jacket of the book to know that the author of this slender volume of hardly a hundred pages has been in turn, King's Counsel, Fellow of All Souls, Director-General of the Ministry of Information during the Second World War, Lord of Appeal in Ordinary, arbiter of the boundary between modern India and Pakistan, draftsman of an admittedly abortive constitution for Cyprus, head of the recent commission on monetary and credit problems, and author of the now classic Reith lectures on The Problems of Power.

From internal evidence, *The Law and Its Compass* proves its author an incomparable analyst of issues, a sure guide to the core of the dilemma which is to be resolved. Step by step, in fact, perhaps somewhat too smoothly, we are led to the fork in the road, and asked to choose between the avenue of order as the low road of the law, and the steeper path, sometimes called natural law, and more provincially in England denominated public policy, from whose heights one tests whether a particular technical device or a supposed precedent can in justice be applied in the ever-new situations which are the constant stuff from which the growing law is woven.

The progressions in the Radcliffe lectures march in stately, if muted, measures. They start with the setting of the Christian religion and mediaeval unity whence emerged the English common law. They continue with the efforts by Lord Mansfield to move the bench from too narrow an outlook, molded exclusively by forms of ancient writs issuing out of Westminister, into a broader atmosphere, lighted by Roman and commercial principles of equity and natural justice. They explain that the ideal of tolerance has aspects far more significant than its origin in conflict among sectarian religious groups, or its defense, by Mill and his fellow Utilitarians, as a negative disposition of self-restraint by the powerful. The more modern view of tolerance, for which Radcliffe pleads, is the awareness of its affirmative virtue — its acceptance as a practical premise that each man has a positive contribution to make to the common life, the almost sacred belief that the spiritual significance of man's journey on earth is the ever-widening opportunity offered to each traveler to make his own choices; to grow in width and depth of experience, to accept responsibility, and to achieve character consequent upon choice.

For an American reader the penetration of this new classic of the law — a work not one whit inferior in imagination and idealism to Cardozo's *The Nature of the Judicial Process* — may perhaps be best revealed if the third lecture be the first read. In its pages are most quickly discerned the reason why Lord Radcliffe regards his topic as falling within the wide ambit of a study of liberty. Here is the explanation why, with the *double entendre* implicit in the word compass, Lord Radcliffe selected as his title *The Law and Its Compass*. Here are the unforgettable German letters reminding us that no study of law is sufficient if it attends solely to the problems of obedience to law, and to the force of inertia implicit in the habit of obedience, and if it neglects the even more difficult problems of disobedience to law when it no longer is a reflection of the Pillar of Fire, and when it has ceased to represent that moral force by which alone sovereigns reign and the law rules.

This third lecture is the long-awaited answer to the doubts to which Justice Holmes and Judge Learned Hand have left us heirs. While not unmindful that the law is inevitably, in part, a merely arbitrary system of preference, a necessary instrument of order, Radcliffe quite rejects the suggestion that law is *never* more than the interest of the stronger arrayed under the form of prescribed regulations. Immanent in the law are principles of justice. No doubt from area to area, and era to era, those principles expand and alter. Yet they are the warp which gives the pattern durability and distinction. With us, it is the firm faith in fraternal love, in individual initiative, in a common purpose to draw boundaries beyond which no terrestrial power shall impair the mighty moral vision of men in quest of a meaningful life.

In the United States the Constitution and especially its annexed Bill of Rights are the reminders of the grand place of justice as the presiding genius of the law. A Roman or a mediaevalist might in similar fashion have referred to the classic doctrines of the natural law. An Englishman would once have seen the law as parcel of the public regime nourished by the Christian religion. Thereafter for a time the Englishman had the possibility of using the looser standards of public policy to recall, in grave cases, the essential relation of law to the right ordering of society and the furtherance of individual spiritual needs. But the perhaps too professional outlook of a calling concentrated on its daily technique, and conservative in its method, prevented a full appreciation that the garment on which it daily labored covered social and moral aspirations far beyond court and chambers.

What, however, is important for the future is how law appears not alone to judges and to advocates pleading before them, but to legislators, to administrators, perhaps, above all, to lawyers in chambers, those men who draw the contracts, corporate resolutions, collective bargains, trusts, and estate plans which govern so much of our modern civilization. Guiding our citizens to make their choices, will our bar, will our legislatures and administrative agencies, make them sensitive to the long reach of the issues before them?

Will they, like the sophists Thrasymachus and Gorgias, teach that the law is only the interest of the stronger? Will they give illustration to those who view, with Marxian acidity, the law as a mere arrangement of dominant economic forces? Or will they perceive as Lord Radcliffe has so superbly done, that that is not law which is only law? For is not law the public face radiant with awareness that it is the reflection of men's deepest and noblest ideals?

From *Northwestern University Law Review*, 1961

III

A Great Public Calling

The Young Men in Washington

I AM going to take as my subject tonight "The Young Men in Washington" — why they are there; how long they will last; and what their significance is from the point of view of the country and of schools like Exeter.

To any one of you who has been in Washington in the last year I do not have to plead the timeliness of my subject. Whether you came to secure approval for an NRA code, or to register a new security, or to borrow from the RFC, you probably met not one but a dozen young men who were not merely novices in their particular jobs, but also novices in political life.

Like Mark Sullivan, you may have felt that they were engaged in a subtle, subversive campaign to overthrow the established order. Or, like John Maynard Keynes, you may have come away with the impression that the presence of these men is the most hopeful sign of the New Deal because it means the beginning of a permanent civil service composed of unusually intelligent, well-trained, and enthusiastic minds.

To me, both of these impressions seem to fly in the face of devious, stubborn facts. I do not believe that the young men in Washington are going to duplicate upon our soil either Russian Communism or the English civil service. And I suspect that both the fear and the hope are accounted for

by a failure to face with brutal frankness a preliminary
question: Why did these young men come to Washington?

Before I try to answer my own question, I want to stress
one general *caveat*. In making crucial decisions (be it about
a girl or a job) few men are in the habit of articulating all
the reasons for their choice. Most of us pick a wife or an
employer partly for reasons we admit; partly for reasons
we recognize, but do not admit; and partly on a thoroughly
inexplicable hunch. This general principle of selection applies to those of us who have recently picked Uncle Sam as
our employer, so that it is never easy to isolate and analyze
all the considerations that brought us into government service.

But though I do not pretend that I could give a complete
and adequate explanation of the decision in any individual
case (my own included), I suggest that the group of young
men can be divided according to motivation into four divi-
sions, which, of course, overlap.

First, there are those who came on account of the excitement in Washington. The bank closing, the blue eagle campaign, the new legislation, made Washington instantly appealing to those of an adventurous turn of mind. And, as
the saying goes, "they came for the ride" (and the newspapers are giving it to them!).

Second, there are those who on account of the depression
could not get jobs in private life, or who could not get jobs
that paid as well as government posts. This is a constantly
increasing group, especially in the New Deal agencies that
pay high salaries.

Third, there are those who came because they recognized
that government offers unlimited opportunities for personal
growth. In private concerns young men are rarely given the
important tasks that develop imagination, prowess and self-
reliance. Usually older men are available, and there is a nat-

ural reluctance to allow a youngster to risk the capital and prestige of the concern or its clients. The government is not so hesitant. There are enough big tasks for everyone. And on the least showing of ability, a very young man may find himself entrusted not merely with the power of decision, but with the power to plan large undertakings, to manage large staffs and vast funds, and to assume full responsibility for results.

Fourth are the men who have always wanted to make the public business their private concern, and who are now being given their chance. This, I sincerely believe, is a large proportion of the total, for the second Roosevelt, like the first, has fired the enthusiasm of those who are anxious "to spend and be spent in the public service."

If I have correctly analyzed the motivation of the young men who have recently entered government service, it is easy to give an answer to my second question: How long will these young men last?

The man who came for excitement will, as political life returns to a normal routine, be directed by his adventurous spirit into other channels. The man to whom government service meant a better job will, as business picks up, and as his special talent begins to command a wider market, take another post. The man who came for self-development and personal growth will, after he has tested his powers and acquired what Ruskin has happily described as "an education which shall enable him to ring with confidence the visitors' bell at double-belled doors," return to his private career. For each of them will have accomplished his purpose, which was to get ahead in the road by cutting out of line.

Of course, a few in each group will stay, and together with them many of those who came out of a genuine desire to serve the common weal. Though even in this last group I suspect that most will return to serve their local communities, for they will have come to feel that it is the man who has deep roots in his own state who has not merely the greatest political weight, but also the surest perception of the profound currents that move people and events.

In short, I doubt the correctness of those who share Keynes's vision of an American parallel to the British civil service. To me the differences between Great Britain and the United States seem too fundamental. At the bottom is the difference in our attitude toward and our experience with industry and finance. In England there is a greater recognition of what Veblen has called *The Theory of the Leisure Class,* and in some quarters it is still regarded as more fitting for a gentleman to engage in political than in economic activity. Another difference is that in England an enterprising man may feel that in business merit is stifled by vested interests — a feeling quite contrary to what has been and what, I venture to predict, will be, the case in America. And finally, and perhaps most important, our schools have not been prepared to emulate the English public schools and universities in pointing toward a career of government service.

Up to this point I have tried only to analyze the phenomenon of the young men in Washington. There remains the ultimate task of evaluating it. What is its significance? Was the experiment, on the whole, satisfactory? Is it worth repeating?

I contend that even as a short-term investment these men were worth having. Indeed, in some respects I am prepared to urge that they were even more valuable as a short-term investment than they would have been as a long-term one.

To the old-line departments they brought not only a broader educational background than the ordinary civil servant, but particularly a flexibility of mind, an intensity of effort, and an enthusiasm of spirit characteristic of youth.

Yet if they were indefinitely to prolong their stay, their stimulating effect would wear off. As they became more expert they might have become mentally more rigid and temperamentally more bureaucratic. The essence of their elixir can be duplicated, but perhaps it could not be sustained.

That is the negative side of the picture of their departure. But there is a positive side of more importance. The young men who have been in Washington will return to their local communities and private callings with a new insight. They will to a degree have mastered the method of government in the same way that men who go to a school like Exeter master the method of academic education. And also like men who have been at school or college, they will have an abiding affection for and loyalty toward the institution where they were educated and to whose glory in some small measure they contributed.

And that patriotic feeling, that understanding of and participation in governmental processes is a matter of the greatest significance to a democratic government. For it is of the essence of a true democracy, whether it be a Greek city-state, or a colonial New England town, or the modern America, that supporting and scrutinizing the officers of the day there should be a body of citizens informed on public questions, and prepared from personal experience to advise and participate in their solution.

If you agree with this thought, and if for these or other reasons you want to see a new crop of young men come to take the place of those who will leave, you and the government will have to plan accordingly.

Tonight I have not time even to sketch in outline the possible terms of that cooperation, but before I close I want to offer for your further thought a few suggestions.

On its part, the government might profitably create a

number of special posts, with relatively brief terms, intended for young men of general education. These posts might be biennially filled by appointment by Cabinet officers, in a way not unlike the method followed by some Justices of the Supreme Court in selecting their law secretaries. Or they might be filled by methods similar to those pursued by the Rhodes Scholarship authorities.* Or for these posts annual, non-technical civil service examinations might be held.

Whatever method the government used, it could not succeed without the aid of older men, like the alumni here tonight. For young men, however conceited and cocksure they appear on the surface, ultimately turn to you for guidance, and will not take governmental posts unless you urge them to do so. It will be up to you to point out the advantages of these posts to them, both as individuals and as part of the community. And in particular you will need to elucidate for them one paradox — that though you as representatives of the business world and the general public uniformly express contempt for "politicians" and "government clerks" collectively, you are apt to value an individual man more highly if he has held a responsible public post where he has acquired the technique of handling and explaining major issues, and where he has gained self-confidence and a certain prestige.

Finally, in any program, the schools and the universities will have a dominant role. I do not plead for courses in civics — for myself, I suspect that if books ever breed great public servants, the volumes are not school texts but biographies and works like Plato's *Republic* or Zimmern's *Greek Commonwealth*. Nor should I ask for the revival of what seems to me the anachronism of debating societies. In-

* The Congressional Fellowships are only one example of how this course is being followed in 1964.

stead, I propose a more subtle, and perhaps a more adult, device. I suggest that the students be more frequently given the stimulating opportunity of hearing, not across a platform, but in the Lantern Club or the study of some teacher, a man with the winning charm and modesty of the Governor of New Hampshire, John G. Winant, or a young man of ability and promise like my distinguished classmate at Exeter, Larry Duggan, who, as you perhaps know, was one of the chief negotiators of the reciprocal trade treaty we have recently concluded with Cuba.

My specific suggestions may seem visionary. But they are offered as a challenge to you to produce more practical methods of approach, and they are submitted because I believe that through the young men who have been in Washington, and the young men whom you can persuade to come, the democratic institutions of this country will be strengthened, and there will go out from the government into private life a group of citizens with greater capacity, broader vision, and deeper patriotism.

Notes for an address to the Exeter Alumni
Association of New York, 1934

The Lawyer's Relation to Recent Social Legislation

LAST month a friendly and distinguished publicist said to me: "The lawyers of this country are today as far out of step with the country as a whole as the bankers were in the period from '29 to '33; and they may soon become their successors as the scapegoats of public opinion."

This struck me as an arresting challenge. And, though, as you will see, I do not subscribe to my friend's conclusion, I think the challenge is worth examining carefully and not unsympathetically. For the quotation, if it is not a fair analysis of present-day conditions, may serve as a timely warning as to future dangers. At any rate, I shall take it as my text.

Since the beginning of this century, if not before, there has been a gradual reorientation of a large part of the bar of this country. In this analysis, my description and my criticism will be weighted so as to take principal account of the metropolitan part of our bar. I think that my line of approach is warranted for several reasons. In the first place, the bar is in large measure judged by its conspicuous members, and, with a few notable exceptions, such as the Government's ranking advocate,* who has been fittingly drawn from your own community, our best known, if not ablest,

---

* The Honorable Stanley Reed, then Solicitor-General; later a Justice of the Supreme Court of the United States.

lawyers are practitioners in the big or at least middle-size cities. In the second place, in present-day American society the metropolitan area is becoming an increasingly important fulcrum, and it is there that the leverage of the lawyer class as well as of other classes has been most effective. And, finally, though, to my way of thinking, the population of small towns and rural areas yields to no other part of the population in character, in intelligence or in fundamental soundness, it is often more difficult to detect there than in metropolitan centers the first signs of new intellectual movements and trends.

Turning then with this acknowledged bias to an examination of the bar, I think the fact which strikes us at the outset is the degree to which the bar is associated with, and has become almost part of, the business class in the community. Admittedly this association has always existed to some degree. But the emphasis has been increased of late. A hundred years ago the connection between the bar and any particular other group was so far from noticeable that an acute foreign observer of our scene, De Tocqueville, remarked in his book on *Democracy in America* that the lawyers were a "party [which] extends over the whole community, and penetrates into all the classes which compose it." This description is plainly not accurate today. Now the bar is, or at least its leaders are, much more closely tied to business than, shall I say, to labor, or to agriculture, not to mention other groups.

The forces which led to the peculiarly strong association with business are numerous. For one thing, businessmen have more complicated relationships with themselves and with society than do persons otherwise gainfully employed. Since relations between man and man, man and property and man and the State are the very fabric of which the law is woven, it is only natural that those who have the most complicated relations have the most legal business to offer. In other words, businessmen call more frequently than their fellows do on lawyers. Moreover, as a consequence of scientific advance, economic factors, and world conditions that need no summary, business has been going forward at a rate faster than that at which the community as a whole has advanced. In this march at double-quick time, business has been attractive to many vigorous and adventurous men. Men trained in the law, like other men, have seen that this is the corps in the army of society which has offered the largest experience and greatest rewards. Thus lawyers have gradually been becoming, at least in sentiment, a part of the business class.

This closer association has had some very desirable results.

Clearly business profited. Lawyers as a group are not only intelligent, that is, intellectually wide-awake; but they are educated, that is, reared in a formal discipline. Therefore, until the relatively recent rise of the graduate schools of business, it was principally to them that business turned for general analysis, organization, and guidance. No one who has the slightest familiarity with a corporate law office would underestimate the role of the business lawyer. Valuable as is his knowledge of the technique of case-law and statutory regulation, that knowledge is only a small part of his contribution to the business world. I take it that it is no accident, but a formal acknowledgment of long standing *de facto* rule, when lawyers are made executives or directors of a corporation. Instead of guiding a business from a law office, they guide it from the offices of the business itself.

And not only business profited, but in some aspects society profited. Without the technical skill and the sober habits of thought that characterize so many lawyers, our nation could never have been so rapidly industrialized, and our civilization so successfully enlisted in the competitive struggle.

Moreover, without the constant cross-fertilization of new business concepts and old legal concepts law would have become only a minor social science without profound influence on the development of our dynamic and vital society.

But the association between law and business has also had its undesirable results.

The fact that corporate law seemed, nay was, such an energetic and such a lucrative practice, drew the best lawyers more and more from the courts into office practice. Today how many acknowledged leaders of our profession are barristers? Today how many of our outstanding lawyers are equipped to be, or have any desire to be judges? What has happened is obvious enough. We are devoting less and less of our best brains to the particular processes which improve the *judge*-made law and adapt it to modern needs. Perhaps it is partly on this account that the relative position of the common law and of statutory law has begun to change, and that more and more of our law is on the statute books and not in the reports. Perhaps it is partly on this account that the law schools and the law teachers have been steadily gaining in importance and influence, and that with this increase in the influence has come an increase in the citation of law review articles and textbooks in judicial opinions. I shall not stop to elaborate these ideas. It will be enough if I have raised in your minds a question whether by emphasizing his role as an office adviser to clients, the modern practitioner has not withdrawn from certain essential fields of the law in favor of the legislator and the teacher.

An even more significant, and to me even more undesirable, consequence of the increased association of law and business has been its effect upon the independence of the bar. In this country we have never had the precious tradition of the English bar which forbids a barrister to have any permanent business connections. But formerly we could boast that our leading advocates were not definitely tied to a particular interest or group. The lives of Luther Martin, Jeremiah Sullivan Black, Reverdy Johnson, Benjamin R. Curtis were but magnified examples of the average lawyer's independence. In their time it was not the fashion to accept a permanent alliance. It was then recognized that clients would receive, no less than lawyers would give, the best legal advice and the best legal arguments only if each lawyer was familiar with different types of clients and different branches of the law. Today the practice is different. And though I do not for a moment charge that the lawyer of today *intends* to be less independent or detached in judgment than his predecessor of yesterday, I cannot help believing that the character of his practice necessarily makes him so.

I have until this point been talking with convenient generality about the lawyer's association with business, and its broad advantages and disadvantages. I now propose to turn more particularly to the effects of this connection within the last four or five years. In doing so I intend rigorously to adhere to your own rule that on occasions of this sort partisan discussion is taboo. But, I feel that without violating the letter or the spirit of that wise ordinance, I can properly remind you of certain political consequences and repercussions of the *entente cordiale* to which I have adverted.

Without passing any judgment upon the soundness of their views, we are all aware of the obvious fact that a majority of the lawyers in this nation have in the last five years been of a different political complexion than a majority of their countrymen. The lawyers have come to be looked upon not merely as definitely partisan but as definitely "agin the government." And I believe that you would ad-

mit, something that I do not charge, namely that as a consequence there has been shown a remarkably factional spirit
in many recent arguments on constitutional law and other
branches of public law.

Of course, cacophonous political discord between the
lawyer and the politicians is hardly a novel event in our
history. Anyone who peruses that amusing volume *Jacobin
and Junto*, by the distinguished legal historian Charles
Warren, will see that it is not new for lawyers to find that
in "Affairs of State" the times are out of joint, and that it is
not new for politicians to find that lawyers are men of small
spirit and lesser minds. You will remember that the lack of
mutual respect between the two groups reached such a
pitch that when he was dying, George Washington, to
show his spite of professional lawyers, drew his own last
will and testament and specifically directed that if any question should arise as to its construction the matter should be
set before three arbitrators whose decision on the points in
controversy was to be final.

The members of a bar which only 125 years ago was held
up to ridicule as a group of pro-monarchy, pro-English pet-
tifoggers and yet survived will in all probability weather
the present stormy era in which they are belittled as a group
of reactionary servants of the vested interests whose special
function is the exaltation of property rights over personal
rights.

Though I do not doubt that we shall weather this like
other storms, I wonder whether there is not in the current
criticism of our profession some kernel of truth worth dis-
covering.

Perhaps the clue may lie in Dean Pound's now famous
aphorism: "The law must be stable, and yet it must not
stand still." In that quotation the second clause is usually
emphasized, at least by those who write of the progress of

the law. But I am of the opinion that in that aphorism the first thought is at least as important as the second, and may indeed embrace it: "The law must be stable."

Some of us have come to think of stability as a state of rest. But in a fast moving world perhaps the only way to remain stable is to move, and to balance against new forces, new controls. We as lawyers have been contributing to an upbuilding of the forces of private power. We have been, as I already pointed out, to a large extent the architects of new business aggregations. Have we been acute enough to observe how our private construction has thrown out of adjustment the ancient equilibrium of private and of public right? Have we recognized that for the new forces there must be new controls unless our society is to cease to be democratic?

If we have not noticed the maladjustment, our fellow citizens have. And at the polls, local and national, they have determined to redress the balance. This determination is one of the factors which lay back of much of the social legislation in Washington. It is also one of the factors which lay back of much of the social legislation in the States. And such State legislation has been considerable. In some quarters it is the fashion to say that recent State social legislation is nothing but an echo of the sound and fury in the National Capital. But no view of recent regulation could be more mistaken. I need mention only one example to point the fallacy. Is the regulation by taxation of the chain-store business a phenomenon dictated by Washington — or is it a spontaneous local manifestation of the desire to eliminate the alleged social disadvantages of expanding big business in the merchandising field?

In this advancing wave of regulation the lawyers were caught off guard. The reason that we were caught off guard is, it seems to me, and I speak hesitatingly, that we were too loyal to a *part* of the community to see the new problems in the light of the *whole* community. Our *entente cordiale* brought us into a war on the side of one of the contending parties, and once in, though we, of course, fought like good soldiers, we lost our great opportunity to serve as mediators, which is our historic role in society.

The war into which we plunged was fought on a broad front. But everywhere one side carried the banner of "laissez faire" and the other side marched under the slogan that "all private business is affected with a public interest."

Although the war is not over, and I, who stand enrolled in one of the armies, cannot claim to be an impartial observer, I venture to predict that the struggle is drawing to a close.

At first it may have looked as though the advocates of *laissez faire* were to win. They scored some notable victories. But as the smoke clears and we trace the course of battle, I think we shall come to think of the *Schechter* case and the *A. A. A.* litigation as the legal equivalents of Bull Run and Chancellorsville. The forces of the Union received a bad drubbing. To a skeptical observer, it looked as though they could not regain their strength, but they have rallied and now with the decisions in the Wagner Act, Social Security Act and Ashwander cases behind us it may not be presumptuous for Government counsel to be optimistic about the cases involving the PWA, the holding company statute, and the TVA.

If all or substantially all of these future battles do end with the National Government on the top side, and if the States can maintain the outposts to which they advanced in *Nebbia* v. *New York* and *West Coast Hotel Co.* v. *Parrish*, then we shall have come to the end of what I regard as the

third great period of the constitutional development of the
United States and we shall be ready for a new phase of public law.

The three periods to which I referred will, I dare say,
occur to you readily. In the first period, which began with
the Constitutional Convention itself and continued until the
1830's, Marshall was the dominant figure, and his famous
opinions following so closely Webster's equally celebrated
arguments, gave to our Constitution its peculiar and authentic stamp of greatness. The second period of constitutional development was achieved not in the courtrooms of
the nation, but on its battlefields. In the Civil War, with
much blood and sweat, the Constitution written by the Framers, and interpreted in their spirit by Marshall, was given
an enduring strength by the bond of unionism. And finally,
in our day, in what I have called the third period, the ancient powers given to and preserved for the Union have
been invoked to make a democratic government function in
a modern world.

Though you may readily agree with my classification as
to the three periods of constitutional growth which I have
described, you may be wondering as to the description of
the new phase of public laws which I have been bold
enough to say lies ahead and is about to come upon us.

The three great periods of the past involved struggles between nation and state and between legislative and judicial
power. Ahead I see a different sort of contest, and one in
which the lawyers have not yet enlisted, and in which I
hope and later shall plead that they will not enlist as partisans.

It seems to me that in this dawning era the issues in public
law will turn on questions of administrative justice and the
technique of the administrative process. Social regulation is,
I believe, here to stay, and our first problem is to make that

regulation orderly, equitable, and such as to appeal to the average man's sense of fairness. The importance of these standards cannot be overestimated. If administration is disorderly and arbitrary it will be ineffective. That will mean chaos, not government. More important, if the administration of new social regulations is unfair, it will alienate public opinion. And in the last resort public opinion is the only durable support that any government can have. Tyrants may rule for a day, but he who would have his political influence endure must be sparing in his resort to force or authority. His only satisfactory weapon is persuasion, and men are persuaded only if they feel that they are being treated fairly, and that the power to which they yield is one which is not only rational but aware of limitations.

This the Fathers of our country, and their ancestors in England, knew. The phrase "due process of law" epitomizes their wisdom. And it is that phrase, now happily freed by the *Nebbia*, *West Coast Hotel*, and two *Railway Labor* cases from the spurious doctrines engrafted upon it, which contains the seeds of the new legal growth that I see ahead.

Already there are signs pointing the way. Those of you who follow with care the work of the Supreme Court of the United States will have observed the drift in that direction. Recent litigation arising under the Packers and Stockyards Act furnishes one among many ready illustrations. I do not intend to state the facts or the holdings in *Morgan* v. *United States* and *St. Joseph Stock Yards Co.* v. *United States* but they are significant of the trend. The Chief Justice who wrote those cases and who penned the earlier decisions in cognate fields, *Crowell* v. *Benson* and *Panama Refining Co.* v. *Ryan*, has shown an awareness of the emerging problem, and has at least laid the lines for future exploration.

Indeed, even before there were on the docket of the Supreme Court many cases concerned with topics such as the fairness of administrative proceedings, the method of giving notice and opportunity to be heard, the process for arriving at judgments, the manner of publishing determinations, and the scope of judicial review — these topics were mooted in the law schools. Our students of comparative law have kept their eye on England and the Continent, which in these matters have an experience at least one generation greater than ours. Law teachers have known that the problems of the *Arlidge* case (*Local Government Board* v. *Arlidge*) would soon cross the ocean; and they have been warning us to avoid castigations like those embodied by Lord Chief Justice Hewart in *The New Despotism*. They have seen in what direction constitutional law would turn.

It is only a parochial mind that supposes that the lawyer's constitutional function in relation to a statute comes to an end once the courts have upheld it. This is only the beginning. Otherwise, in a country like England, where the courts cannot set aside an act of the legislature, there would be little constitutional law. But in England, as every man knows, there is a vast body of constitutional law, and here there will be an equally large body of constitutional law, even if every act that Congress passes is either sustained, or, under a new dispensation, exempted from the rigors of our accustomed scrutiny.

I suggest that the critical question for us is how the members of our profession will act with respect to the newly developing body of public law. Unlike my publicist friend whom I quoted at the outset of my remarks, I prefer to judge my profession by its attitude toward the future. I do not think it altogether fair to judge it by its immediate past, by the conduct of a majority of its membership in the recent period of constitutional law from which we are emerging. In that now swiftly ending war, the lawyers were acting under the stress of social forces which they could not fully see, or if they saw could not, because of the emotional aura in which they were enveloped, properly evaluate. To them these new forces seemed to threaten the very economic institutions which were the special handiwork of the lawyers. And against such threats and assaults the bar, no doubt largely from motives of loyalty and conviction, fought hard.

But that fight is lost. And it is time to forget the bitterness and the passion of the struggle and to work for the reconstruction which always follows a war, no matter who wins. In this reconstruction, in this new avenue of public law, is our profession to lag behind or is it to put its shoulder to the wheel, and to aid in the achievement of an administrative system which will not merely satisfy elementary standards of fairness, but will carry to the average man the conviction that the foundation stone of our commonwealth is "equal justice under law"?

There are unique reasons why we as lawyers are needed. I do not pause over the obvious technical advice which we can give. Nor shall I dwell on our experience with national and local regulatory bodies like the Interstate Commerce Commission, the Federal Trade Commission, the Securities and Exchange Commission, Workmen's Compensation tribunals, public utility commissions, or taxing authorities. This special knowledge is but a small part of our peculiar fitness.

We are in name, and I think in fact, engaged in a learned and honorable calling. To us the practice of consulting history, economics, philosophy is a professional habit of mind. We are used to making a broad survey of the province of human knowledge in order to bring every relevant fact to bear upon our problems.

And we have learned the complementary art of focusing

attention on the particular facts in the case before us. We know that a broad vision is of value only in its concrete application, and that such application requires minute adjustment.

Furthermore, I think that, at least in this company, I shall not be regarded as boasting if I say that the discipline of the law sharpens our powers of analysis, and aids us in clear oral and written statement. Our training is such as to make us fit not only to understand but to communicate our understanding.

And then, finally, we have been accustomed, in our office practice no less than in the courtroom so to act as to preserve a record of our conduct — not only in order that at some future day we may be able, for purely personal ends, to summon from the past the experience which we have accumulated, but also in order that if in legal tribunals or elsewhere we are called up to answer for our actions we have available for scrutiny by any duly qualified investigator the basis upon which we have proceeded.

These practices, of broad inquiry, of attention to detail, of clarity of statement, of preserving self-explanatory records, are the very practices which differentiate good from bad administration. They not only are *relevant* to, they are themselves the stuff from which are evolved the standards of due process of law.

And yet, though we are peculiarly fit to aid in the evolution of social regulation, are we willing to serve?

So far, you will confess, the record is not an encouraging one. With the exception of a few fields such as the regulation of banks and utilities and the administration of tax laws (in each of which the financial rewards loom large), the more celebrated members of our profession have not distinguished themselves in administrative law.

You know as well as I that the administrative practices in

workmen's compensation cases, in immigration proceedings, and in labor disputes are notoriously unsatisfactory. Only the more glaring abuses are corrected. And then usually only after litigation. Does the bar with any real zeal watch the administrative handling of the average case? Is much time devoted by our foremost practitioners to securing more than the minimum of decency for the poor whose most important interests are at stake in these administrative hands?

But you may say that harsh as are administrative practices in these special fields, their influence on the general body of the law is negligible.

Even if we assume that every denial of fair play is not a blot upon our professional honor, and even if we take a narrowly selfish view of our role as lawyers, I suggest that each denial of fairness should concern us. For these practices have a generative force that we do not always perceive. Have you ever taken down the volume of Sheppard Citations to opinions of the Supreme Court of the United States and with it traced the history of a doctrine first enunciated in an immigration case? If not, I suggest you do so, and you will find to your surprise that a point of administrative practice first applied to an unfortunate alien, suddenly crops out again to be applied to restrain the liberty of an aggrieved citizen. In a law built on precedents every case may be a big case, and every administrative law point may be of consequence to every lawyer.

The rule of analogical growth applies to statutes no less than to court decisions. The events of the current year supply a convenient example. In April the Supreme Court of the United States upheld the National Labor Relations or the Wagner Act, an enactment of the national Congress. By the end of May, New York and Wisconsin had on their statute books, and the legislatures of Massachusetts, Pennsylvania and New Jersey were on the road to enacting, state Labor Relations Acts of the same type as the National Labor Relations Act. Now the point which I wish to make is not that the state legislatures copied the national legislature. That is a fact that has its interesting implications; but it is not the fact with which I am now concerned. Nor does it concern me now that each of these statutes represented a further step toward protection of the rights of labor. My point is much more technical. What I note is that the administrative pattern, the type of tribunal established and the mechanics of court review established in the national act have been sedulously copied into state acts. And once on the statute books of a state this administrative pattern will, I feel confident, reappear not only in other *labor* legislation in that state, but in all sorts of *regulatory* legislation.

And what I have predicted with respect to the Labor Acts I think could equally well be predicted with respect to administrative patterns evolved in those parts of the Social Security Act dealing with unemployment compensation and grants-in-aid.

In connection with this analogical growth, what part is the bar playing? Has any group of lawyers, indeed have many individual lawyers, who are not retained by a governmental agency or engaged by a law school or research foundation, shown any real interest in this administrative pattern except as it affects a particular case or controversy? Is there any vigilant body of practitioners who care enough about the larger aspects of the calling we profess to devote their time to a disinterested analysis of these patterns? Have bar associations formed committees to advise these new administrative tribunals how to perform their functions more effectively and more fairly?

I throw out those rhetorical questions in no spirit of hostility. I cannot say that were I a lawyer in private practice I should have been prepared with answers of which I was proud. I interject these questions solely for your examination and your consideration. In your hands they may be turned to some useful purpose. They may serve to light the backfire which will meet and overcome the burning challenge which I have taken as my text.

But though I do not criticize, I am tempted to interpose a *caveat*. If to this new challenge the lawyers and their bar associations do not respond, it will be not only the public, but also the bar that will thereby be the loser. Administrative tribunals and administrative law will go on despite the indifference of the bar. They may go on, as Charles Muir suggests in his provocative little volume *Justice in a Depressed Area*, under the tutelage not of lawyers but of social workers and other laymen. And in time we may find that to the eyes of some unprejudiced social scientist it will appear that the law has broken into two big segments: the one a domain of private right in which the professional lawyer still speaks with authority; the other a domain of public right in which the professional lawyer is regarded as an avowed partisan peculiarly sterile in making significant contributions, and peculiarly biased in forming judgments.

Though this division of legal authority is possible, and, if possible, is a danger, I personally do not expect to see it occur. I count not merely on our professional pride to save us. More than that I count on our idealism. We are engaged in a great public calling. Whatever limitations we may have urged in cases argued on behalf of our clients and their occupations, no one of us would urge on our own behalf that ours is an occupation not affected with a public interest. On the contrary, we rejoice in our public duties. We reserve our greatest honors not for those among our brethren who earn the largest fees but for those among us who serve the public best. And there is no distinction that we more covet, no compliment that we more desire, than to be regarded as an honorable, an independent, and a public spirited bar.

An address delivered at the Centennial Celebration of the University of Louisville School of Law and before its alumni and the Kentucky Bar Association, 1937

The Future of the Bar

You and I, even the youngest of us, have been living in one of the great creative eras of the law, in quantity at least. This age will compare with that of William the Conqueror, or Edward I, or Lord Coke, or Lord Mansfield, or John Marshall. For ours has been an age in which fundamental concepts of the law have been revised, not necessarily to our liking. On that obviously we may differ. But that it is a fecund age and one of the great creative ages of the law, none can deny. We have seen in our own time a shift in the federal structure of the nation, so that it is plainly rather a national federalism than a balanced federalism. We have reached a stage in which legislative supremacy in the field at least of social and economic relations is virtually conceded.

The law of master and servant has yielded to the law of labor relations. The alien, the indigent, and the criminal have acquired an importance in constitutional law formerly occupied only by interests of property. Through statutory enactment and judicial decision we have seen the venerable rule of Anglo Saxon law that a man must bear the loss he suffers unless he can plainly point to another as the cause of his loss, disappear as the controlling rule of liability in fact. We have observed public control increasing over businesses which were formerly thought not to be affected by a public interest.

Now, I have no intention of discussing that whole trend, but I want to point out to what extent, partly as a result of that trend and partly as a result of other factors, we have come to an era of specialization of the bar. I need hardly say that specialization is not a peculiarity of the legal profession of the twentieth century. It is a general phenomenon, existing in industry, in commerce, in agriculture, and in the professions, in education, in medicine, in engineering. It is to some extent a general result of the industrial age. But the specialization of the bar is also due to some peculiar factors existing only at the bar. Of the general causes which have made themselves felt upon society as a whole, and upon the bar, not the least is the element of bigness in American society. Whether or not, like Mr. Justice Brandeis, you regard bigness as a curse, it is plainly one of the dominant characteristics of the America that we know. And we shall be most unjust if we attribute that bigness to the inflated vanity of some capitalistic megalomaniacs, for bigness is our deliberate choice as a people. Without bigness, could we have harnessed atomic energy? Without bigness, could the labor unions of this nation have succeeded as far as they have in eliminating cutthroat competition and sweatshops? Without bigness, could the mass of people have the machines and gadgets which to them, whether we like it or not, are a material part of their vision of happiness? And if bigness of enterprise is essential, then lawyers specializing in the business of those bignesses are inevitable, for every such large enterprise requires of necessity lawyers who will devote their whole time to the affairs of that particular enterprise.

But specialization has other causes in so far as it manifests itself among us at the bar. First we live in an age when, though we may still be guided by the spirit of the common law, the body of the law is statutory. Of course, it is truer in the federal courts than it is in the state courts, yet all of us know that the bulk of our business finds its root today in enactments of legislatures and not in decisions of common law judges. It was possible when the common law was the main staple of our business, for a man to become a master of very nearly all of it during his lifetime. He could at least know the leading cases, gain some familiarity with various fields of activity, acquire the habit of what Lord Coke told King James was artificial reason, and supplement his deficiencies, if there were any, on the eve of any trial or any consultation with the client. But such preparation and such knowledge are impossible with respect to the type of statutes with which we deal. I think it fair to say that statutory construction is without principle except the principle that you must be familiar with and, if you like, prejudiced with respect to evils which were supposed to exist and the benefits likely to be secured by the legislation. In other words, you must know the field, and such precise knowledge of many fields is far beyond the capacity of any one lawyer.

Connected with that primary cause is a secondary cause that almost all these new social and economic measures have been entrusted to administrative agencies for their enforcement. And administrative agencies have built up their own rules and regulations, even their own rules of admission to their own bars. And the rate at which they issue opinions and regulations and orders in comparison with even the most productive of courts is like a comparison between the rate of output of a newspaper publisher and a book publisher. None of you, I am sure, can keep up with more than two or three loose-leaf services; and only, I dare say, a judge is in the habit of dipping with any regularity in more than three or four such services. Thus the very framework of our time creates a situation in which specialization has become almost inevitable. Today, in fact, almost all of you could be divided into labor lawyers, or S.E.C. lawyers, or tort lawyers, or criminal lawyers, and so forth, down the line. I know so far as your wives and legal stationers go, you are lawyers engaged in general practice. But in your hearts you know that there are only so many subjects, so many specialties, which you handle. And whether you know it or not, your clients believe it. I think they act unwisely, but most clients have the to me ill-founded view that when they look for counsel they want the man who has tried a parallel case previously, rather than wanting the man of general wisdom and common sense. And that ingrained habit of the client shows itself in the work we get.

Is it a disaster that we have become so specialized a profession? I suppose many people would give an offhand yes to that. They would reply with the old saw about knowing more and more about less and less, or they would speak of the intellectual and ultimately the spiritual imbalance which comes when a man devotes himself to a thorough knowledge of one subject rather than a well-rounded competence. They might point to the dangers that a man will become a cog in a machine of corporate society. And if no other argument occurred to them, they might speak of the misery of a man's feeling of his own unimportance. And yet, would these critics propose that we should do without atomic energy and motor cars and old age pensions? Not a one of them. A pragmatist would think there must be something wrong with a criticism which proposes no plan of reform, no uprooting of a situation which has been criticized. And I for myself refuse to accept that argument and that criticism, since I find them bootless. Tonight I propose to enter before you an appearance on behalf of specialization.

At the outset I will admit that if I were living in the age of the Renaissance I should be quite content to set before you the rounded work of Leonardo da Vinci or Francis Bacon as a model. Even if I lived one hundred fifty years ago and could emulate Benjamin Franklin and Thomas Jefferson, that would be a rich and rewarding kind of ideal. But those are not careers which are possible for any of us. And I am going to suggest that in the life that we have today at the bar and will have tomorrow, there is for the man who has the eye to see it and the zest to pursue it, as much intellectual excitement and as much spiritual adventure as there ever was in the old days.

I am going to begin my argument with a parable which those of you who have had training in science will already know. It may not be a literally true story, but it crystallizes a symbolic truth.

A young Harvard graduate student came to study under Louis Agassiz, the famed naturalist. Agassiz welcomed him, and the graduate student asked what he was to do, and Agassiz said, "Here is a stone. Take it and come back after you have studied it." The graduate student came back after a fortnight and Louis Agassiz said, "Sir, you are not ready to talk with me yet. There is much more to that stone than a fortnight's work."

The law, the modern law and its problems, are like that stone. To a certain extent, of course, the law is a mere technique for deciding cases. But it is something more. To a certain extent, the law is a jargon to be found in documents and pleadings, but it is something more. Essentially the law is one of the, perhaps the best of, the mirrors for the reflection of the social process. Each legal problem has a reality which is reflected in that mirror. To know that problem you must know its adjacent neighbors and its whole setting. Let me give an example.

Suppose you are the lawyer to draw a collective bargaining contract. You are a mere apprentice, if all you know is in three red fabrikoid volumes and two or three black volumes of a loose-leaf service. A labor problem to a master in the field presents the whole background of American labor history. It presents the problems not only of the particular industry, but the wage and price level of the country. It involves a knowledge of political trends, not only those disclosed in the daily newspaper but in the liberal weekly, in the trade union press, in the publications which come out not only of Washington but of the United Nations and the International Labor Organization. And there is even more. There is the whole field of industrial psychology. You think I exaggerate perhaps, with that last recondite example, and yet I think I may prove my point with it. How often when you represent an employer in a negotiation with respect to a labor contract, the employer says to you, "Why isn't it possible with respect to labor contracts, as it is with respect to material contracts and sales contracts, to have a standard form which you use year after year with a mere alteration of a number of articles and of the price and some minor details about terms? Why is it necessary to go through the whole process each time?" I commend to your attention a little volume by Professor Elton Mayo, the Australian, who for a time taught both in Massachusetts and in England, and who made a study of the practices at Western Electric's Hawthorne factory. He and his colleagues, for example, increased the illumination in a particular room. The workers produced more than they had before. Strangely enough, in the next room, which was being used as a basis of comparison, the workers also increased their volume of production though there had been no change in the lighting. And then they removed the lighting in the first room and once again the production went up. And why? The answer was that when workers knew that an intelligent interest was being taken in their production, and they were sharing and being associated in the experiment, they responded. The same is true with respect to other phases of the human relations involved between labor and management. And the annual bargaining process is a part of that pattern. I have taken an example, and a rather extreme one, perhaps, from the labor field. But I certainly could argue that the social and economic knowledge, the knowledge of related disciplines and sciences, are required in many other fields.

You have an antitrust case. Is it enough to present the facts with respect to the particular company and to subsume those facts under the headnotes of all the cases decided by the Supreme Court of the United States since the rule of reason was promulgated in 1911? Of course not. The judge and you must know something about the industry, the alternatives open, and the whole field of competition and economic and social considerations which bear upon the problem. Is your field rate regulation? Surely you have not satisfied the demand if all you presented is an analysis of a particular company, its acquisitions, its prospects. They must be centered against a much broader background of prediction and analysis of the whole economy. And if you are a criminal lawyer whose case comes before a judge who must sentence the defendant, certainly it is your business to know the history and policy of the statute under which the offense is laid; the whole background, sometimes psychiatric as well as otherwise, of the defendant; the types of sanction which are available and which are suitable.

No matter what your specialty is, it has become richer because of the complications of the world in which we live. It presents a challenge to any man who has intellectual curiosity, who has any adventure of spirit and who cares to be associated with other men in the creation of a free and open society. Are we less fortunate than the men whose interests were debt and detinue, assumpsit and indebitatus assumpsit, trover and case? We have turned from a profession which was, because of its worship of precedent, primarily a backward-looking profession to a forward-looking profession concerned with consequences. And ours is as new a logic as Dewey's or Russell's in comparison with Aristotle. We have moved into an entirely new method of thinking.

So far I have talked about the intellectual aspects of the age of specialization. I now want to go on to another point. Quite without our being aware of it, as business has moved across national boundaries so have we. We have come into an era in which comparative law and international law have stolen upon us without our knowledge. As recently as when I was in law school men looked at the course in international law as though it were fit only for those who were going into the Department of State or some like activity. But today in many fields the international ramifications have begun to make themselves felt. Let me take the traditional A, B, C method of approach. I care not whether you take aviation or banking or copyright and I haven't intended to be artificial in my selection — I could have taken equally well admiralty, or bills and notes, or criminal law. In each instance I could point a finger at a recent important international arrangement which affects the specialists in that field. I will be content by taking one of the cases an earlier speaker today, Mr. Reeve, cited.

On April 4 of this year in *Farrell* v. *United States*, an admiralty case, the issue was settled with reference to Convention No. 55 of the International Labor Organization, which the United States had ratified, unknown to most of you, in 1936. The question as to the right of a workman employed at sea to medical care, was determined by an international treaty.

You may think that I speak of unimportant details. And yet, I suspect that it is through international cooperation

upon technical detail that ultimately such world organization as is effective will be achieved. May I remind you of a
very fine essay written by the greatest of our legal historians,
Frederic W. Maitland, who, summarizing the nineteenth
century, made references to the importance of action taken
in 1847 by the then multiple German principalities. There
were, as you know, at least half a dozen different states. The
first action they took toward unity was in 1847 when they
agreed upon a uniform law of bills of exchange. If you will
remember that at the present time the American Law Institute Committee and the Commissioners on Uniform State
Laws headed by Illinois's own Dean, Albert Harno, are engaged in drafting a commercial code, and that it is proposed
that that commercial code shall be adopted possibly by
UNESCO, or another affiliate of the UN, possibly by Latin-
American states which have taken a principal interest in the
subject, you will realize as concretely as I can make my example that specialization in the law may have the most important international consequences.

If I were to stop here, you might think that I looked
upon the lawyers as a mere congeries or heap of specialists
without much in common except the fact that they all went
to law school and all were admitted to the bar. I do not
regard the bar and our profession as a mere opportunity for
a philosophical mind, nor a chance to act as a road builder
for the peace and the polity of the future. We have another
strong interest which is our common bond. We are the
great teachers of government and of justice. No civics
teacher, no orator on platform or on radio, has the chance
which you and I have when we deal with clients, with juries, and with others concerned with law cases. We show
just where the garment of society covers a point. Our concrete lesson outlasts a hundred speeches. All of us in these
contacts with clients and with jurors and with witnesses

have an opportunity with respect to the governmental and social system under which we live. We inevitably discuss the reach of a man's rights and the obligations that he owes to society. We are engaged in a calling in which we are bound to convey the lesson that the surest test of the legitimacy of power is the willingness of power to acknowledge limitation. We are inevitably dedicated to the proposition that, save in exceptional circumstances, the individual citizen should not feel the coercive pressure of public authority, but should direct his life in accordance with the moral element within him and around him in society. We believe that civilization, in Whitehead's great phrase, is the maintenance of the social order by its own inherent persuasiveness, and that recourse to force is the surest evidence of the failure of civilization. So long as we remain true to those ideals, so long as we engage in what Mr. Conant calls the wise restraints that make men free, for that long we shall be what we were when we were called to the bar, an ancient, an honorable and a unified profession.

An address delivered to the
Chicago Bar Association, 1949

The Independence of Lawyers

THERE is never an independent judiciary without an independent bar. Yet it is very easy for us to talk about the independence in the judiciary without penetrating to the more serious aspects of the independence of the bar.

The independence of the judiciary does not exist. Indeed, only six weeks ago I had that point emphasized when I was in Belgrade talking with the judges of the Supreme Court of Yugoslavia, two or three lower court judges, the Attorney General, the Procurator General, and a couple of law professors.

About a dozen of us were in the room together, and the discussion was complete and candid. I shall not review it all; but at one stage I was asking the judges of the Supreme Court whether they felt the same freedom that I feel in deciding an important political case against the prosecution. This question was being put in the presence of the Attorney General and the Procurator General, and there was a good deal of buzzing among the judges before they answered.

Then one of them spoke out in perfect English and replied: "You will see my brethren are not in agreement as to the answer to give you. But may I remind you," now, these are his words, "that Pericles said, 'The secret of liberty is courage.' And my brethren differ in the amount of courage they have.' "

It is fair to say that independence of the judiciary requires only courage. Independence of the bar requires a great deal more. The judge — at least the Federal judge — lives in a protected world. Corruption aside, it is almost impossible to get rid of him. And he has this feeling of great security which no member of the practicing bar can quite share.

We are all aware that it leads often to the material disadvantage of members of the bar to be independent. I come from a state in which it is not forgotten that William Thompson, who represented Sacco and Vanzetti, lost a substantial part of his practice thereafter. And I think it fair to say that in general, disinterested public service is not usually financially rewarded. Mr. Charles Curtis drafted our Fair Employment Practices Act, a very useful piece of legislation which I am sure did not bring him any affluent clients.

The whole problem of the independence of the bar turns to some extent in this country upon a willingness to undergo a degree of financial loss beyond the loss of time.

I know that lawyers serve on boards of charitable institutions, on hospital boards, on university boards, and in other philanthropic causes; and in those aspects give their time. But some objective observer might say, however noble the motive, such association may have as its by-product some professional advantage.

The kind of service of which I am speaking has no advantage materially, and often is very expensive. Our tradition does not show that a person like Sir Stafford Cripps can be a radical politically, and have conservative clients come to him on the basis of his professional merit. A man indeed may be a great lawyer with a great practice before he be-

comes a public servant, like Dean Acheson, and may as a
result of political service find that those who previously
thought him an excellent lawyer no longer are so sure that
they want to give him business because of his political
views.

We must be realistic enough to recognize that when we
deal with the problem of public responsibilities of the bar,
we are involving ourselves in something more than the work
of a good Samaritan.

I am not going to talk much about the lawyer in court,
and yet there are some things which I should like to refer to
in passing, both on the criminal and on the civil side. We all
know that not only by virtue of the Constitution but by
virtue of any standard of fair play, men who are indigent
are entitled to be represented in criminal matters, whether
they are charged with political crime or merely with that
type of wrong-dealing with property which has no political
overtones.

And yet with a few conspicuous exceptions such as the
service of, as he then was, Mister Medina, in regard to a
treason trial, how many lawyers of first rate quality have
been willing to serve in political criminal trials on behalf of
the defendants?

With respect to civil matters, I think we do somewhat
better, and my impression is that referral agencies and other
types of work distribution which have evolved in Chicago
and Boston and elsewhere, on the whole take care sufficiently of the more pressing cases. Indeed, I am not sure I
wouldn't be prepared to say that under our system, plain-
tiffs get at least as good legal representation as they are entitled to.

But how diligent are we as a profession in watching the
judges? How much courage do we as a group of lawyers
have in dealing with those members of the bench who are

not dispensing the kind of justice to which the community is entitled?

Judge Clark will remember an occasion on which he and I sat next to each other after he had a message from C. C. Burlingham which required a certain judge to retire or risk Mr. Burlingham's exposure of him. How many C. C. Burlinghams are there among us who would willingly stick out their necks to point out the obvious failures in integrity and efficiency on the Bench? Very few!

We all know — and the deans of law schools here know better than I — that surely two-thirds of those men whom they graduate will almost never go into a courtroom. They will be either working in private law offices or in government law offices or for private companies, but will have remote — if any — relationship to the courts.

I think it fair to say that it rarely occurs to the large offices in the several cities what their responsibility is with respect to the whole bar. It is very easy indeed to criticize people because at the age of thirty-five or forty-five they are "shysters." It is very easy to forget that it may be because they were sons of aliens, or members of a minority group, or of a non-white color, or for some other reason like that, they never had a chance adequately to learn the standards of the profession under masters in their calling.

There was a time when our bar, like the English bar, was an apprenticeship bar. There was a time when George Wythe in Virginia, and Theophilus Parsons in Massachusetts, and other men in your various states, took the young aspiring lawyer and trained him.

I do not mean to say that we have lost on net balance by going to a system of law schools instead of individual teachers and the apprenticeship method. But though we have not lost on net balance there is one kind of loss we have sustained, and that is the kind of direct moral influence, the awareness of responsibility which men get from a direct contact with an elder at the bar whom they admire and respect.

All of us know what a succession of judges' law clerks owe to the judges of the Supreme Court and of lower courts, not in the way of technical education but in the way of moral example and high standards. Is it not true that the same might happen with respect to the practicing bar? Do we not in part owe Philip Jessup to Elihu Root? Do we not in part owe Joseph Eastman to Louis Brandeis?

And is it not true that if the large law firms were more willing to take in for short periods of time — one or two years — a larger number of lawyers whom they did not intend to keep permanently and whom they said they did not intend to keep permanently, but to whom they were willing to give the benefit of the moral and professional climate of that office, we would all be the gainers?

Is it not part of the professional responsibility of the large offices to act as the judges of the high court have acted, as the teachers of men who are really not of much use when they are being taught? No one who has had a law clerk fools himself that during the first few months he gets as much out of the law clerk as he gives. But he may in the long run say that of all the things he does, being a teacher is the most rewarding. This task of being a teacher is not confined to the professors. It is open to everyone in dealing with the young.

A quite different aspect of the public responsibilities of the lawyer interests me, and that is the relationship of the lawyer to the problems of the law dealt with by the legislature as distinguished from those dealt with by the courts.

We are in a world quite different from the law world of a hundred years ago. We all know that the larger part of the law with which we are concerned, is not judge-made. We are amused when we are told that Dean Langdell did not think it worthwhile to collect statutes because the law was the law in case books and cases. We know perfectly well that Professor Herbert Wechsler was right when he said that we used to look at the statutes through the window of the judicial case. But no longer do we — if we are wise — look at the statute in quite such limited terms.

We are faced with one of the great challenges of judicial history: whether legislation can be on as high a plane intellectually, jurisprudentially, as case law. Professor Schulz, the author of one of the most famous books on Roman Law, said — and it is on his authority I must rely, for my own knowledge does not reach this point at all — that there never had been a law-inspired nation which was statute-inspired — that all great legal systems emerged from case law.

Whether this be true or not, we are faced with the challenge as to whether in our society which is becoming increasingly a statutory society, we can have as high principle, as evident concern with jurisprudence, as exists in a common-law or judicial system. And that is the problem not only of the law professor and legislator, but the problem of the bar.

I am well aware that there are some steps already taken with respect to this type of concern. The American Bar Association has its working connection, for example, with criminal law. The American Law Institute has its working connection with the Commercial Code, the Penal Code, and other matters. The Association of the Bar of the City of New York is concerned in studying conflicts of interest, security and loyalty, and other such problems.

But is there as yet a widespread awareness of the breadth of this problem and the degree to which the bar must attend to the elevation of standards in the legislative process? Do we have that kind of continuous attention — and I mean not only to the Congress but to the forty-nine separate legislatures of the forty-nine states?

We have the Annual Notes about what the Supreme Court of the United States is doing. We have local notes about local courts. But which review, which journal undertakes to concern itself with the legislative process and its impact on the law with such a steady attention, with such a critical eye, as we devote to the much less important work of the courts?

There are other areas that will appear to all of you. There is the problem of criminal sanctions and other types of sanctions. Who has undertaken to review in any comprehensive method the great variety of sanctions now on the statute books with respect to different kinds of offenses, the usefulness of treble damage suits and qui tam suits? Is there at the bar any such attention to this topic as it deserves?

What about the position of voluntary associations, those characteristic American forms of group activity which have excited the interest of men like De Tocqueville and Maitland? What group at the bar has been concerned with methods of entry into the dismissal from such organizations, and fair play within such organizations?

Is it not correct that we have occasional outbursts of Congressional inquiry as to one particular area, but no such overall study of this problem as its dimensions would warrant?

Take the problem of privacy. Lord Acton said that *in radice* all questions of liberty were questions as to what was immune from state inspection and action. We all know that there are special problems which arise from time to time as to which members of the bar or bar associations concern themselves, but the overall development within and effect upon our society of privacy, which may very well be one of the keys to both fraternity and love, is an aspect of the law to which no one is giving the weight which the subject merits.

And what of taxation? I do not mean the kind of tax study which deals with the problems recited in a C.C.H. or a Prentice-Hall survey. I am talking of the social effects of various types of taxation.

Let us take our own profession. Is it not true that any sophisticated person fully aware of the force of the tax laws of the United States, and interested in his material advantage, would decide that he would come off best in association with a large group of practitioners in a common firm in a way that would level out his earnings over a long period of time and not run the risks which independent practice presents, of very large windfalls one year, most of which would go to the tax collector, and small returns another year?

And are we not through our indifference to the social aspects of the tax law, undermining the most precious of the characteristics of our calling—our independence?

What I have said was merely intended to be illustrative. It is the responsibility of the leaders of the bar to develop among the juniors of the bar and the profession as a whole, an awareness of the very deep questions — whether this takes the form of seminars, whether it takes the form of stimulating in each of the states reviews of legislative as there are reviews of judicial action, I do not say. But I am convinced that we are dealing here with a problem of the most challenging nature, in which our responsibility to the community is best performed by our being aware of our responsibility to the young people in our calling.

I am told that Judge Learned Hand concluded the other night with a quotation from Wordsworth. Wordsworth was concerned with the "might of souls and what they do within themselves."

An address to the Arden House Conference on
Continuing Legal Education for Professional
Competence and Responsibility on the topic
of the independence of the bar discussed
earlier by Judge Learned Hand,
John Lord O'Brian, Esq., and
Dean Erwin Griswold, 1958

The Age of Discretion

EVEN the most casual observer is aware of the trend of our law toward flexibility and discretion. One sign is that since the crisis of 1937 the Supreme Court of the United States has more broadly interpreted the United States Constitution, as a result of which the powers of the President, of the Congress, and of state legislatures have been expanded, at least in the economic field. Another indication is the greater willingness of judges to disregard precedents in all types of cases. A third is the increasing tendency to give to administrative agencies the power to adopt from time to time different regulations, the power to interpret technical statutory terms, the power to find facts, and the power to shape remedies deemed appropriate.

I do not intend to discuss whether these trends have been desirable or undesirable, avoidable or inevitable. My intention is to concentrate on how these trends affect the nature of American law and the future of the practice and the teaching of the law.

There are some who say that the nature of American law has been fundamentally altered, that it has lost its characteristics of certainty and stability and has escaped from the bonds of professional discipline into the unrestrained area of politics. In support of their charge they note the extent to which controversies are now submitted to executive authorities who often lack legal training; and the degree to which these authorities are sustained in their substantive conclusions, provided they observe a few minimum procedural formalities. They note that even where controversies are still determined not by political agencies but by courts, frequently the judges, according to their own brethren, do not follow rules established by their predecessors. And these critics ask whether in the light of these developments it cannot fairly be said that we are living under what they characterize as a Marxian concept of law — that is to say, a frank recognition that today law is little more than one of the political processes by which the group which is dominant at the moment manifests its power and achieves its ends.

But there are others who say that there has been no basic change from the American law of yesterday to that of today. They begin by stressing the fact that there is a common misunderstanding as to the characteristics of yesterday's law. Let us assume, they say, that as Judge Cardozo reported in his *Nature of the Judicial Process* the law laid down by appellate judges was in Cardozo's day relatively certain and that in the overwhelming majority of private cases only one result was possible for judges who were of good will and of adequate intelligence and education. Nonetheless, appellate decisions were but a small segment of the picture. The great bulk of judicial work was done by trial judges. In any particular lawsuit their contribution was often unpredictable and either theoretically unreviewable or practically unreversable. In many ways the trial judge had a nearly unlimited discretion, for example, in criminal sentences, in reorganization plans, in the shaping and timing of equitable relief, in the manner of conducting a trial, and in conveying indirectly, if not directly, his view to the jury. No one who ever had a suit before a trial judge would agree that the judge was "confined from molar to molecular motions," as Holmes said of judges generally in *Southern Pacific Co. v. Jensen.* Moreover, say those who assert that there has been no basic change in American law, not only were the trial judges always more important than the appellate judges, but the legislators and executives were always more important than either trial or appellate judges. Just because legislation and executive action were not customarily studied so much as judicial decisions in yesterday's law schools, it does not follow that in practice legislation or executive action was then unimportant or certain or stable or predictable. In short, so runs the argument, there has been nothing more than a normal evolution from the past with a moderate increase in the amount of discretion entrusted to those who always possessed and exercised it.

My own view stands between these two extremes.

It seems to me to be an understatement to claim that there has been only a gradual evolution, or to say that there is only a continuation of an earlier situation where judges wielded less legal power than legislators and executives. In my opinion the authority of the judiciary and the place of judge-made law has undergone a sharp and a decisive decline. I do not want you to suppose that I am leveling a charge against any judge or group of judges. I am not ready to cast any judge in the role of Pope Celestine V, and, like Dante, indict him for *"il gran rifiuto."* All I say is that today the role of judge-made law is distinctly secondary.

But from the premise that the judiciary has declined in importance, it does not seem to me to follow that we are subject to arbitrary discretion, or, to borrow a caustic phrase, that we "live under a whim of iron." I suggest that although legislators and administrators today wield larger discretionary powers than ever before, they are not in reality free to wield these powers in an arbitrary and capricious manner. Consciously or unconsciously, they are governed by certain standards and norms.

In speaking of standards I am not referring to constitutional limitations such as those embodied in the "due process" clauses of the Fifth and Fourteenth Amendments. Nor am I considering specific restrictions that may be inserted in so many words in a particular statute. I do not even mean to emphasize the extent to which a public official sets standards for himself; how from force of habit, from laziness, from lack of time, from lack of capacity, from a desire to appear to be fair, he establishes his own precedents and routines to which, often unconsciously, he adheres. My thesis is that regardless of the discretion with which an officer or legislator is vested, he is in fact controlled by technical norms which have been developed for each subject and also by general norms which are basic to the society in which he lives. You will notice that I have used the word norms. I do not say that these norms are themselves law in the sense of being enforceable commands of the sovereign. I say that they are among the important sources and materials of which the law is made; and they are limiting factors in the exercise of each discretionary power. Let me make my meaning plainer, by discussing first the technical norms, and later the general norms.

After one has worked for any length of time in a particular field he acquires a sense of what considerations have a legitimate bearing upon problems in that field. I do not merely mean that the legislator or administrator becomes aware of particular individual and group pressures, and recognizes, as it were, the parallelogram of partisan forces in which he is caught. My point is somewhat more subtle. He comes to have an appreciation of the history and grammar of his specific topic; to understand which objectives in that field public opinion over a long term of years has sought to promote, and which to discourage; to foresee the probable evolution of his subject; and to grasp the values which inhere in that process of growth.

But an executive or legislator in exercising his discretion is aware of more than the criteria of his own specialty. He is constantly reminded of the broader standards that lie at the base of the whole of our society. Some of them are our heritage from the great philosophical and the religious thinkers. In his *Adventures of Ideas,* Professor A. N. Whitehead traced the ideals of liberty from Periclean Athens through the Stoics and the lawyers of republican Rome through Clement of Alexandria and the Early Church Fathers to Locke and the French philosophers and our own Founding Fathers. Other standards lie embedded in Anglo-American history: they are the sediment of the struggles between parliaments and kings, between colonies and the home country, between the "ins" and the "outs" in a century and a half of American politics. They are recorded not only by the great historians of the world, Thucydides and Tacitus, Acton and Bury, Andrews and Becker; they are the constant theme of American literature, today no less than in the times of Emerson and James Russell Lowell.

This complex of ideas does not, of course, constitute a corpus of "natural law" in the old sense of that term. It does not form a set of measuring glasses so minutely divided as to gauge each exercise of legislative or administrative discretion. But nonetheless, these philosophical, historical, and literary traditions become limitations of which those in authority are properly reminded whenever they are tempted to take summary action, or to proceed without a full consideration of all relevant factors, or to act capriciously, secretly, or spitefully.

In short, I submit that while in our day the law has been fundamentally changed by the increase of discretionary powers and by the decline of the relative role of the judiciary, it is not true that those who have been given discretion are free of normative standards or are unaware of professional discipline. To be sure their discipline is not identical with that of the common law, nor with that of the bar and the bench; but for all that it is the sort of discipline with which lawyers and law students are concerned.

That lawyers are concerned with the exercise of administrative and legislative discretion I need hardly argue in this assembly. Your calendars reveal how much more of your time today is devoted to engagements in Washington and before regional offices, and how much less to appellate and trial courts. Your managing clerks and librarians constantly remind you how much more of your office expense and office space is devoted to loose-leaf services, administrative reports and legislative documents. And there is not one of you who would deny the gift of prophecy to Mr. Justice Holmes for his statement made in 1897 that "For the rational study of the law the black-letter man may be the man of the present, but the man of the future is the man of statistics and the master of economics." We have gone a long way from the view of Roger North, the seventeenth-century English Solicitor General, that "it is not necessary for counsel to know what the history of a point is, but to know how it now stands resolved."

Today you as lawyers devote, I suspect, little of your time to considering how far the courts will allow executives or legislators to regulate your clients. You are concerned not with what the executive or legislative branch theoretically can do without being reversed by a court, but with what it actually should do if it is to be affirmed by public opinion. Thus, like those who themselves wield authority, you who appear before them are most concerned not with judicial cases but with what I described as the technical norms of the subject and the general norms of society, that is, both with the history and grammar of the particular topic and with the underlying creed of our society.

In an era where the bar spends most of its time in administrative and legislative forums and most of its thought upon the wise and sensible exercise of discretion, how stand the law schools?

The bulk of teaching in the law schools is still devoted to the study of cases decided by appellate courts. This form of instruction has great advantages. It has given generations of students an unequaled training in logical analysis, in the precise use of words, in exposition, and in the professional habits of thought characteristic of centuries of lawyers. And these judicial cases have been taught in a spirit of intellectual excitement and adventure that none of us can forget. When in his essays on *Universities and Their Function* Professor Whitehead said that "the justification for a university is that it preserves the connection between knowledge and the zest of life, by uniting the young and the old in the imaginative consideration of learning," he gave the justification of the Harvard Law School as we know and as we love it. No one who knows the case system in operation would ever supersede it.

But in this age of discretion is it not important to go further than we have in supplementing this type of study of judicial cases? I am not unaware that in a few exceptional courses on special topics, such as corporate finance, the materials now studied embrace more than extracts from judicial reports. Yet I believe I do not overstate the situation when I say that the overwhelming majority of present-day candidates for the degree of Bachelor of Laws receive no training in the Harvard Law School in the norms or standards which they would properly take into consideration if as administrators, legislators, or lawyers they were concerned with the exercise of discretionary powers. Might not some modern Socrates say that our instruction bears too close a resemblance to what the ancient Socrates condemned in the Sophists of his day?

To meet this possible charge and to prepare students for this Age of Discretion, I suggest that it is worth considering two possible lines of reform in our legal education.

In the first place, it seems to me that in the teaching of what are sometimes called the public law courses, courses such as labor law, antitrust law, and public utilities, the instruction should be based upon the premise that the most important material lies outside of judicial reports. I know that someone will say that while it is true that important data are in economic treatises, in Congressional debates, in legislative hearings, in pamphlets, in monographs, in histories, in private agreements, and in a dozen other places, such material should be studied in the college or somewhere else in the university but not in the law school. I take up that challenge. And I do not take it up on the limited ground that college training is apt to be fragmentary, to be pitched to a level of relatively less mature minds, and to be studied with less serious purpose. My point is that the consideration of economic, political, historical and sociological material for the purpose of exercising discretionary power is different from the consideration of the same material for the purpose of pure scholarship. When we consider this material for the purpose of the exercise of discretionary power, we are not interested in what is eccentric or obsolete; the emphasis is on the normal and the dynamic. What we are interested in is not in a recital of how this material has affected the past, but in how it is likely to and how it should affect the present and the future.

In addition to broadening the basis of instruction in these particularistic courses such as labor and antitrust law, it seems to me of the greatest consequence to allow any undergraduate to elect, and possibly to require him to take, several courses in the fundamental norms of administrative law, of legislation, and of jurisprudence.

At present, if I understand correctly, administrative law is taught primarily in the light of court cases. To my way of thinking, such instruction overlooks the fact that what an administrator wants to know and what he expects to hear from a lawyer is not merely what he must do but what is the sound and desirable method for him to proceed. With all their merits, the doctrine of judicial review enshrined in our constitutional system, and the doctrine of the rule of law, to use Professor Albert Venn Dicey's phrase, are not the only touchstones as to how an administrative process should be conducted. We need to develop for administrative law canons of fairness and tolerance, of orderliness and stability, of change and of growth — and the law school is the place to begin that development.

The same need for developing standards of legislation has long been apparent. In the sixth of the lectures which he gave twenty-nine years ago at Johns Hopkins University, published as *Standards of American Legislation*, the late Professor Ernst Freund discussed "The Meaning of Principle in Legislation." That lecture would still serve as an admirable prolegomenon for a course in legislation. And such a course would serve the uses not only of those who were drafting or interpreting statutes but of those who were concerned with the preparation of any sort of document that was to govern on a large scale the relations of numerous persons, private or public. We have been much too slow to admit that a definite part of legal science is the study of the non-logical aspects of regulatory schemes, the aspects which are sometimes treated as though they were the exclusive province of psychology, or semantics, or philosophy.

And not least of all I should hope to see in the law school of tomorrow a greatly increased interest in courses in jurisprudence. I can sense that some of you are already prepared to raise an eyebrow. The time of a law student is short, and bread-and-butter courses come first, you say. Jurisprudence is all very well for the philosopher or for the teacher or, if he gets time after his day in court, for the judge who has to make a bar association speech. But, you ask, what has jurisprudence to do with Wall Street, or Pennsylvania Avenue, or Main Street? To that pertinent question I think I have an answer. When the world is in turmoil the study of first principles is not a luxury but an essential. Take any important change of the last dozen years in your special field of activity. Was it the Securities Act of 1933, or the Public Utility Holding Company Act, or the National Labor Relations Act, or the Undivided Profits Tax? Is it not fair to say that when you came to interpret that act, to advise your clients, to make your argument before the administrative agency concerned and before the courts, you were attentive to more than the letter of the statute and the precise facts of your client's case? Did you not consider and did you not expect to have others consider a host of imponderable factors drawn from comparative law, from basic social principles, from the history of the struggle for liberty, and from the traditions of our people? Was there not at the base of your whole inquiry a search for a calculus of fundamental values? And was it not to jurisprudential considerations that you finally turned?

It is because we have always known that in the last analysis what counts in the law are not technicalities, not mastery of routines, not mere craftsmanship but a sense of justice, that we call the law a profession. With the churchmen and with the schoolmen, we stand as one of the great professions, entrusted with the task of shaping and transmitting the values of civilization. We have a major role in preserving what Werner Jaeger, borrowing a classical Greek term, has called the Paideia — the cultural spirit — of our society. To preserve that spirit and aid its growth is the high mission of the Harvard Law School, a mission that it has performed so well that the great English legal historian F. W. Maitland in the Rede Lecture for 1901 spoke in one breath of "the glory of Bourges, the glory of Bologna, the glory of Harvard." Let our school always have the intellectual vigor, the broad understanding, the spirit of tolerance to keep that reputation untarnished.

An address delivered to the New York
Harvard Law School Association, 1944

IV

The Living Streams of Value

By What Measure?

THERE is a famous saying which has been attributed to the first Lord Shaftesbury: "What is your religion?" "The religion of all sensible men." "And what is the religion of all sensible men?" "Sensible men never tell."

It is undeniably rash to depart from this prudent reminder and to discuss the ultimate standards by which one measures life. For the audience is certain to have radically different views. And, more important, it requires not only frankness but humility to admit how baffling are the problems and how inadequate the answers. When we wrestle with the ultimate, all of us, like Jacob of old, feel that we are touched in the hollow, and the hollow is strained; but few of us extort the blessing that we seek.

At the outset one must candidly admit that, in our own era, there is a substantial body of opinion to the effect that it is meaningless to talk about questions of ultimate value. According to this opinion, the life of man is lived in a welter of conflicting interests; each of these interests has some value; some of these interests are tinged with and expressed in terms of emotion; but none of these interests has any resemblance whatsoever to those eternal ideas of which Plato spoke and which, for him, possessed a clarity and universality similar to mathematical principles. We are reminded that when a man speaks of the values he cherishes he inevitably shows the bias of his animal origin, his economic status, his early emotional experiences. The eternal Republic of Plato, we are told, has fallen before the assaults of Darwin, Marx, and Freud. And the new utopia is pictured as one where men's needs and desires are first tested for stress and thrust, and then as many of them as possible are satisfied by that type of statesman appropriately called "a social engineer."

Lest you think I exaggerate the degree to which a severely empirical, materialistic approach has caught us in its grip, let me recall three conspicuous examples of contemporary thinking in international, national, and personal spheres.

In a penetrating diagnosis of American diplomacy, George Kennan, our highly qualified ambassador to the U.S.S.R., concludes: "I see the most serious fault of our past policy formulation to lie in . . . the legalistic-moralistic approach . . . the assumption that state behavior is a fit subject for moral judgment. . . . Our own national interest is all that we are really capable of knowing and understanding."

A like philosophy animated the opinion of the Supreme Court of the United States in dealing with the most critical issue of civil liberties presented in the last decade. "Nothing," wrote Chief Justice Vinson, "is more certain in modern society than the principle that there are no absolutes . . . a standard has meaning only when associated with the considerations which gave birth to the nomenclature . . . all concepts are relative." And, in a field quite different in scope from these political examples, the field of personal moral conduct, we find a similar willingness to discard what might be called the test of idealism in favor of a stark realism based upon self-interest. I refer to the obvious change in sexual morals which is both portrayed in, and accelerated by, a book like the Kinsey Report.

Now it is not my plan to examine the soundness of the particular assessment of interests made by Ambassador Kennan, Chief Justice Vinson, or Dr. Kinsey. My object in citing them was to illustrate the degree to which major problems in our society tend to be viewed in strictly pragmatic terms. And in using the adjective pragmatic, I mean not to combat a particular philosophical school, but to show the extent to which, in some quarters, the emphasis is not on idealism, but on utility and self-interest as the measure of one's life.

No one of you will suppose that empiricism is a novel doctrine. Twenty-five hundred years ago, Protagoras taught that "man is the measure of all things." And every generation, to some extent, revolts against the ideals of its fathers. In so far as the Ambassador, the Chief Justice, and Dr. Kinsey help us acknowledge that our ideals have changed, and thus save us from hypocrisy, so much the better. There is no more corrosive corruption than continuous proclamations of allegiance to a tradition which one secretly despises and practically disregards. For my part, I welcome so much of the pragmatic revolt as avowedly discards the values we are not prepared to embrace; and I favor keeping an open house for the spirit of truth in the realm of human action no less than in the realm of physical science.

But the empirical rejection of a particular tradition and opening the door to free inquiry do not show that no ideal element whatsoever should enter into the assessment of human conduct. Most of us are aware of a tension between what we are and what we would be. It will not do to say that this is a mere psychological residue from our childhood when we were under the authoritarian control of a parent, teacher, social group, or religious body. It is well-nigh universal experience that there is a need to put a bridle upon what the medieval world called the three lusts: the lust for knowledge, the lust for sensation, and the lust for power. The classical world warned against *hubris* and the Christian world lists pride as the first of the seven deadly sins. And for us of the present generation these admonitions have particular force. Not only have we observed the extent to which vaulting ambition has debauched the Nazi and the Russian state machines, but our own American accession to a place of predominant power has filled us with, quite literally, an awe-full sense of responsibility. The repeated citation of Acton's dictum of the corruption of power is indicative of our consciousness that, unless we are restrained, we shall encounter our nemesis. Indeed, is this not the basis of the great appeal of Reinhold Niebuhr's doctrine of the sinfulness of man and the irony of attempting to seek an escape within the framework of history?

Yet the awareness of the need of moderation in conduct and humility in thought does not, by itself, satisfy the deepest craving of our time. We have witnessed, as perhaps no other generation has, new disclosures of the mighty forces of nature and of the weakness and unreliability of man. For we have been contemporaries not only of the discoverers of nuclear fission, but of the defendants, here and abroad, who conspired to betray their countries' most precious secrets. From treason itself we have learned how deep a role idealism can play. And we demand a true faith responsive to those affirmative adventurous pulsations which emanate from the mystery of life.

Some would have us return to the bosom of an orthodox church, there to imbibe a revealed religion. No one can deny the appeal of this call and the degree to which it answers a widespread yearning for spiritual security. It offers a settled discipline that comes with the credentials of a long past and the promise of an everlasting future. Blessed are those who are prepared for that road. But for some of us there appears, at least initially, to be a barrier foreclosing the path to this refuge. We believe that in the world of the ideal, as well as in the world of fact, the door to further inquiry must never be closed. Any dogmatism is, by definition, unacceptable to us since, in our view, the journey of man on earth must always be in terms of search rather than discovery. Perhaps it was of this that the seventeenth-century French Catholic Malebranche was thinking when he said that, "if God held in one hand truth, and in the other the pursuit of truth, he would say 'Lord, the truth is for thee alone, give me the pursuit.' "

Others urge us to turn for guidance to the humanistic tradition — to classical Athens, or Renaissance Florence, or Augustan England, or to some synthesis of "the best that has been known and thought in the world." This approach has been familiar since the time of Matthew Arnold, though it has been given new currency by lists of the hundred best books and courses in so-called general education. While every insight of the past has its precious contribution to make to the enlargement of men's vision, this predominantly retrospective assessment of men's ideals has within it the seeds of great danger. It is, by definition, a philosophy of conservatism — the saving of the values of the past. Thus it gives minor scope to the adventurous and creative aspects of the present. Moreover, as Alfred N. Whitehead warned: "Nothing does more harm in unnerving men for their duties in the present, than the attention devoted to the points of excellence in the past as compared with the average failure of the present day."

This is not to say that history has not much to teach us.

But its first lesson is that effective idealism is the consequence not of great doctrines, not even of great men, but of great societies. And the way societies produce greatness is by the deliberate cultivation of a sense of style. In using the word "style," I mean more than fashion — I intend to emphasize the architectonic nature of virtue: the construction of an image of man's role in a social framework. Greek literature, Greek art, Greek politics, Greek science, even Greek medicine, as Professor Werner W. Jaeger reminds us in his book entitled *Paideia*, bear the impress of the Athenian concept of *arete*: "Originally an *arete* was any kind of excellence," but later it became "a combination of proud and courtly morality with warlike valour . . . the idea of *arete* is the quintessence of early Greek aristocratic education."

A quite different sense of style characterized the civilization of mediaeval Florence, but without it Dante could never have had his vision of the eternal realms or his standards to measure out damnation and salvation.

The point that I am endeavoring to make is that morality is, as its etymology indicates, a result of social structure. Ideal standards are not to be found in copybooks handed down from father to son or church to communicant. Dynamic ideals are an ennobling of particular social, economic, and other material conditions. Each age must make its own measure suitable to its own material. The task is not one of discovery of some standard already laid up in Heaven, or previously used on earth. Indeed, it is not a problem of discovery at all, but of artistic invention, or, if you prefer, poetic creation. But this does not mean the search for morals is illusory. Being a work of art, moral idealism is as real and enduring as a sunset or a song. This accords with Spinoza's propositions: "first that values are essentially relative to men and are in this sense human inventions; goodness and beauty do not belong to things apart from their relation to men; secondly, that while relative to men they are founded in the nature of things and are not arbitrary."

Someone will say this is all very well as a preliminary skirmish, but come now, tell us what kind of form or style is or should be characteristic of our age. What is this ideal interpretation which we should stamp upon the external world we know, and which, though it will not last *semper ubique* as a model for the action of other societies, will nonetheless so mold our time as to give it imperishable glory? How may it be attained?

Let me begin by reminding you of the dominant external characteristics of the society in which we live. Scientific technology, proceeding by way of the industrial revolution, has broken up the unities familiar to our grandfathers. It has converted the man of general competence sometimes into a professional, but more often into a specialist carrying on a task so esoteric, or at least so sharply defined, that its true nature is not understood by one's children or one's neighbors. Modern methods of production, communication, and transportation have created ever-larger areas of effective business, social, and political control, with the consequent decay of those smaller communities and enterprises where virtue was nourished according to time-honored formulas, and subjected to never-ceasing local vigilance. More and more our population has moved into, or adjacent to, metropolitan centers of varied racial and religious backgrounds. Separatism has become a theme of our social life in a way totally unfamiliar to those who knew American democracy in terms of the New England colonial village or even of the Middletown of the last generation. And while technology has tried to balance this divisive current by the cementing forces of motion pictures, radio, television, magazines whose circulation runs into the millions, and newspapers reporting instantaneously significant events from all over the globe, newer methods of communication exert a broadening rather than a deepening influence. We soon become aware how thin and superficial is this new knowledge, how much better it satisfies our appetite for sensation than it satisfies our thirst for understanding.

There are those who propose that to give a society so seriated a sense of purpose, it is necessary to impose a new unity — one built chiefly on a single system of primary and secondary education, bound by successively extracted oaths of allegiance, and perpetually renewed by declared conformity to an expressed commitment. To most of us, however, this has strange echoes of the totalitarianism we deprecate. If our society is to evolve a style that is to be remembered, it must be founded on diversity. That is the root character of our population, of our specialized work, of our urban life, of the freedoms which we have cherished.

And so I suggest that, in its search for value and style, the first task of our free society is to encourage each individual to seek within his own task, his own background, his own social life, a deeper significance. This suggestion will perhaps strike you at first as almost trivial; or at any rate a quite inadequate prescription. Yet once one begins to look upon one's own work imaginatively, becomes concerned with its history, its methods of reasoning, its social impact, its growth of purpose, not only the work itself but the whole universe seems to light up. One is led to seek resemblances in neighboring fields; and as one proceeds, the definition of neighborhood constantly expands so that there emerges an almost common set of ideals. Spinoza taught us that "the supreme fact is that somehow things are one." Indeed, I think that those who study the intellectual development of the great seers of the twentieth century, whatever their professional discipline — Poincaré the mathematician;

Schrödinger the physicist; Eddington the astonomer; Holmes the judge; Osler the doctor; James the psychologist — will find that they were initially led to the sense of values which they finally developed from an intensive study of their own specialized tasks. So I say that the first element by which our society will be measured is its capacity to induce its specialists to seek meaning in the details of their daily work, and to communicate that meaning to their fellows in other specialties.

Let me underline the duty of communication to which I have just referred. There are, I know, those who distrust, or at least regard as of secondary importance, the specialist who seeks to increase popular understanding of his professional knowledge and criteria. But a technician from whose work can be drawn a generalization applying beyond his own field has the opportunity to make the most significant contribution to civilization. What began as an inquiry into the problems of a livelihood becomes by subtle transformation a disclosure of a way of life. Out of the complex comes that simplicity of purpose which is the core of all stability, in societies no less than in individuals. If what I have said seems abstract, let me recall to your mind Cardozo's *The Nature of the Judicial Process* or Hadamard's *An Essay on the Psychology of Invention in the Mathematical Field*, each in its own way drawing from a specialized field the materials which help explain those values underlying the creative process.

So far, I have spoken of those ideal values which may be extracted from an imaginative understanding of the logic, history, and purpose of our specialized vocations. But the principle of a common outlook achieved through a study of detail has a much broader application. Indeed, does it not furnish a clue to realizing the potentialities of the cultural diversities characteristic of the heterogeneous racial, religious, and social groups within our land and perhaps within the world? Hitherto we have alternated between two policies — one of urging them to conform to a narrowly defined democracy; the other, and more usual, of tolerance, but a tolerance tending in practice to be nothing more than indifference based on the belief that each man's ideal pattern is important only to himself or his own group. But spiritual growth rarely results from either imposed conformity or isolated coexistence. The vitality of ideals depends upon the individual's escape from solitariness and his sense of participating membership in the community of mankind. That comes only when his cultural diversity is not merely tolerated, but treasured as a gift to the common account. And the society which lays up such free gifts of the spirit will have a richer store from which to draw when it fashions its pattern of ultimate value.

What the precise pattern of our society will be, and how each of us will enter into it, I have not told you and cannot tell you. What I have tried to make you feel is that though there may be no absolute standards governing the human race from the day of creation to the day of final judgment, yet every man who searches may apprehend beyond the perceptible facts of his own self-interest which he comprehends, a world of ideals evolved from and forming the style of the society in which he lives. This world of ideals he only dimly discerns, but his insight increases as he ponders deeply over the significance of the details of his chosen work and of the nature of the "rock whence he is hewn."

And let him not suppose that the path to which I have been pointing, though it fails to supply definite rules for conduct, or to formulate a creed with concrete content, is inconsistent with a religious life. For religion, as Alfred N. Whitehead taught us, "is the vision of something which stands beyond, behind, and within the passing flux of immediate things; something which is real, and yet waiting to be realized; something which is a remote possibility, and yet the greatest of present facts; something that gives meaning to all that passes, and yet eludes apprehension; something whose possession is the final good, and yet is beyond all reach; something which is the ultimate ideal, and the hopeless quest."

Baccalaureate Address at Massachusetts
Institute of Technology, 1952

The Phillips Exeter Academy: An Appreciation

THE essential function of the great boarding school is (in the words over the portal of the Academy Building at Exeter) to train boys who enter there to become men. In divers ways the school aids a boy to gain mastery of himself. He is instructed in mental and physical pursuits so that needed skills become habitual and the instruments of later development. He forms such intimate associations with his fellows that his standards and his taste are forever affected. His imagination is incited by gifted teachers, poets speaking with an inner authority, historic figures of deserved renown, understanding coaches whose sportsmanship implies a code of gentlemanly yet hard competition.

Enduring this process is rarely an entirely pleasant experience. It is uncomfortable to emerge from the cocoon of boyhood, to face the distress of growing into adult responsibility, and to surmount the first major crisis in a search for identity. Hence most perceptive authors, American and English, who faithfully portray their schoolboy days usually report their loneliness, their maladjustments, and the depth of their despair. They reject the view that their years at boarding school were crowded with gay hours spent with a wholly attractive company of youngsters in a cheerful, country club atmosphere, fulfilling the dreams of Plato and John Phillips.

Many honest, sensitive, detached Exonians would not deny that their own lives at the Academy reflected this ambivalence of growing self-mastery and bitter self-distrust. If I recall correctly, once, walking to the Exeter Inn from a trustees' meeting in the Faculty Room, Tom Lamont, Francis Plimpton, John Cowles, John Nason, Dudley Orr, and I agreed that none of us would say that our days in the Exeter Yard were our happiest. Yet, maybe, they were our most rewarding. They taught us that, after Exeter's testing of our mettle, there was nothing of which we need be afraid. Our steel had been hardened by a cleansing fire. We knew what it was to face without sham or hope of successful evasion the judgments of our elders and, more important, of our peers, and, most important, of ourselves.

Exeter was not in my day, and I do not believe it is now, a satisfactory school for every boy of accomplishment, promise, initiative, and independence. For some, Exeter offers too early, too intense, and too painful an introduction to self-discipline. For some, its education represents too severe a buttressing for the particular strains to which they are subject. Such boys are by no means to be classified, even provisionally, as second-rate. But Exeter's mansion should not be their boyhood residence.

Yet in the nineteen-twenties, I know, and in the nineteen-sixties, I believe, that the Phillips Exeter Academy was the most incandescent place for a boy who was ready for the world's most stimulating teaching — the kind of fire that burned in Frank Cushwa and struck with lightning force the wicks of a hundred waxen lads. It was the place for a boy who, at, admittedly, long range, could feel the charm of Lewis Perry, and nonetheless absorb his doctrine to "beware of the man with magnetism." It was the place for a boy with the inward drive to express imaginatively, in writing, in art, in music, his first glimpses of the inner purposes of life. It was the place for a boy who envisaged self-restraint as the most commanding form of power. It was the place to gain religion, in the profound sense of Whitehead's insight, the capacity to deal with one's own solitariness.

Those are the principal reasons that I cherish Exeter with an affectionate loyalty, which is hardly less than love. There are, of course, secondary reasons — especially, that Exeter prepared me for the larger companionship and richer learning of Harvard College and the Harvard Law School, and that, as an Exeter alumnus, I had bonds with Exonians, like Judge Augustus N. Hand, John Cowles, Tom Lamont, and Bill Saltonstall, who drew me into fiduciary relationships to Exeter, to Harvard, and to the Ford Foundation. Yet the chief debt I owe to Exeter is that I entered a gangling youth; I left with a vision of what it was to become a man.

Written in response to a
request from H. Darcy Curwen
to contribute to a book about The
Phillips Exeter Academy, July 21, 1964

Sentinels and Stewards

IT is sometimes said that Communism and religion are the two ends of the stick of authoritarianism. And when one is caught red-handed grasping one tip, the only course is to turn the stick around in one's hands, grab firmly the other end, and poke the man who was your companion with that point of the stick you just had held so close unto your own heart.

But the reason that I am going to talk about Communism and religion in one speech is not because of their alleged mutual, authoritarian implications, but because they are from different vantage points the most revealing measuring rods of the quality of man's inner stability and courage.

And I choose this forum as the place for this talk not unmindful of the man whom Harvard sends here as its first representative, and the man whom Yale selects as the speaker for its governing body. For Mr. Pusey was chosen, in part, I think we may all proudly boast, because he understands these deep currents of religion which now swell in a new and healthy growth, and Mr. Acheson, true to the bishop who was his father, stands to all of us as the ideal representative of faith and courage, a man who in the practical world has shown that he understood not only how to contain the Communists, but how we ourselves could preserve our integrity and spirit in the daily struggle here and abroad with the reckless foes our democracy encounters. Our two universities, and more particularly Harvard (though Yale in its Law School has not been granted full exemption), have been faced with Congressional inquiry and public scrutiny because some of our less distinguished teachers have been charged with misconduct occurring entirely outside the classroom. And though I have no doubt that we reached the right result in retaining these members of our faculty, I have the temerity in this gathering, and before some of those who must undertake responsibilities for future decisions in the same field, to examine with you the correctness of the reasoning upon which these commendable results have been achieved. If I find fault, the fault will lie at least in part with my own earlier timidity and confusion. For when last spring I had a chance to be heard, my voice was not so clear and certain as I hope it will be now.

I begin with usual, but nonetheless sincere, proclamations. I believe in legislative inquiries as one of the informing agencies of our vital democracy. I regard resort to the Fifth Amendment as a gravely doubtful determination by any teacher. Often he has no legal right to invoke the privilege. Usually he makes a decision which strongly suggests that he has broken the law. Almost invariably his action injures him, his university, and freedom. For all would stand better if he revealed his past and present beliefs and conduct.

Moreover, I look upon Communism as the most reactionary form of despotism of the present day. Like all of us, I discern its military aspect as a threat to the United States and to the free world. I know beyond any reasonable doubt that it is a mechanism for utilizing both knowing and unknowing American agents for espionage, and if need be, for sabotage, and in time of war, for treason. Its corruption goes to the central core of man's virtue, and is to be viewed with that horror which we reserve, not for mere wickedness and evil, but for that utter nihilism which sweeps away the whole roots of man and society.

And yet even these proclamations do not go far enough. I acknowledge that the record shows that on occasion I have been unable to tell a criminal when I saw one. This experience prevents me from feeling any over-confidence in my own capacities of detection. But it has also illustrated for me a lesson which is often forgotten: private judgments are most unreliable when made in the absence of a permanent investigating staff, in the absence of compulsory subpoena process, in the absence of confrontation, in the absence of cross-examination, and without public trials cabined by specific issues, findings, and conclusions.

However, having admitted the magnitude of the Communist evil, I do not admit its immediacy. I do not concede that there is any proof that at the moment we are in such a state of emergency as to present even a plausible case for the suspension of civil liberties. I recognize the temptation to move more expeditiously, dramatically, and drastically than is contemplated by judicial process. We seek to show our alertness to the ultimate implications of the dread conspiracy. We are avid to demonstrate that we are not fools, nor laggards, nor apologists for a materialistic creed we detest. We are tempted to equate eternal vigilance with vigilante action. And yet I submit that each of us individually, as well as the organizations with which we are associated — the university, the bar association, the labor union, the motion picture company, the broadcaster, the private corporate employer — should deal with the Communist menace within the framework of our historic procedure without panic or the slightest departure from either the formal guarantees of due process or the customary, if unguaranteed, methods of imposing punishments, curtailing benefits, or revoking licenses.

Our moral and our political task is to persuade those at home and abroad that we have the strength, self-confidence, and steadiness to be the champion of the Western tradition. And in that tradition, the rule of law and the common consent of our forefathers established standard techniques for the ascertainment of guilt, and even of unworthiness of office. These techniques do not, as is sometimes asserted, promise archaic and cumbersome procedures more helpful to the enemy than ourselves. No informed critic asserts that to remove a person from public or private responsibility there must be an indictment by a grand jury and a trial by a petit jury. Nonetheless, there are standards for even such removals — standards emphasizing our belief that principle rather than expediency is the arch of justice; standards based upon the democratic presupposition that free men give their loyalty when they are persuaded, not merely commanded. It is, for example, clear that any procedure is arbitrary in which men suffer punishment or deprivation without notice of the specific charges against them, without opportunity to be heard, and without the right to hear and to test the full evidence offered in their cases. And these points the governing authorities of Harvard and Yale have always recognized.

Furthermore, men should not be disciplined for beliefs which they are not prepared to translate into pernicious action. The freedom to believe as one wills was more than the rock which the Pilgrims found on the barren coast of New England. It has become the touchstone for determining the true character of a society; if absent, the so-called democratic structure has a false facade; if present, the political and social order embodies a true commonwealth.

But it is asserted that the problem presented to the governing boards of Harvard and Yale is of quite different dimensions than those I have sketched. It is contended that what concerns us is not the broad political and social order, but the university as a private body, the university as an employer, the university as the educator of the young, the university as the mother of its devoted alumni, and the university as the symbol of intellectual integrity.

I agree that the university stands on a footing different from any other institution. Sometimes this difference has been summarized in the nebulous phrase "academic freedom." But that phrase lacks a precision which fully reveals its implications. A university is the historical consequence of the mediaeval *studium generale* — a self-generated guild of students or of masters accepting as grounds of entrance and dismissal only criteria relevant to the performance of scholarly duties. The men who become full members of the faculty are not in substance our employees. They are not our agents. They are not our representatives. They are a fellowship of independent scholars answerable to us only for academic integrity.

We undertake the responsibility for handling infractions of university codes occurring within the times and places where our certificate operates. On these matters we possess the best available evidence, we have familiar canons to apply, and we have established processes of judgment and punishment.

What faculty members do outside their posts, we should leave to outside authority. This is the teaching of Bologna, of Paris, of Oxford, of Cambridge, and I fervently hope of Harvard and Yale.

But I hear someone object that Harvard or Yale, unlike the European university, is a social as well as an intellectual community, a parent as well as a teacher, a club as well as a guild. And we are told that we have the right to exclude those who are not like ourselves, and others who embarrass us by their manners, or their lack of patriotism, or their low concept of civic duty, or their philosophies, or their effect on our financial supporters, or the hostility they arouse toward our institution and ourselves. If the troublemakers are persons we would not have as partners, why must we have them as associates incurring liabilities at our expense?

To this the answer lies in the basic noble conception of a university. It is not and must not become an aggregation of like-minded people all behaving according to approved convention. It is the temple of the open-minded. And so long as in his instruction, his scholarship, his relations with his associates and juniors a teacher maintains candor, and truth as *he* sees it, he may not be required to pass any other test. *Veritas* is his shield and defender.

If we allow ourselves to emphasize our immediate concern, and to assuage as we suppose, the imperative demands of our society, or to seek protection of those who are young, it is my prediction that, in the long run, we shall not preserve but rather undermine our interest, our national safety, and the character of our students, the three considerations which we allege as the basis for any summary action we take. For students and societies alike grow by their power to deal candidly with ideas of every kind without fright, or suppression. Openness is the climate for intellectual advance. Exposure is the road to maturity of character. Thorough examination and cross-examination are the best techniques as yet devised for uncovering false doctrine as well as false witnesses.

So far, what I have been saying was addressed to issues of liberty and of justice. And though these are great considerations, they are not the greatest consideration of man on earth, nor are they the greatest interest of our universities, nor lie they nearest and dearest to the matters with which we are charged not merely by our fellow alumni, but by far higher authority.

Most of us sitting in this room went through our university careers singularly uninterested in religious problems. We hardly knew that we were victims of the *Zeitgeist*. But not only were we caught in the backwash of Darwin, of Marx, and of Freud, but we sat complacent on the edge of a long period of Victorian optimism only slightly dented at the periphery by the struggle of World War I. Our hope, in our undergraduate days, was centered on the material world, and our material capacities to deal with it. While our poetic taste may not have been so jejeune as to have been shaped by Kipling's "If," or Henley's "Invictus," few there were among us who understood the book of Job. We had had his prosperity, but not his suffering. Even if we had his sense of discipline, we lacked his awareness that discipline, prudence, humility are all inadequate. Yea, all — even humility!

Our philosophy left no places for those inexplicable cruelties and unwarranted blessings which experience has now taught us govern so much of our lives. We knew little of the nonrational, not only in our enemy, but in ourselves. And indeed, if we ever thought of what it was that we could not explain, we supposed that some day a scientist, or a doctor, or a psychoanalyst would be able to uncover the territory wherein lay the secret to which we did not then have access.

But now we, long out of college and far wiser in the ways of the world, know that there is that which we shall never know, and that this which lies behind the veil of mystery will always be for man the very condition subject to which he lives and dies.

What we now know, our sons have learned earlier. Witness the large undergraduate audiences attracted by Niebuhr, Tillich, and the other gifted preachers of our day. Note that increased demand for counseling on spiritual sub-jects, and the almost bashful yet nonetheless intense desire of each man to examine the roots of his personal religious background and the forces that shaped the congregation whence he emerged. You who observe this generation of university students could document in convincing detail the early stirrings of a deep religious revival. The nourishing of this fervor is a principal business which we, as trustees of these two universities, have before us. This, indeed, I sub-mit, is one of the reasons we at Harvard have selected Mr. Pusey, and have high hope of his administration.

We are, it is true, the treasurers of the funds, the build-ings, and the other tangible assets of Yale and Harvard. We are, it is true, the final board of scrutiny looking into the qualifications of those appointed to guide our young. We are, it is true, the sentinels to protect men of learning from being interrupted by petty, political, partisan struggle. But above all, we are stewards of two of our Father's many mansions whence in the past have issued forth, and whence in the future shall issue forth, men of courageous faith.

An address delivered at a dinner of the governing boards of Harvard and Yale upon the occasion of Nathan M. Pusey, President of Harvard, receiving an honorary doctorate at Yale, 1954

The First Hurrah

M Y first pleasant duty today is to congratulate those of you who have won prizes. No doubt there is not an absolute correlation between success in school and triumph in later life. Yet, as Justice Holmes said in a famous tribute to his predecessor, Chief Justice Walbridge Field of the Supreme Judicial Court of Massachusetts, those who run fastest on the prepared cinder track are apt to do well in the races of the outside world. And in a more homely fashion the columnist Franklin P. Adams, who once adorned the page opposite the editorials in the New York *World*, wrote that the race may not be to the swiftest nor the battle to the strongest, but it is better to bet that way.

At the same time that I congratulate and make a favorable prophecy with respect to the prize winners in the class, I should like to make it abundantly clear to those who do not today receive formal recognition of their excellence that the odds are overwhelming that in the quarter of your class which will be most outstanding in twenty-five years, over one half will not have won any prizes at these exercises.

A careful analysis of my own graduating class at the Phillips Exeter Academy and at Harvard College and at Harvard Law School, and a comparison of those records with other records kept by academic authorities, has persuaded me that while the bottom drawer may not become the top drawer, there is a very high percentage of men who started low in the estimation of their teachers and classmates who ended up with most glorious records. Indeed, if there is one caution above all others that I have drawn from experience and observation, it is not to trust present prosperity or the apparent immediate benevolence of the gods. So far as I have observed life, those whom the gods wish to disappoint, they first supremely endow with good fortune.

Almost no person and no society has the character to maintain high principle and unflagging energy when he or it is the spoiled darling of good fortune. The classmates I had who came from the best stock and with the most favoring environment rarely had the internal drive or the external motivation which kept them in trim, intellectual and moral. Of the partners whom I have had in later life, few who began with conspicuous success resisted *hubris*, the overweening, arrogant pride against which we have been warned from the days of the early Greeks.

What I have seen in Ceylon and Sicily has taught me that natural advantage, a favoring climate, rich resources, and a sunny sky, may be far less stimulating to maximum achievement than the rock-bound coast and the inclement weather of New England.

What I have said has special relevance not merely to the risk which the now leading members of your class will run in after years, but to the dangers faced by each one of this group of graduates who come from such prosperous backgrounds, have lived such favored lives at home and in this school, and are marked by the red badge of early achievement and widespread acclaim.

What do you really know of the society in which you live and the times in which you are growing up? To be sure, you have from the weekly magazines and such daily

papers as you take time to read some quick superficial reports of the revolutionary forces now marching in full
swing. You know at least the outline of the Negro up-
heaval, of the yellow man breaking loose from the imperial
sway of Western powers, and of the dissolution in Africa
and in the Middle East and elsewhere of those European
empires which colored in red or blue the map of the nineteenth century. You are aware in at least a general way of
how fast privilege and special license are being dissolved by
the growing revolt of the masses. You have heard your parents complain of taxes. You know that the tribe of servants
imported from abroad or from the South no longer takes
care on the same extravagant scale of the supposed needs of
the rich. Those of your parents who are in professions have
complained in your presence of the demand that their special monopolies should be dissolved and admission granted
to people who deserve scholarships and financial assistance
on the basis of their merits and who will preclude your getting any special advantage either in the admission to a university or in entrance in any vocation or profession.

Yet while these progressive steps to undermine the un-
earned advantage characteristic of the upper classes are familiar verbally to you, how much do you really understand
of what makes these revolutions so certain of themselves, so
assured of the soundness of claims which they will turn into
legal rights?

You may say that you know from school, or from the
playing fields, or from summer jobs, or from casual contacts at various social events, more about the colored man
and the alien and the typical member of minority groups
than I am giving you credit for knowing.

I do not believe any suggestion that you are in fact familiar in the deepest sense with men not of your group unless
they are non-representative, non-typical of the groups from

which they come. We usually know our neighbor only if he is either of our clan or so assimilated to it as to be on our boundary, mentally as well as physically. What you know of the Negro, or the Jew, or the foreign-born, or the Asiatic generally depends upon your contact with that member of that group who is most like yourself. The very fact, however, that the man is like yourself is a fair indication that he has ceased to be representative of the vital center of his own group. The Irish Catholic who serves as a partner in a Yankee firm is not often the kind of man who thinks the way the Cardinal or the Mayor of Boston thinks. The Jew who belongs to your father's club is not apt to be a devoted adherent to the welfare of the State of Israel. The Negro with whom you can carry on a conversation of apparent intimacy is rarely a Muslim, and would hardly speak to you of his ambitions in terms as realistic as those described by James Baldwin.

What is the use of my telling you what it is that you and I do not understand about our neighbors? My object is to make you realize, as I hope I now do, that in our pluralistic nation, and even more in the pluralistic world in which we live, we must constantly be on our guard lest we assume that our immediate reactions and our instant value judgments are a completely safe basis for charting a course of conduct.

Nor is it enough for us in a Laodicean fashion to proclaim our tolerance, that is, our willingness to let each grain grow until the harvest. We are not entitled to the divine prerogative of allowing men complete latitude to develop as they see fit at their own peril and at their own reward. We are, in some sense, our brother's brother, but not necessarily his keeper. It is our function to enlarge not merely our own spiritual nature but the creative possibilities of all with whom we are in contact. We have the moral duty and be-you will have sons with allowances too large for their own good and substitute parents in the form of nurses and coaches.

But how many of you will live the reality of the liberty about which you have learned in the Funeral Oration of Pericles, or the Gettysburg Address of Lincoln?

For how many of you will an important element in your lives be your citizenship?

Oh, in time of war you will no doubt be the first to form and participate in a Plattsburg Movement, or to join a flying escadrille. There is no question that if offered a post in the Cabinet of a President, or a place on the Supreme Court of the United States, or a brief tenure as Ambassador to the Court of St. James's, most of you will immediately see in such a possibility glamor, glory, and grandeur.

But what will you do in your own city or town? What will you do to put yourself in the mire of state politics, to run for the state legislature, to take the jibes and taunts of your friends and neighbors, and the heavy blows of your political opponents?

One day this week, walking to my office, I passed on the Boston Common the monument raised to the *Arbella* and its crew, that vessel which brought in 1630 for the first time European man to the port of Boston. I could not help recalling that two decades ago a St. Mark's graduate of whom you have every reason to be proud, John L. Hall, referred in an argument he made before me on behalf of the Curtis Publishing Company in a libel suit brought by James Michael Curley, to that monument which he, like myself, passed every day as he walked to work. Without malice, and with, I believe, most appropriate candor, he noted that on that monument there stands a quotation from John Winthrop to the effect that "We shall be as a city upon a hill. The eyes of all people are upon us, so that if we shall deal

yond that the possibility of moral gain inherent in
tion of what would otherwise be an underdevelo

For us the glory of life is the opportunity it gi
enter into the deeper feelings of those whom chanc
to our door, or to whose door we come by chance.
we would understand those whom we meet and, ind
we would understand our own deeper self, it is not ei
to raise our hat, and in courtesy merely to greet in g
manly terms the stranger as he passes. For in our lives
is the possibility of a merger, not of ambition nor of spe
purpose, but of a spiritual awareness founded in part u
our deep consciousness that we are all together enwrapp
by an unfathomable mystery, imprisoned within the flan
ing ramparts of a world we did not build, and bound by a
experience of suffering, permanent, dark, and obscure, which
partakes of the nature of infinity and yet is illlumined by
gleams of flashing light leading us forward with a sense of
mission like that which guided those who searched for the
Holy Grail.

I am certain that there are among you, and particularly
among those much younger than myself, many who feel
that the kind of message I have so far tried to give is a
second-rate repetition of the kind of sermon to which you
have listened all too often. But what I have tried up to now
to do is to make you recognize that the kind of life which
opens up before you is governed by something other than
what William James called "the bitch goddess, Success."
From this room will go forth many boys who will become
rich and powerful men. Not a few of you will have assets
which reach seven figures. Not a few of you will be the
presidents of large corporations. Not a few of you will own
yachts and belong to the most fashionable country clubs and
town clubs. Not a few of you will go on the opening night
of the opera with wives bedecked with jewels. Not a few of

falsely with our God in this work we have undertaken, we shall be made a story and a by-word throughout the world." Mr. Hall was drawing to the attention of the jury in the libel case the high standard which we expect of ourselves and of those who could be our leaders in moral, as well as in political, life. With a commendable discretion which I am not going to imitate, Mr. Hall did not refer to the fact that the monument had been built in the administration of James Michael Curley and that with unbelievable gall Mr. Curley had had his own face sculpted into the monument as the face of one of the companions of John Winthrop. Mr. Curley thought he was having *The Last Hurrah* and that we in Massachusetts were content to allow the high tradition to which we were heirs to be defiled by men who care only about power and pelf.

Gentlemen of the Graduating Class, in your era, in the age you will dominate in the next fifty years, who is going to have *The First Hurrah* and *The Last Hurrah?* Men like Winthrop or men like Curley? What are the prizes which you are going to esteem? Money in the bank, memberships in exclusive clubs, corporate offices, or the greatest office which is open to you — citizenship in the brotherhood of man?

Notes for a speech at
St. Mark's School, Prize Day, 1964

The Living Streams of Value

BEGINNING in 1914 we have faced a succession of up-
heavals in the established order following multiple wars
and revolutions. Two colossal powers, the U.S.A. and the
U.S.S.R., have been drawn out of isolation to face each
other in a world struggle. The framework of daily living
has been shaken by scientific development. For the first
time in history spoken words move with the speed of
light, and transportation moves with the speed of sound.
Men are enticed from the smaller rural communities that
nourished a customary virtue, and now find their source of
livelihood in large-scale urban private and public enterprises. Property has lost those ancient qualities summarized
in the legal phrase "right, title, and interest." As a consequence, power has become an attribute of a managerial
rather than an owning class.

Some there are who regard this evolution with despair.
They deplore the rise of "the mass man." Like Rathenau,
they fear "the vertical invasion of the barbarians." With
Valéry, they are alarmed at the operation of a new social
theorem in social history, the rule that in the world of
affairs mass equals force.

The decay of the elite as the source of authority, these
pessimists observe, has been accompanied by a widespread
pragmatic revolt in all branches of knowledge. Standards of

an earlier age have been challenged as meaningless. Notably, this has been true in philosophy. The instrumentalism of John Dewey has been followed by the logical positivism of Wittgenstein, who has taught that the word "value" has no meaning, except as a description of an emotional attitude. Likewise, in economics, the tenets of moral philosophy which underlay earlier masters like Adam Smith are not regarded as solid ground. The prevailing notion is (to copy the phrase that Professor Schumpeter borrowed from Mrs. Robinson) that economics is a mere "box of tools." This same utilitarian, descriptive, and amoral approach pervades all the so-called behavioral sciences. No clearer example could be found than the writings of that university professor — Kinsey — who is today most widely known to the American layman — a professor associated in the public mind with the statistical survey of current practices in a field where the previously accepted criteria were ethical, not scientific.

The fundamental problem presented to the men and women of your generation has thus become whether you agree that there are no values beyond those of your self-interest, and that your only search should be for greater power in promoting the causes which emotionally appeal to you.

Some voices that speak with a background of impressive knowledge say that the task ahead of you is limited. You are to be concerned not with value, but with operational efficiency. At least, this is how I read the address delivered two months ago to the American Academy of Arts and Sciences by Professor P. W. Bridgman, the Nobel Prize winner. Making a bold extrapolation from Gödel's theorem, Professor Bridgman suggested that there is no possibility of finding within any system of knowledge a critical standard adequate to test its assumptions. The argument is that Gödel showed that "no system can ever prove itself free from contradiction." From that proposition Professor Bridgman derives the corollary that there is no meaning to the Socratic teaching "Know thyself." "The 'Know thyself' of Socrates presents a special case of a system dealing with itself."

Despite the powerful presentation of Professor Bridgman and those who think like him, I come here to urge you to look for value, for purpose, for meaning in your lives. And yet I do not come with an authoritative table of ultimate measurement. Indeed, I do not believe that I or any other man can give you an undeniable scale of values. You must find them by seeking them out in your own way.

But I start with the faith that in a life well spent, there is something more than the mere release of energy, and an increase in operational efficiency.

To be sure, energy by itself may make for external success. There is truth in William James's analysis of the qualities leading to material rewards — force of character, passionateness, and doggedness.

I concede also that external success turns more on chance than choice. Much is attributable to the accidents of physical and mental health, and to the unpredictable consequences of companionship with one's mate in marriage, one's first employer, one's work associates.

But taking the tricks offered by fortune does not promise to bring the durable satisfactions of life. The grand prize is not place and power, but the values and visions that mold your inner self.

Down what avenues shall you commence your search for these values? I propose that you explore four complementary approaches.

Undoubtedly the first one is religious. I give this a top priority though I recognize that the religious approach is usually possible only if one has had early nurture in a specific creed, or the mature experience of a sharp emotional crisis unsettling one's early self-confidence, or some other variety of experience not easily subsumed under any rational category. Probably few men achieve faith merely by a willing suspension of disbelief. Yet though restraint, reason, and ritual unaided may not lead to religion, nonetheless religious values for those who see them have an unquestioned primacy. And in our times the number of men who have this vision is increasing. Consider the disciples of the historian Toynbee, or the poet T. S. Eliot, or the to me most helpful philosophers, Whitehead, Alexander, and Jaspers.

For the men to whom the religious set of values is not immediately open, another path suggests itself. Are final standards to be found by collating, comparing, and condensing the experiences of separate civilizations, and separate patterns of culture? A few optimists have high hopes that from a diligent study of comparative practice, ultimately, anthropologists, scientists, and scholars of literary and artistic traditions will develop a core of humanistic values, "the best that has been known and thought in the world." Frankly, though I wish well to the intellectual descendants of Matthew Arnold, I cannot say to you that this approach seems to me to promise practical results of affirmative significance. Its worth is chiefly prudential — a guard against provincialism and pride. Was not Herodotus right in his analysis of the experience of Darius? Darius found that no money would tempt the Greeks "to eat the bodies of their fathers when they died," and that no sum would induce that race of Indians "called Callatians . . . men who eat their fathers" to "burn (as did the Greeks) their fathers at their decease." And so Herodotus concluded that there were no universal standards of sound practice and that positive or customary "law is the king o'er all."

If value is not to be found exclusively from a comparative study of civilizations, is it to be distilled from the history and purpose of the particular society in which a man dwells? Is there, in other words, an American set of values which may serve as your bench marks? To an extent, the answer is affirmative. There is an American creed of which we may justly be proud. In the opening chapter of his magnificent treatise on *An American Dilemma,* Gunnar Myrdal described our faith, its emphasis on freedom and thought and expression, its guarantees against arbitrary arrest, its respect for "due process" and the rule of law, and its representative republican procedures. Myrdal pointed out how fortunate we in America were that our national declaration of belief was accepted alike by the conservatives and the liberals. The conservative honors the creed because it is the eighteenth-century testament of his ancestors; the liberal endorses the creed because it is the most radical, revolutionary creed for the betterment of man that the world has so far produced. And yet, let me warn you that worthy as is the American creed, it is not a pattern valid *semper et ubique.* Take heed of the bitter experience of Nazi Germany, symbolized in the fate of your sister college, Heidelberg University. Once on the pediment of its library was inscribed the motto, "To the Living Spirit." Under Hitler the dedication was altered as a tribute "To the German Spirit." And this chauvinistic change, this emphasis on parochial pattern, marked a decisive step in the decline and decay of the virtue of a great people.

There remains a fourth potential source of value. You may at first regard it as trivial in comparison with what the other avenues open up, but to me it has untold possibilities of development. It is the attempt to derive from the detail of your daily work a set of principles and values which will give not merely your calling and your career, but your character that kind of style which does you honor.

This approach will at first, I am sure, seem strangely in-
congruous, as you enter upon your professional work. For in
our complicated modern technological society each of us begins in a small corner, charged with an infinitesimal segment
of some vast undertaking. Routine, regularity, self-denying
rhythm seem the road to advancement. And perhaps the
first steps toward promotion do come more easily if one
conforms to his fellows and closets himself within specific
diurnal tasks. But the highest reaches of a calling are certainly never attained by the men who simply believed that
"leg over leg, the dog got to Dover." The summit of each
profession is reached only by that type of man who has
concerned himself with the history and the philosophy of
his discipline, and its place in relation to neighboring disciplines. The only sort of interdisciplinary growth in which I
have confidence is individual. The great developments
come from interdisciplinary individuals, who have made up
their minds not to be satisfied with the small coin of their
own callings, but to carry in their pockets the gold and sil-
ver of many different mintings. This is one road toward
realizing Pasteur's dictum that "success comes to the prepared mind."

The man of wide interests is not only more likely to gain
personal success, but to promote the ultimate welfare of our
people. For the rounded society at which we aim will be the
result not of a miscellaneous assortment of segmented men,
but rather the reflection of the enlarged spirit of men of
broad sympathies, wide acquaintance, and tolerant outlook.

What I have tried to say has been phrased much more
poetically in a letter which at the time of my graduation
from college I received from Mr. Justice Holmes:

However a man feels about his work nature is likely to see
to it that his business becomes his master and an end in itself,

so that he may find that he has been a martyr under the illusion of self-seeking. But we rank men partly at least by the nature of their dominant interests, and we think more highly of those who are conscious of ulterior ends — be those ends intellectual ideals, to see the universal in the particular, or the sympathetic wish to help their kind. For your sake I hope that when your work seems to present only mean details you may realize that every detail has the mystery of the universe behind it and may keep up your heart with an undying faith.

On this wind-swept day with its overcast skies, may I in closing quote to you two lines from the *Song of Roland* that came to my mind as I drove over your rolling countryside and across the Cannon River into this lovely campus.

High are the hills, and huge, and dim with cloud.
Down in the deeps the living streams are loud.

Commencement address delivered at
Carleton College, 1954

The Anatomy of Courage

I SHOULD like you to consider with me a characteristic and fundamental phase of the structure upon which our society is built — its morale. You have no need to be reminded that the last generation has been living in what W. H. Auden has called the "Age of Anxiety," what T. S. Eliot has described as "The Waste Land." In our own lifetime we have watched the disappearance of the easy optimism of the nineteenth century — a Darwinian confidence in the inevitable progress of mankind. It is not merely that in horror we have had to reckon with the retrograde cruelties in the Germany of Hitler and the Russia of Stalin. There is in us an awareness — which our parents often lacked, though our more remote forefathers had it — that within every man there is irrational evil as well as irrational good. Whether or not this irrational evil is labeled with the theological term of "Sin," it is an aspect of man which seems not to disappear, and hardly even to diminish, as he gains in technological mastery.

This awareness of an irrational dimension, vivid as it is to us who have lived in the years just before and the years of World War II, is even more evident in the youth in our universities. No teacher who speaks from any scientific or humanistic platform attracts a wider audience than religious leaders like Tillich and Niebuhr. They, without all the apparatus of compulsory attendance and regular examinations, draw to the chapel many times the number that go to any classroom.

While mindful of this religious revival among students, and indeed in a wider circle, I do not propose to address myself immediately to the fundamental concern which disturbs them. Rather, I shall approach my topic indirectly by considering courage in a fourfold aspect: physical courage, emotional courage, social courage, and spiritual courage.

Of all types of courage, the one which etymologically and historically leaps first to mind is physical courage. From childhood we have known the lionhearted man of mediaeval knighthood. And as we advanced in school we were taught that this brave figure traces his lineage to the Spartan soldier. This is the model whom Plato in *The Republic* glorified as the warrior who obeyed the guardians and shepherded ordinary folk. The warlike courage of this Greek type furnished substance for one of Aristotle's four cardinal virtues. And the pattern which Aristotle discerned was refined by Cicero and even more majestically by the Stoic philosophers.

There are those who believe that in our altered social life, physical surroundings, economy, and technological circumstances we of the West have become too effete to retain our physical courage. Are reckless gallantry and a willingness to subordinate personal physical survival to the ideal of a great cause less compelling motives for men of the West than for men of the East?

For myself I have no doubt that in the final showdown our brothers and our sons, and we oldsters ourselves, will fight with as much vigor as any people anywhere. Remember the debate in the nineteen-thirties in the Oxford Union when a majority of that house resolved that under no circumstances would they fight for king and country. Yet Hitler soon learned that what men will do when faced with danger bears no resemblance to the way they boast of indifference before the beast attacks them. Of course it is always braver to face up to danger before it leaps upon us. Archibald MacLeish was clearly right in the famous essay in which he has exposed the reckless pusillanimity of the undergraduates of twenty years ago.

But we need not rely merely upon what happened in World War II. We already have convincing evidence that today our generation has men of physical courage. Consider Captain Carlsen and his pertinacity in saving his tanker. And shortly after Edmund Hillary climbed the highest peak in the Himalayas last summer, Americans from New Hampshire boldly attacked the second highest peak. Whatever doubt there may be as to where the Carnegie and other foundations should spend their general resources, no one has ever felt a paucity of deserving candidates for medals.

The problem of emotional courage is a more subtle issue. The basic nature of emotional courage has long been understood — by none better than Dürer, whose plates of *Melancholia* and of *The Knight, Death and The Devil* reveal the two extreme phases of men's dispositions. Yet new light in our lifetime has been cast by Freud and other psychiatrists and specialists in the sciences of human behavior. Today most men recognize that it takes more than habit, more than training, more than will, to be courageous. Men enter this universe differently equipped; and long before they are consciously educated in any scholastic system, they are conditioned by early experiences. These, if not indelibly marked on their lives, are at any rate as difficult to erase as to decipher.

So it is that some among us, perhaps most, fluctuate in

our capacity to summon forth our maximum strength. But some of the greatest contributors to our civilization and welfare have had periods of great emotional instability.

Lincoln is a familiar case. Less well known is the example of Charles Evans Hughes. Merlo Pusey was the first to draw the veil to let us see that the great Chief Justice whose majesty impressed us during his lifetime in person, as it has since then in marble on the front of the Supreme Court Building, was actually a man in a state of exquisite tension who balanced his years of unbelievable intellectual activity with months when he found it necessary to leave his family and his work and go mountain climbing here and abroad. What we know from the uninhibited Boswell and from Dr. Johnson himself shows that both the Great Cham of Literature and his more volatile biographer each had his alternating moods of elation and despair.

And in this company, I need hardly remind anyone of the autobiographical experience — described, to be sure, under the fiction of a French character — which William James narrates in *The Varieties of Religious Experience*. When seized by the green terror, James nearly succumbed. Yet as time elapsed, he not only regained his balance but dared report to the world at large the depth of his dismay. By his understanding and self-revelation he has aided all who have followed him to master their own personalities.

Indeed, have we not learned that candor in revealing one's own limitations and acknowledging one's own struggles is the first prescription for increasing emotional courage? What Lincoln, Hughes, Johnson, Boswell, and James described, they described not for themselves alone, but also for us. Every man has it in his power deeply to increase his fortitude by facing his weaknesses and taking those elementary precautions of rest and withdrawal which will give him serenity and assurance.

A type of courage much to the front in current discussion is social courage, occasionally called civic courage.

Ours is a very different world from that of the Colonial Fathers. In the smaller societies of early New England, as in the Athens of Aristotle, every man was inevitably a political animal dwelling with his neighbors in a common concern for the welfare of a community which he could see with his eyes and understand with his experience. We live in an entirely different world: each of us is so hard pressed to earn his daily livelihood in the particular compartment where his skill is at a premium that we rarely discern the scope and nature of the social organism of which all of us are a part.

And yet no society will ever be made by a mere collection of professionals. He who is only an editor and not a citizen, or a lawyer and not a citizen, or a judge and not a citizen, cannot by being added to the heap of other men similarly narrow in their professionalism give that foundation from which will grow a cohesive and meaningful structure. A society is not a sum total arrived at by adding individualists. It is the large *S* which reproduces on vaster scale the small *s* within each of us.

But how, in the circumstances of our time, can each of us develop so that he will be a fully conscious social being contributing to the common weal? Two answers — neither adequate, but both perhaps suggestive — may be given.

The first is that in American society, and indeed in all the Western world, the method by which men grow in social stature is through participation in voluntary associations — the university, the church, the labor union, and that host of private groups whose early rise was discussed by De Tocqueville, whose local history has been depicted by Professor Arthur Schlesinger, and whose legal significance Maitland described in immortal terms. These voluntary associations in society give man a chance to expand his social nature and to feel his common ties. These associations do for a peaceful society what military association does for a belligerent society. This thought has been strikingly developed in a perceptive Phi Beta Kappa address by Harlow Shapley, who took his theme from William James's celebrated essay, "The Moral Equivalent of War."

The very nature of voluntary associations demands that they must be self-generated. They cannot be sponsored by the state and articulated into its corporate existence. For this is the road toward totalitarianism. The associations of which I am speaking result from independent creative activity. Their members' desire to contribute to the common weal must spring from the adventurous spirit of man and not be dictated by any terrestrial power. To be sure, some of these associations may not conform to the dominant views in a community. Some may be composed of protestants. And others may be regarded as wayward. Indeed this has long been recognized as one of the dangers of voluntary associations. The political tyrants of Greece outlawed them. The mediaeval glossators observed that both Imperial and Papal powers frowned upon associations unless they were licensed. But in America, at least until recently, we have always said that except when an association is criminally conspiratorial in character, or unlawful in its means or its ends, we would take the risk of divergence and dissent, and count this all a gain for democracy and development. We have agreed with Heraclitus that "from different tones comes the finest tune." McCarthyism, in its generic sense, is a denial of that principle. It is the urge for conformity. And in its effort to solidify us to withstand atomic war or preparatory espionage, the supporters of the newer concept of so-called Americanism seem to me to have sapped one of the roots of social courage.

A second and perhaps more fundamental method of

achieving social courage is to recognize how far each one of us bears responsibility for the well-being of our society and the climate of opinion in which we live. We cannot, like the *Hausfrau* who believes herself charged only with duties toward *Kinder*, *Küche*, *Kirche*, turn our backs on the politics of our day.

Can I put my views better than by reminding you of the magnificent illustration of Karl Jaspers reopening the Medical Faculty at Heidelberg in 1945? You will recall that he said to those assembled that all in the room, himself included, were responsible for the Nazi evil, if for no other reason than the fact that they were still alive: "We who survive have not sought death. . . . We preferred to remain in life for the weak, even if justifiable, reason that our death would not in any way have helped. It is our own fault that we are still alive. . . . It demands that we should take on us the consequences of being alive in such conditions." This, as Sir Walter Moberly said, in his profound study of responsibility, "is not the language of hysteria but of insight."

And now I come to the fourth division of my topic, spiritual courage. We have been living for centuries upon the spiritual capital bequeathed to us by the men who dwelt in Palestine, in Greece, in India, and in China from 800 B.C. to A.D. 200 — the so-called Axial period of our history. The Hebrew prophets, Jesus and his immediate followers, the Greek founders of philosophy, the authors of the Upanishads, the Buddha, gave us a rich store from which we have constantly borrowed. And although our account is not overdrawn, our own contributions to the total fund of faith have been small indeed.

It is plain that, without going further back, from the Age of Reason at the end of the eighteenth century the depletion has been extravagant. What began as a movement of deists outside the Church and was aggravated by the development of a nihilistic outlook from the time of Nietzsche has been intensified by the extremes of an existentialist movement which, in its origin under Kierkegaard, was perhaps the most original Christian activity of the last hundred years.

And now as we come face to face with a threat of a strictly materialist philosophy from the Communist states, we are on the verge of spiritual bankruptcy. And indeed nothing reveals this more clearly than our attempt to treat as though they were spiritual principles the political maxims of democratic liberalism — maxims which are and were meant to be negative restraints on abuse of power, not affirmations of the ultimate ends of man.

But, under the surface, another current has begun to tug at our society. Already I have referred to Tillich and Niebuhr and to the audiences which they have attracted. Men of science, no less than men of the cloth, at last proclaim that there are and always will be limitations imposed upon the mind of man. There lies beyond his reason a territory of mystery. The further man progresses, the more man is aware that the boundary lies beyond any steps that he and his followers can ever take. How men in the future will deal with these spiritual problems that lie beyond man's capacity to analyze and define, no mortal dares predict. The very meaning of a mystery and of nonrational considerations is that they do not lend themselves to a plan. For a plan is by definition an intellectualization of something fully understood.

Nor is even the general direction of the way in which we shall go something that lies within my personal capacity to discern. Only one who wishes to play the role of a false Messiah could set himself up before you as a prophet of the spiritual future.

And yet, without rashness and with due humility, one may believe that philosophers like Jaspers are in general right in their emphasis on the crucial importance of each man looking into his own background of spiritual tradition. Isaiah said to us: Be "mindful of the rock of thy strength," "the rock whence ye are hewn." Turning to our origins nourishes those emotions which make us receptive to spiritual influences.

It may be that the spiritual influences of the future will come in shapes quite different from those we and our ancestors have known. But familiarity with the older vessels will make us better prepared for what the future may hold.

From the *Atlantic Monthly*, 1954

This I Believe . . .

SOLITARINESS is the core of every man. And what he believes lies at the core. When overcome by emotion this inner loneliness vibrates, and its secrets can be discharged by love, by prayer, by meditation. But no one can stand deliberately before a microphone and make that intimate revelation from which emerges the understanding peace that surpasseth knowledge.

I can, however, try to give you the atmosphere in which my deeper self dwells. When I pause for reflection, I am aware of bi-polar tensions. All the different aspects of me are arrayed on one side and are drawn to one magnetic field. Pulling at the other end are all the forces in the universe that are not part of me. And yet I feel not merely this separateness, but a strong togetherness between me and everything else that is. So that simultaneously I am in the world and apart from the world.

I wish I could say that this view of my relationship to the universe had made me humble. Humility is the noblest fruit of introspection. It establishes defenses against pride — that sin which the orthodox church justly stamps as the foundation of all evil. But when I become concerned about the miserable creature that I am, I do not draw closer to God, or to the magnificence of His creation. I am only inflating my own importance in my own eyes. I am augmenting, not mitigating, my pride.

Yet self-assessment is not self-defeating. Through intimate analysis, man recognizes more clearly that he is weak, and that he lives without protective boundaries, always dimly apprehensive of the impenetrable beyond. If man is to comprehend this further territory he must summon as his guide not reason, but mystic insight. And there is no guarantee that a reliable guide will come when called. Not having had any mystic experience myself, I formerly thought I could overleap the limitations of my knowledge, my reason, and my discernment by developing fortitude. I supposed that by inhibiting my desires and training my will, I could become immune to shock. But self-knowledge and self-discipline did not yield me a Stoic virtue and equanimity.

Therefore, I no longer am unreservedly optimistic. Yet I still believe that by inward scrutiny, resolution, and courage man can strengthen his fabric, and give design and style to his life. He can refuse to overvalue the inexplicable boosts and buffetings of fortune. And he can allow for the existence of non-rational evil, and likewise, non-rational good.

But experience prevents me from assuming that by mere volition, practice, and restraint, without grace, man can become his own commander. No matter how tight he holds the governing rein, his mental, emotional, and spiritual forces will not run sedately in harness. The fickleness of his human disposition stands prey not only to outside disasters, but also to internal pressures that he cannot distribute according to advance order. Nay, the order itself may produce not obedience, but revolution.

Have I then no authoritative answer to the universe's ultimate question? I have none. Indeed, I take it as inherent in the human dilemma that no mortal can have an answer that will fully, and permanently allay doubt. And yet I dare to feel confident that to be even partially satisfactory, an answer must bear the seal of religious faith.

And what do I mean by religious faith? Surely more than a creed, a commandment, a metaphysical scheme. It is that inner compulsion persuading us that we are implicated in an enveloping mystery. It is that search for meaning, which though it never reaches its goal, gives life a structural unity. It is that constant nourishment of our own personal and community roots as the emotional source of spiritual courage. It is that inexpressible yearning toward the fulfillment of the undiscoverable purpose of the universe — a purpose which when we are tuned to our most excruciatingly sensitive pitch, we firmly believe is unfolding before, and, in small part, through each of us.

Broadcast on radio program, *This I Believe*,
by Edward R. Murrow, 1954

Index